Created in Our Image

Created in Our Image

The Miniature Body
of the Doll
as Subject and Object

Kitti Carriker

Lehigh
University
Press

Bethlehem: Lehigh University Press
London: Associated University Presses

Associated University Presses
440 Forsgate Drive
Cranbury, NJ 08512

Associated University Presses
16 Barter Street
London WC1A 2AH, England

Associated University Presses
P.O. Box 338, Port Credit
Mississauga, Ontario
Canada L5G 4L8

The paper used in this publication meets the requirements
of the American National Standard for Permanence of Paper
for Printed Library Materials Z39.48–1984.

Library of Congress Cataloging-in-Publication Data

Carriker, Kitti.
    Created in our image : the miniature body of the doll as subject and object / Kitti Carriker.
        p. cm.
    Includes bibliographical references and index.
    ISBN 0–934223–54–8 (alk. paper)
    1. Miniature dolls in literature. 2. Doubles in literature. 3. Split self in literature. 4. Literature—Psychological aspects. I. Title.
    PN56.M5363C37   1998
    809'.93356--dc21   98–10777
                                                                            CIP

PRINTED IN THE UNITED STATES OF AMERICA

Contents

Created in Our Image

1

Created in Our Image: The Miniature Body of the Doll as Subject and Object

Little attention has been given to the problematic role played by the handmade doubles, the three-dimensional, tangible figures such as dolls and puppets that fictional characters and craftsmen create in their own images. Especially when created in miniature, it seems that dolls appeal to the reader's fascination with and fear of images made in human likeness. Viewing the doll, the robot, and the miniature as manifestations of Freud's notion of The Uncanny, Lacan's Discourse of the Other, Julia Kristeva's concept of The Abject, and Susan Stewart's juxtaposition of The Miniature and The Gigantic provides a way to explore the psychological implications of their creation and the extent and the limitations of the power they hold, if indeed any, over the humans who have served as their models and creators. The images treated in these works are neither those placed ready-made in the text by the author nor those metaphysical in nature, but those that the fictional characters themselves have designed, created, and brought to life.

The motif of the man-made double can be traced through several centuries of literature, looking primarily at British fiction and poetry from the latter half of the eighteenth century to the present and, where pertinent, at examples drawn from the American literature and the Continental fiction of the same periods. Of particular significance is the reflexive nature of figures that have been made to imitate the appearance of their human creators and the way in which, as doubles, they stand in relation to their originals.

The complicated relationship these figures share with their creators combines the themes of the double, the doll, and the miniature. In chapter 1 of this work, Swift's *Gulliver's Travels* and short fiction by Goethe,

9

Tolstoy, and Clarice Lispector are used to illustrate the significance of size, proportion, and perception. Chapter 2 begins with an explanation of both Freud's Uncanny and Lacan's Discourse of the Other. In light of these psychoanalytic concepts, the literary automaton can be seen in several works as a manifestation of the created other whom the subject attempts to erase from existence: Mary Shelley's *Frankenstein*, a selection of short fiction by E. T. A. Hoffmann, and Carlo Collodi's *Pinocchio*. In chapter 3, the doll is viewed as material icon and symbolic counterpart of the semiotic subject. The critical theories of Freud, Kristeva, and Lacan offer alternative ways of reading Yeats's poem "The Dolls"; and "The Captain's Doll," by D. H. Lawrence, is analyzed in light of the semiotics of Umberto Eco and Michael Riffaterre. In chapter 4, Kristeva's theory of abjection is applied to short fiction by Tommaso Landolfi, Edna O'Brien, and Margaret Atwood in order to portray the body of the doll as an imperfect imitation of the human subject it represents. Chapter 5 looks at ways in which the miniature and the doll figure are attempts to attain perfection in uncanny surroundings. First, some particular aspects of Freud's Uncanny are applied to "The Doll's House" by Katherine Mansfield; second, and in conclusion, Angela Carter's novel *The Magic Toyshop* is explored in terms of both the Uncanny and Lacan's idea of the Mirror Stage.

The Double

The motif of the double, whether of miniature, gigantic, or "normal" size, has been well established as a literary tradition by such theorists as Otto Rank and, more recently, Masao Miyoshi and Tzvetan Todorov. In his classic *The Double: A Psychoanalytic Study* (1914), Rank deals with such qualities as narcissism, spirituality, and the supernatural, treating the evolution of the double from both a literary and an anthropological standpoint. Freud, in his essay "The 'Uncanny,'" refers to Rank when explaining the connection between fear of death and fear of the double: "For the 'double' was originally an insurance against the destruction of the ego, an 'energetic denial of the power of death,' as Rank says; and probably the 'immortal' soul was the first 'double' of the body." However, Freud goes on to explain, once the stage of primary narcissism has been surmounted, "the 'double' reverses its aspect. From having been an assurance of immortality, it becomes the uncanny harbinger of death."[1] Miyoshi also identifies this simultaneous "craving for and fear of the encounter with the second self—each of which has its archetype in a traditional version of the double: the Platonic, or epipsychean, longing for unification of the severed halves of man, and the folkloristic fear of the double as an omen of death."[2]

Miyoshi deals with a metaphysical rather than a material form of the double. He defines as "the thematic or ideological" mode of self-division that which pertains to the self-aware, self-knowledgeable, self-conscious writer who tailors such themes as "the self-duplication of the doppelganger, the double, and the Romantic ideal, or the self-division of the Gothic villain, the Byronic hero, and the Jekyll-Hyde split personality."[3] He uses the terms "metaphysical" and "aesthetic" to describe some of these variations (and others such as the epipsyche, the self-portrait, and the monster). He suggests that self-consciousness (or "the consciousness aware of itself") implies doubleness, requiring both a subject and an object; the object (itself), being reflexive of the subject, becomes an embodied other.[4] Hardy's *Jude* and *Tess*, for example, are novels that he analyzes along these lines. What clearly defines this category of the divided self, he says, is "their embodiment of the self-consciousness."[5] Yet, Miyoshi's emphasis remains on the abstract consciousness and not on the concrete body. In addition to fictional characters and dramatic persona, he includes concepts such as Arnold's "Hebraism and Hellenism" and Ruskin's "two paths" as manifestations of self-division. My focus, while sharing Miyoshi's thematic and ideological orientation, will veer away from these metaphysical conceptions, centering instead on doubles that are material creations, apprehensible by the physical senses.

Todorov classifies the double as both a mode of discourse and an exemplary fantastic phenomenon. Of Todorov's various fantastic themes, the theme of the self and the theme of the other are both significant to his treatment of the double. Where the relationship of human beings to their world is the focus of themes of the self, their relationship to desire is the focus of themes of the other; these are often themes of doubling, concerning as they do the perception-consciousness system, the structuring of the relation between people and the world, and the definition of these relations. Where vision is the key element of themes of the self, discourse is the key element of themes of the other, since "language is . . . the structuring agent of man's relation with other men." To show the connection between the governing principles of the two themes, Todorov refers to Henry James's "The Question of Speech": "All life therefore comes back to the question of our speech, the medium through which we communicate with each other, for all life comes back to the question of our relations with one another."[6]

Of course, even in its conventional sense the term *double* is many-sided and complex; it is more applicable to certain examples of literary dolls, puppets, automata, and miniatures than to others. When discussing the subject's creation, by artifice, of the other it is necessary to establish the idea of the concrete and palpable doubled image as distinct from the doppelgänger, the subject's abstract or ghostly "double-goer." Robert Rogers addresses the ambiguities and uncertainties in the definition of *double* and the concepts identified by this word. He attributes our difficulty in marking out boundaries for the term to a "casual familiarity with the double in literature [that] has bred a strange mixture of contempt and awe, contempt for what seems like a facile device of melodrama and awe at the uncanny feelings which exposure to doubles can evoke." He goes on to describe the conventional, diabolic, antisocial double that clearly, yet perhaps stereotypically, represents "unconscious, instinctual drives."[7]

It is true that the carefully fashioned miniatures studied here are motivated by or exist as a result of the motivation of such drives. They also aptly illustrate the powerful link between the uncanny and factors such as doubling and repetition. However, they are neither stylized, farcical, nor melodramatic in a predictable or conventional mode of easy resolution. Instead, these creations capture and convey a melodrama of unease and contradiction. They represent so many variations of the "antithetical self" that their "intriguing features" cannot be easily reduced to stereotype; Rogers calls for "a broad, generic definition of the psychological double and a taxonomy of the numerous subtypes," which will eliminate the confusion provoked by the term *double*.[8] Offered here is a detailed analysis of one of these numerous subsets of the double—the doll or living doll that the subject creates in his or her own image and then contends with. Surprisingly enough, while studies on the double abound, those on the doll are in short supply.[9]

The Doll

The interest here is twofold: the appeal of the double and the appeal of the miniature. As Karl Miller points out, "in playing with his dolls an author is playing with his doubles . . . a favourite doll has been the orphan and his opposite."[10] Worthy of a brief mention here is the somewhat dated but painstaking piece of nineteenth-century research *A Study of Dolls* (1897), by Hall and Ellis. Their study is organized around data gathered from numerous surveys of school children: Did you ever play with dolls? Did you enjoy it? At what age did you begin and stop?

and so on. The questions, both psychological and pedagogical in nature, address names, discipline, hygiene, sleeping and eating habits, weddings and funerals, and clothes and accessories for dolls. The goal of their inquiry is to shed light on the role dolls play in the socialization of children and their continuing signification in adult society:

> what is the best form, size, material, amount of elaborateness or mechanical devices, dress, paraphernalia, degree of abandon in play, proper and improper imitations of human life, whether doll play was instinctive with and good for boys as well as girls . . . the age at which the doll instinct is strongest, whether paper dolls precede, follow, or co-exist with dolls of three dimensions, doll anatomy, doll psychology, the real source of the many instincts that are expressed in doll play . . . whether it is related to idolatry.[11]

The work aims to be nothing if not comprehensive! In their introduction, they lament the lack of attention to such issues and "the meager and fragmentary doll literature": "Indeed, this paper, imperfect as it is, is the first to call attention to the importance of a strangely neglected, new, but exceedingly rich psychogenetic field."[12] In almost a century, very few studies on the topic of dolls have followed the groundwork laid by Hall and Ellis.

Of particular interest for today's reader is the similarity between a sampling of their conclusions and the contemporary views of the miniature and the minute formulated by theorists such as Susan Stewart and Naomi Schor, who are doing much to establish and advance an aesthetic of littleness and detail. Hall and Ellis tell the reader, for example, that "on every hand we see that a large part of the charm of doll play is the small scale of the doll world, which . . . focuses and intensifies affection and all other feelings. A large part of the world's terms of endearment are diminutives, and to its reduced scale the doll world owes much of its charm." Like Schor, they comprehend the latent power of the small and trivial; and like Stewart, they appreciate the miniature's power to delight and torment. They write that "to make small will always be of itself alone a most effective pedagogic method, and will always exert a potent fascination."[13]

The set of literary figures, including dolls, puppets, miniatures, mannikins, mannequins, and homunculi, draw their potency from two sources: they are both a subset of the double and a manifestation in literature of the uncanny, eerily repetitive, begrudgingly recognized, familiar yet unknown. A new theoretical approach is required to explain the varied roles of such automated and supplanting figures in our literature, for they differ widely from the more traditional conception of the double as a character created in juxtaposition to the original and placed into the text by the author himself. In many ways, the creation of the other by characters within the narrative is analogous to the novelist's creation of characters. In the opening lines of her story "The Loves of Lady Purple," Angela Carter suggestively describes the similarity between the signification of language and the manipulation of a marionette:

> The puppet-master is always dusted with a little darkness. In direct relation to his skill, he propagates the most bewildering enigmas for, the more life-like his marionettes, the more god-like his manipulations and the more radical the symbiosis between inarticulate doll and articulating fingers. The puppeteer speculates in a no-man's limbo between the real and that which, although we know very well it is not, nevertheless seems to be real. He is the intermediary between us, his audience, the living, and they, the dolls, the undead, who cannot live at all and yet who mimic the living in every detail since, though they cannot speak or weep, still they project those signals of signification we instantly recognize as language.[14]

Self-reflexivity, self-referentiality, and allegorization all play a part in the reflexive text's aim to make readers uneasy with their naive or unexamined worldview. This aspect of self-reflexivity suggests an element of the uncanny (another source of uneasiness) in a fictional character's creation of an "opposite," an "other," a "self-representation," or a "signature." The character has (or is given or desires to have) the ability to redouble herself/himself, much as a reflexive fiction can redouble upon itself, imitating, repeating, or parodying its own substance. The fictional puppeteer is such a character: "The master of marionettes vitalizes inert stuff with the dynamics of his self" (Carter, "Lady Purple," 254).

Worthy of exploration in both psychological and semiotic terms is the reason not only why authors portray doubles in their works but why the author would choose to portray the subject's creation of its own small double, especially when such a creature displaces the author's position. Besides displacing its creator, the doll also has the capacity to assure the viewer, at least temporarily, of physical wholeness and integrity. This approach takes into account the element of self-knowledge that the reflection or the double yields. Not just the traditional "harbinger of death," the double may also herald self-awareness.

A case in point, the complex impulses of animated fictional creations such as Carter's "Lady Purple" demand an analysis more elaborate than those which identify them as metaphysical emissaries of death. However, Carter's fiction does take into account the automaton's connections with the world of the dead, and so does Stewart's theory of the miniature, which describes a duality that is similar to the traditional double's ability to cross boundaries and to participate in either mode of existence. As the narrator of Carter's tale points out, these three-dimensional, man-made, visual representations may impersonate death, but they do not embody it; the marionettes may fall to their deaths at the end of one show, but they rise again "in time for the next performance. . . . All complete, they once again offer their brief imitations of men and women with an exquisite precision which is all the more disturbing because we know it to be false; and so this art, if viewed theologically, may, perhaps, be subtly blasphemous" (Carter, "Lady Purple," 254). Conceived in the mind of an "Asiatic Professor" and created by his hand, Lady Purple is a being not from the land of the dead but "from the dark country where desire is objectified and lives. She gained entry into the world by a mysterious loophole in its metaphysics." Nor are she and her creator knowing antagonists, though in his expertise he has imparted to her a gift that he himself is denied—immortality. This means little to her, however, "for, since she had never aspired to mortality, she effortlessly transcended it"; and the Professor, harboring no fantasy that he may defy aging, gracefully accepts the discrepancy between their two natures: "Her miraculous inhumanity rendered their friendship entirely free from the anthropomorphic" (Carter, "Lady Purple," 262–65).

It is important to establish what visions of self are at stake and what psychological implications are inherent or suggested by the creative impulse that yields the double in any of its various forms: doll, puppet, robot, miniature. Of the miniature, Stewart writes that "like all objects, the miniature locates a version of the self, but our attention must be drawn to the particular versions of the self invented by such particular objects."[15] In this study, I turn my attention to the object, the detailed replica, investigating the contradictions, conflicts, and complications that arise due to the double's creation and the expectations that are either fulfilled or frustrated by its existence.

Jonathan Swift: *Gulliver's Travels*

Intrinsic to this definition of the double and delineation of the self-made image as an uncanny and fantastic subset of this class is an analysis of size, proportion, and perception. Based on the premise that "the body is our mode of perceiving scale . . . stating conventions of symmetry and balance on the one hand, and the grotesque and disproportionate on the other," Stewart's intriguing study explicates the importance of relative size in the creation of the self-made double.[16] She uses Swift's Gulliver as a figure who aptly illustrates the significance of relative size. Although Gulliver falls outside of the category of a double or a double created by a fictional character, he does provide an excellent example of what it is we may be seeking in our preoccupation with miniature figures.

Gulliver's Travels, first published in 1726, is a story about perspective. Swift renders the familiar unknown by altering Gulliver's perception and launching him on a voyage of the fantastic. His satiric ends are served by making Gulliver appear first as a giant in the land of the Lilliput and then as a tiny midget, a Lilliputian in Brobdingnag. In this narrative, Swift experiments with the human body and the body politic, illustrating the peril of trusting in social and political institutions, or in technologies that are doomed to fail. Even more perilous is man's pride in the strength and beauty of his body—a body whose betrayal of its owner is inevitable. Through a series of perceptual illusions, Swift implies that we are charmed by miniaturization because it makes us omniscient, giving us power over the body and control over the mechanizations of the environment. The miniature is a tiny machine—diminutive, inorganic, and manipulatable.

In the opening paragraphs of "Part II: A Voyage to Brobdingnag," Gulliver states: "Undoubtedly philosophers are in the right when they tell us, that nothing is great or little otherwise than by comparison."[17] Then he begins his account of living among the giant Brobdingnagians. He imagines that to them he must seem as an insect, a rodent—or a Lilliputian, even—might seem to the normal Englishman. Reminding himself that human creatures tend to be vicious and predatory in proportion to their bulk, he expects at any moment to be seized and eaten. He begins his adventures in Brobdingnag feeling like a small, helpless animal, and he repeatedly suggests that he is treated and responded to as if he were a weasel, a frog, a toad, a spider, a sparrow, a rabbit, a kitten, a puppy. But, even though Gulliver must consort with animals, he comes to exist in Brobdingnag much more like a doll in a dollhouse than like an animal. Especially in his relationship with Glumdalclitch, Gulliver is treated like a doll; and the Queen of Brobdingnag has an elaborate dollhouse built for him.

Initially, he fears that he might easily be stepped on, but soon he is discovered and lifted up by a servant who, as Gulliver says, "considered a while with the caution of one who endeavors to lay hold on a small dangerous animal in such a manner that it shall not be able either to scratch or bite him, as I myself have sometimes done a weasel in England" (Swift 71). Gulliver is ill at ease, for the servant who holds him captive has over him the power of life and death. Gulliver knows that he could now be treated as he has treated bothersome little creatures in his past: "For I apprehended every moment that he would dash me against the ground, as we usually do any little hateful animal which we have a mind to destroy" (Swift 71). He may even recall his own recent temptation to "seize forty or fifty" Lilliputians and "dash them against the ground" (Swift 19).

Gulliver's life is spared, however, just as he spared the Lilliputians. The servant delivers him to the farmer, who takes him home. But, at the farmer's house, Gulliver continues to perceive that he is being treated like an animal (and, worse, that he may be eaten). He is terrorized by just about every member of the household. The farmer's wife screams at the sight of him "as women in England do at the sight of a toad or a spider" (Swift 72). The baby wants him for a plaything, grabs him, and puts him head first into her mouth. The son's behavior causes Gulliver to think on "how mischievous all children among us naturally are to sparrows, rabbits, young kittens, puppy dogs" (Swift 73).

Not only is Gulliver subject to the treatment usually reserved for small victimized beasts, he is also subject to abuse from these creatures themselves. He is harassed by the monkey and carried off by the Spaniel; he defends himself and his host family against annoying flies and wasps; he triumphs over a linnet and frog who intrude on his territory. Perhaps most ludicrous of all, he fights off the rats on his first afternoon in Brobdingnag. He wakes from a nap disconcerted and trapped on the huge bed, "eight yards from the floor," only to discover that two rats have made their way up the curtains to stalk him (Swift 75). Gulliver becomes a heroic Nutcracker, valiantly wielding his sword and battling the army of two Brobdingnagian rats. He fells one of the enemy; and the other one, fearing for his life it seems, makes his escape, but not before being painfully wounded by Gulliver.

Despite his new diminutive stature, Gulliver views his relatively petty accomplishments as a source of pride. His pretentious courage and bravado gradually become laughable to the Brobdingnagians, but this early exploit does elicit some mild concern. After his near-tragedy with the rats, Gulliver is given over to the care and keeping of his "little nurse" Glumdalclitch, the farmer's nine-year-old daughter; she is small for her age, "not above forty foot high" (Swift 77). Immediately, instead of battling with rodents and being treated as one, he is catered to and babied as a little doll. Seeing Gulliver in juxtaposition to the giant child bears out Stewart's assertion that "although the miniature [a Lilliputian, for example] makes the body [of Gulliver] gigantic, the gigantic [Glumdalclitch] transforms the body [of Gulliver] into miniature," thus emphasizing its toylike qualities.[18] Glumdalclitch dresses and undresses him, sews numerous little outfits for him, and untiringly launders these small clothes for him. She treats him as a little girl would treat a new doll with a new wardrobe. With the help of her mother, she tucks Gulliver into her doll cradle for the night, now that they realize the mishaps that might befall him on a big Brobdingnag bed, and she places the baby bed carefully out of harm's way—where the rats cannot reach him.

No longer a vulnerable and edible morsel, Gulliver has become as a tiny person, a homunculus, a doll. What emerge now are the doll-like traits and qualities, which appear in Gulliver as the reader sees him from the perspective of the Brobdingnagian. Glumdalclitch gives Gulliver a name that is the Brobdingnag equivalent to *nanunculus*, *homunceletino*, and *mannikin*: Grildrig. What distinguishes Gulliver from ordinary dolls is that he is a living curiosity, a talking doll. Glumdalclitch tutors him in the language of Brobdingnag, and before long he can ask visitors "How do you do?" if Glumdalclitch so instructs him. Just as if he were wound up for a series of tricks, he walks, talks, bows, and draws his sword on command. Although the rumors that circulate around the countryside compare Gulliver in size to an animal, the description is of a miniature human, and the resulting image is that of a doll. The little being is "exactly shaped in every part like a human"; he is designed, like some dolls, to imitate human behavior; and, like the more expensive collectible dolls, he possesses "the finest limbs in the world, and a complexion fairer than a nobleman's daughter" (Swift 77).

When Glumdalclitch and her father present Gulliver to the King, who is a student of philosophy and mathematics, His Majesty is struck by what appears to be a mechanical doll, crafted to perfection: "When he observed my shape exactly, and saw me walk erect, before I began to speak, [he] conceived I might be a piece of clock-work (which is in that country arrived to a very great perfection), contrived by some ingenious artist" (Swift 83). Twentieth-century anthropologist Loren Eiseley, in his essay "The Bird and the Machine," accurately describes the eighteenth century's preoccupation with the concept of perfected clockwork to which Gulliver—or Swift—refers:

> Little automatons toured the country—dolls controlled by clockwork. Clocks described as little worlds were taken on tours by their designers. They were made up of moving figures, shifting scenes and other remarkable devices. . . . Man . . . moved and jerked about like these tiny puppets. A human being thought of himself in terms of his own tools and implements. He had been fashioned like the puppets he produced and was only a more clever model made by a greater designer.[19]

The mechanical puppet Eiseley describes here is exactly the type of doll that the king imagines Gulliver to be, until he speaks, and it is on just such a grand tour of the country that Glumdalclitch's father takes Gulliver, showing him off for profit until the King purchases him.

At court, Gulliver is treated more than ever like a doll. The Queen commands her royal cabinetmaker to create an elegant bed-sitting room to replace the rough box that Glumdalclitch had lined as best she could with quilted cloth and furnished with the doll bed for Gulliver. The new room is furnished by a "workman, who was famous for little curiosities." Gulliver is also provided with "an entire set of silver dishes and plates, and other necessities, which, in proportion to those of the Queen were not much bigger than what I have seen in a London toy-shop, for the furniture of a baby house" (Swift 85).

Even though Gulliver points out that his house is miniature only in relation to the houses and furnishings of the Brobdingnagians, he does not seem to be describing dishes and beds and chairs that could be used by an average-sized Englishman. Instead the reader sees an expensive little dollhouse, filled with quaint and tiny collectors' items. In fact, when Gulliver presents two chairs to the Queen, we do not see them as something that we, being no bigger than Gulliver, could certainly sit in; we see them as the Queen does—curious little items to be stored in a cabinet and admired. We become as big as Brobdingnagians for a moment, and we look down at Gulliver, who is no longer our size but is a doll, a puppet with the faculties of speech and reason. Gulliver too begins to identify with the giant Brobdingnagians and to imagine himself "dwindled many degrees below my usual size" (Swift 87).

Though, in an abstract sense, Gulliver loses perspective of his size, he is reminded of it physically again and again. He laments that he has become the laughing stock of the court because of the inevitable mishaps he experiences and because Glumdalclitch, though she loves him to excess, relates his little follies to the Queen for her amusement. He begins to feel trapped and harried, as he did when bound by the Lilliputians and cramped into the Lilliputian dwelling. There too Gulliver was in a dollhouse, but on that particular voyage he was not the doll. In Brobdingnag, his living quarters are indeed correctly scaled to his size. Yet they seem too small because, in effect, he is imprisoned there and kept. Once outside of Glumdalclitch's sight and the safety his house affords, his life is always endangered. Likening himself to a bird in a cage, he contemplates the possibility of escape.[20] Though confined to a cage, he is not an animal; ensconced in a dollhouse, he is not really a doll, as his frustration confirms.

   The King, when granting that Gulliver does indeed have a
consciousness and is more than a perfectly constructed mechanical doll,
classifies him as an animal, not a human (i.e., a Brobdingnagian). After
Gulliver relates to the King the state of affairs in Europe, the king
"cannot but conclude the bulk of your natives to be the most pernicious
race of little odious vermin that nature ever suffered to crawl upon the
surface of the earth" (Swift 107). The King has already, after listening to
Gulliver defend the honor of England "observed how contemptible a
thing was human grandeur, which could be mimicked by such diminutive
insects as [Gulliver]" (Swift 86). The King's pronouncements illustrate
what Stewart calls "the skewed relation of language to physical scale . . .
the fact that description of the miniature and description of gigantic rely
on internal systems . . . and social notions." Concerning the King's
enormous physical body, she says that "a human the size of a
Brobdingnagian may be a physical impossibility, but a fictive human the
size of a Brobdingnagian is absolutely appropriate, particularly in
relation to the physical impossibility and fictive possibility of its inverse,
the Lilliputian."[21] One extreme requires the invention of the other.
   What Gulliver fails to realize is how the two modes of perception are
dependent upon each other. After returning to England, he is plagued by
the inability to put things into proper perspective, although the souvenirs
with which he has returned should make this clear (e.g., the tiny
Lilliputian cattle and the Brobdingnagian comb, made by fixing stumps
from the King's beard into a paring from the Queen's huge thumbnail).
Stewart says that "these souvenirs serve as evidence of Gulliver's
experience and as measurements of his own scale." She points out that
while the souvenirs of Lilliput "are most often whole and animal," the
souvenirs of Brobdingnag "are partial and human." Gulliver's vision of
Brobdingnag has been "partial yet intimate." He cannot see, for example,
that to the giants he himself was little more than a Lilliputian souvenir—
whole and animal.[22]
   He has learned the lesson that "nothing is great or little otherwise than
by comparison," and he reflects, considering the laughter and derision
that his bravery—as well as his mishaps—evokes in the giants, "how
vain an attempt it is for man to endeavor doing himself honour among
those who are out of all degree of equality with him" (Swift 70, 100).
But, blinded by self-deceit, he continues to view himself as a giant. He
thinks that he is a Brobdingnagian with just cause to look down upon his
fellow Englishmen as contemptible creatures. He perceives the literal and
figurative littleness of all around him without sensing it in himself. He
attributes the fact that he sees himself as a towering giant to "the great
power of habit and prejudice" that holds sway after the months of living

with the Brobdingnagians (Swift 121). But habit did not force him to perceive himself as a miniature Lilliputian living among giant Englishmen after his return from Lilliput. More than a victim of habit and prejudice, Gulliver is a victim of egotism. He assimilates himself not to the size of the majority of the people around him (this we could attribute to habit) but to the largest physical being, whether this is a minority of one or an entire community. For him, when it comes to establishing a constant standard of measure, normal equals biggest. Gulliver's willingness to aggrandize himself by belittling others is consistent with Stewart's thesis that the miniature is marginalized and that "to speak of the giant is to take part in the fiction of an authentic body. The giant, its superfluousness, its oversignification, its simultaneous destruction and creativity, is an exaggeration or lie regarding the social status and social integration of the subject."[23] The various internal systems and social notions of hierarchy at work in Gulliver's consciousness are effectively revealed in his own skewed perceptions of relative size.

During his stay in Brobdingnag, Gulliver progresses from feeling like a weasel to feeling like a Brobdingnagian. One way in which the reader can view Gulliver during his transition is as a walking, talking doll. He certainly resembles a doll more than he does any of the numerous animals to which he is compared. He looks like a tiny representation of a human, he wears tiny clothes, he lives in a succession of doll-sized abodes filled with doll furnishings. He is comforted by a little girl who likewise takes comfort in his companionship. All of these characteristics make Gulliver seem as doll-like to the reader as he must seem to the citizens of Brobdingnag. He even impresses the King as being one of the finest examples of eighteenth-century clockwork that he has ever seen. Though the King's final assessment is that Gulliver must represent a race of vermin, still, in the palace Gulliver is treated not as an animal but as a tiny person, for his doll-like traits and qualities inspire the Queen, as they move Glumdalclitch, to treat Gulliver gently and to protect him as they would an heirloom or a precious curiosity.

Gulliver offers the reader an unusual perspective, in that unlike most miniatures he not only takes on the role of being observed but also has the capacity to observe for himself. He is subject and object at once; he can speak and write and recount his experience as a miniature. Illustrating the concept that the human body provides the standard measurement, Gulliver does not become a miniature by shrinking. Unlike Alice in Wonderland, he does not find himself "shutting up like a telescope" on the one hand or "opening out like the largest telescope that ever was" on the other. Rather than changing in size, he changes location.[24] Regarding the shifting perspectives of Gulliver's sensory experience, Stewart says that "the clumsiness of Gulliver, the ways in which new surfaces of his body erupt as he approaches the Lilliputian world, is the clumsiness of the dreamer who approaches the dollhouse"; he becomes gigantic simply by moving among the miniatures and smaller simply by moving about "in the shadow of the gigantic."[25]

The Miniature: Goethe, Tolstoy, Lispector

Perspectives that shift from the giant's huge shadow to the compressed interior of the dollhouse are not unusual in works like Lewis Carroll's *Alice's Adventures in Wonderland* (1865) or Goethe's "The New Melusina" (1817), drawing as they do on themes of fantasy and fairy tales. The world of the ideal miniature is also startlingly evoked in fictions as varied as Tolstoy's "The Porcelain Doll" (1863) and Clarice Lispector's "The Smallest Woman in the World" (1960). These narratives rely on what Stewart calls "Microcosmic thought—the use of the body as a model of the universe and of the universe as a model of the body." In this metaphor, the model "is an abstraction or image and not a presentation of any lived possibility."[26] In "The New Melusina," "The Porcelain Doll," and "The Smallest Woman in the World," the miniature body is struggling against the overwhelming sway of abstraction to present a "lived possibility." But repeatedly the miniature characters are all but vanquished by the larger corporeal bodies of their gigantic companions. Just as the Lilliputian universe demands the invention of a Brobdingnagian world, so too does the conventional standard of measurement require an exaggerated ideal; and the miniature, untouched by death, is the perfect form for the desired ideal—"since on this earth nothing lasts forever, and all things that once were great must grow small."[27]

In Goethe's "New" fairy tale, the rather undeserving hero finds himself in possession of an exquisitely small self-contained world and in the company of a magically beautiful woman who, though subject to death, has limitless resources of wealth that attract his worldly attention much more than any thought of immortality. The woman is the pixie Melusina, transformed into a goddess in order to search for a human mate who will help perpetuate her failing race. Upon learning that the life-sized woman of his dreams shrinks to become this creature of fantasy, the narrator reconciles himself by comparing the relative merits of a miniature lover to a gigantic one: "'Wouldn't it be much worse if, instead of becoming a pixie, she were to become gigantic, and put her man in a casket? How happy all lovers would be if they could possess such a miniature of their beloved! For that's what it is, a miniature, a most artful deception'" (Goethe 208–9). For a time then, he is content to transport her from place to place (in a casket that is rather like Gulliver's traveling closet) in return for her life-sized companionship in the evenings and her unfailing supply of gold and silver coins.

His perception is changed, however, when he is shrunk to Melusina's size, aided by the power of a magic ring. Initially he feels that "as a tiny couple we were just as happy as we had been when we were big"; he is awed by the casket's expansion into a marvelous palace, "roomy, priceless, and in excellent taste"; and he notes with smug and foolish pride "that I was better built than anyone else in this little world" (Goethe 215–16).[28] He finds that everything in Melusina's world is perfectly matched to his new size. "Flacons and goblets were beautifully proportioned for a tiny drinker—as a matter of fact they were better proportioned than *ours*." As this pronoun reveals, even though he is now small, he cannot truly assimilate his perception to the pixie scale. His standard of measurement is determined by his human-sized body; his miniature self does not even seem to be his own. Despite an ideal dwelling, an ideal lover, and his own ideal form, he feels "utterly miserable": "Unfortunately I could not forget my former condition. I discovered within myself the measure of my former size, and it made me restless and unhappy. For the first time, I could grasp what philosophers mean when they speak of the ideal that is supposed to cause mankind so much suffering. I had an ideal of myself and at times saw myself in my dreams as a giant" (Goethe 218). Melusina's unhappy lover introduces this declaration with an expression of surprise that his new life of gaiety, wealth, and perfection is yet so unsatisfying to him. He finds it strange but true that he should tire so readily of these pleasures, the things he was always longing for in his old life: "And now something took place that had never happened to me before" (Goethe 218). For him, it is an astonishing self-revelation to discover that his desires have altered, that the power to become his own double and to embody the miniature ideal of himself means nothing to him but oppression and frustration. He wants his flawed, undisciplined, and grossly human self back again. When he reverses the spell of the magic ring and escapes from the miniature world of the pixies, he says that, had he not stepped outside of the palace "my figure shot up with such velocity that . . . I certainly would have . . . destroyed the whole building with my new born clumsiness" (Goethe 218). If Gulliver's is the clumsiness of the dreamer approaching the dollhouse, his is the clumsiness of frantic retreat. The ideal object is something one wants to possess, not something one wants to be.

This distinction is made clear by comparing his reaction to that of Tolstoy's narrator in "The Porcelain Doll." This character also expresses surprise, but the revelation he experiences is quite different. In fact, he feels quite satisfied, but then he is the one who possesses the ideal object, not the one who has been transformed. He finds it strange yet pleasant that his wife should be miniaturized, and his initial sense of surprise gives way to the conviction that her new condition is indeed "natural": "She is not oppressed by this, nor am I. Strange as it may seem, I frankly confess that I am glad of it, and though she is porcelain we are very happy."[29]

In this story—which is actually excerpted from a humorous letter that Tolstoy wrote to his wife's sister—the narrator recounts the events of his wife's sudden metamorphosis from flesh and blood to porcelain. He thinks he is dreaming when he realizes that she has lost her corporeality: "[She] stood before me immovable. I said: Are you porcelain? And without opening her mouth (which remained as it was, with curved lips painted bright red) she replied: Yes, I am porcelain" (Tolstoy 34). He realizes that, instead of his warm and breathing Sonya, she has become a cold, smooth statue, "planned for external appearance only." Her gown is "all of one piece" with her body, and her body itself is all of one piece with the porcelain tree stump against which she leans (Tolstoy 34). Once her substance changes, as if that were not odd enough, another miracle takes place—she suddenly shrinks to the size of a few inches until he can hold her in the palm of his hand. He stores her behind his necktie for safe keeping, rescues her from the playful clutches of their little dog, and looks for a way to mend her when one of her legs and the supporting tree stump are accidentally broken off. The caring husband pays close attention to the importance that details now hold for his wife, newly small in the same large world. To protect her, he orders a small wooden box whose interior is contoured to her shape, "covered outside with morocco and lined inside with raspberry-colored velvet," and finally covered over "completely with chamois leather" (Tolstoy 35). The fineness of the detailed box emphasizes her role as decorative and ornamental. Cleverly designed boxes and dolls quite often go hand in hand, especially in the world of the miniature. In their *Study of Dolls*, Hall and Ellis report that "the smallest doll in the world is no larger than a pin, and the lid of the box where it is [kept is] a magnifying glass."[30]

Aside from the fact that Sonya still assumes her human form at times (only when husband and wife are alone together does she become small: "In the presence of others she is just as she used to be" [Tolstoy 35]), there is one other unique twist to Tolstoy's conception of the ideal miniature: the boundary between the ideal and the natural world is not at all distinct. Unlike Melusina's lover, Sonya does not achieve perfection even in her small form. Though "planned for external appearance," she is not an object of artful deception: "The fold of her chemise was broken off and it showed brown. At the top of her head it showed white where the paint had come off a little. The paint had also come off a lip in one place, and a bit was chipped on one shoulder. But it was all so well made and so natural that it was still our same Sonya" (Tolstoy 34–35). These miscellaneous flaws serve to remind the observer of the porcelain doll's human, and therefore imperfect, original. The most vivid sign of the natural world is that "her stomach was the same as when she was alive, protruding upwards—rather unnatural for a porcelain doll" (Tolstoy 35). As it turns out, Sonya is pregnant, and her husband wonders whether her various metamorphoses might not harm the child. Sonya's pregnancy, in the inanimate world of the doll and figurine, is a signifier of "all the advantages and disadvantages of that [the human, corporeal] condition" (Tolstoy 33). It is the one factor that still connects her, even when she is stowed stiffly away in her miniature casket, to the physicality of her fully functioning human body. In fact, her husband recalls nostalgically the days when Sonya was in control of her own body and able to move her arms and legs into any position she chose.

At the story's end, her fate remains uncertain—whether or not her leg can be restored, whether she can grow large again if she is not mended, whether her child will arrive without difficulty, whether she is oppressed by her sudden miniaturizations and enlargements, or whether she is as pleased to be a miniature of herself as her husband is to "possess such a miniature of [his] beloved" (Goethe 209). This, of course, was taken by Melusina's lover to be the formula for perfect happiness; but, once turned into an ideal of himself, he learned otherwise. Almost entirely objectified, Sonya remains passive. Her point of view is withheld from the text, and she speaks only once: "'Leva, why have I become porcelain? . . . Does it make any difference that I am porcelain?'" (Tolstoy 35).

Brazilian writer Clarice Lispector explores similar issues in her story of Little Flower, "The Smallest Woman in the World." A mystical story of magical realism, an ironic account of racism, sexism, and perspective, it is also a study of the miniature and the gigantic. As Tolstoy's Sonya must be kept in the lined and covered box for her own safety, Little Flower's civilization is nestled deep in the jungle forest: "And—like a box within a box within a box—obedient, perhaps to the necessity nature sometimes feels of outdoing herself—among the smallest pygmies in the world there was the smallest of the smallest pygmies in the world."[31]

Little Flower then has not shrunk but has been born a member of this miniature tribe; and, like Sonya, she is pregnant: "the rare thing herself had something even rarer in her heart, like the secret of her own secret: a minimal child" (Lispector 388).

Little Flower is not as small as the porcelain Sonya; she is "seventeen and three-quarter inches high, full-grown, black, silent—'Black as a monkey.'" Thus is she described by the French explorer Marcel Pretre, who discovers her and informs the press, sending along a photograph of her that appears "in the colored supplement of the Sunday Paper, life-size. She was wrapped in a cloth, her belly already very big. The flat nose, the black face, the splay feet. She looked like a dog." The body of the narrative is devoted to the reactions of those who see the newspaper account, reactions that range from one reader's case of "the creeps" to another's rush of "perverse tenderness." Much as the Brobdingnagians reacted to Gulliver, it is easy for the "gigantic" viewers to see Little Flower as less than human (i.e., as monkey or dog), because of her size as well as her color. When one girl observes how sad Little Flower appears to be, her mother says that "'it's the sadness of an animal. It isn't human sadness'" (Lispector 385–87). Another girl, automatically relegating the woman in the picture to the class of servant, thinks how clever it would be to have such a small maid to wait on her family's dining table.

A young boy imagines how he could sit Little Flower on his brother's bed to frighten and surprise him. His exclamation corroborates the conclusion of Hall and Ellis that "even feared and hated objects excite pleasure when mimicked on a small scale." They also suggest that "some children fear everything in human shape, perhaps, till they make the acquaintance of a new baby and then love dolls."[32] To the boy, Little Flower serves a similar function. He focuses only on the toylike and insignificant aspects of her body, explaining what is to him a novel and entertaining idea: "'Mummy if I could put this little woman from Africa in little Paul's bed . . . wouldn't he be frightened? Wouldn't he howl? . . . And then we'd play with her! She would be our toy!'" His mother, on the other hand, is reminded of "anxiety, dreams, and lost millenniums." Another reader is "upset all day, almost as if she were missing something." These sensations of loss are countered by a desire for possession. In one household, for example, "in the heart of each member of the family was born, nostalgic, the desire to have that tiny and indomitable thing for itself. . . . The avid family soul wanted to devote itself. To tell the truth, who hasn't wanted to own a human being just for himself?" Even Little Flower, regarding the private tree in which she and her husband live, conveys to Pretre that it is immeasurably "good to own, good to own, good to own" (Lispector 387–89).

Selfishness, sensitivity, or indulgent sentimentality—these various reactions to the newspaper's narrative and pictorial account of Little Flower's existence arise from nostalgia, that "sadness without an object ... which creates a longing that of necessity is inauthentic because it does not take part in lived experience. ... Nostalgia, like any form of narrative, is always ideological: the past it seeks has never existed except as narrative."[33] Such an absence, such a sadness, is allayed in part by the acquisition of miniature objects of desire—like souvenirs and collections. For example, nostalgic longing is countered by the sense of completion or perfection one feels when seeing the smallest doll in the world, encased in a box whose lid is a magnifying glass. Or in the extremely rare case reported by Lispector's narrator, it is a glimpse of the smallest woman in the world that offers such fulfillment. But Little Flower, like Gulliver, is more than a living curiosity or a talking doll; a wife and mother-to-be, she partakes of the lived experience of her tiny race and species, the ever-threatened Likoualas, who are "retreating, always retreating" (Lispector 386). However, the truth of her existence is an experience entirely removed from the life of those who are awed and saddened by her photograph. Their longing is indeed nostalgia, the sadness without an object, a longing akin to the need for unification felt by "the severed halves of man"—the double seeking its other, the subject seeking itself (see Miyoshi, above). For a fleeting moment, they believe they have discovered in this tiny being the object that they lack. Such a conviction is possible only by forgetting the fact of her humanity.

Coming face-to-face with "the smallest existing human thing" for the first time, Pretre feels that he "had unexpectedly reached his final destination": "His heart beat, because no emerald in the world is so rare. The teachings of the wise men of India are not so rare. The richest man in the world has never set eyes on such strange grace. Right there was a woman that the greed of the most exquisite dream could never have imagined" (Lispector 386). Lispector recounts the discovery of the little by the big and observes the varied reactions to such a find. "The Smallest Woman in the World" is an uneasy story, full of conflicting, confusing, and disturbing emotions. The exuberant children, closer to the world of the miniature than their elders, come nearest to expressing the feelings evoked in them by Little Flower. But none of the "gigantic" readers exposed to the tale—and especially to the photograph—of Little Flower can articulate their responses with any accuracy. Even Pretre, the explorer trained in gathering facts and recording "recognizable realities" is at a loss. His skill at naming and classifying fails him when he suddenly and unexpectedly wins the trust and affection of his small subject. In response to her warm laughter, he "tried to smile back, without knowing exactly to what abyss his smile responded, and then he was embarrassed *as only a very big man can be embarrassed.*" He deals with this difficult moment by "wink[ing] several times" and "taking notes. Those who didn't take notes had to manage as best they could" (Lispector 386; 389–90, emphasis added). Taking notes is of course what his readers back home fail to do. While Pretre creates the narrative of their absent past, they must manage as best they can with their nostalgia, seeking in Little Flower (the subject of Pretre's ideological and theoretical research) the objective correlative of their inauthentic longing and objectless sadness.

Little Flower too must manage as best she can, for her people are threatened by the gigantic shadow of the larger, corporeal universe. They live in fear of the savage Bahundes, who catch the vulnerable Likoualas in nets and eat them, and the representatives of civilization, who seek them out in wonderment, tempted by the possibility of possession, which their small size promises. For Little Flower, as for Gulliver, life in the giant's shadow is governed by the constant fear of being swallowed. Stewart identifies "tragedy" in the second book of *Gulliver's Travels* as "the threat of consumption, of having the entire body destroyed by being made into an object or a small animal."[34] Little Flower feels as lucky to have so far avoided this particular tragic fate as Pretre feels to have discovered her. Her good fortune translates into "the ineffable sensation of not having been eaten yet. . . . Not to be devoured is the secret goal of a whole life. While she was not being eaten, her bestial laughter was as delicate as joy is delicate. The explorer was baffled" (Lispector 388–89). From his towering stance, this "very big man"—who has of course never experienced the primal fear of being devoured—cannot well appreciate the elation of the miniature Little Flower.

The confrontation between Little Flower and Pretre illustrates the necessary coexistence of the two extremes of size: the miniature and the gigantic. One exaggeration implies the other, and their juxtaposition is required if the constant figure—the normal, human-sized reader whose position is continually subject to change—is to maintain any sense of perspective. Hall and Ellis describe this juxtaposition in terms of the child who can only with great difficulty take in at one glance the entirety of an adult figure and for whom "the extremes of large and small develop their chief charm well on in the doll period":

> Things large, like things far, fail of exciting interest, and of being comprehended by children, and are almost as effectively out of their range as things microscopic for adult eyes. As the microscope and telescope bring

minute and distant objects within our purview, so a doll microcosm opens up a world of relationship so large, and simplifies things so complex as to be otherwise closed to the infant mind. If we take a large view of the doll problem it thus comprises most of the most important questions of education.[35]

Setting aside for now the question of education and taking instead a large view of the doll problem, or a gigantic view of the miniature, is also one avenue to comprehending an important question of modern fiction and psychoanalytic criticism—the issue of the handcrafted miniature and the role played by the doll.

In the sequence, "Five Poems for Dolls," Margaret Atwood observes that "There have always been dolls / as long as there have been people." Some of these dolls wish "to be dangerous," while others "resent us." The dolls bear witness to our human antics and travel with us to the next world. Could they be gods, the narrator wonders, or "did we make them / because we needed to love someone"?[36] These dolls possess an uncanny wisdom, and the miniature casts an uncanny charm over its beholder. Analyzing this uncanniness leads to such issues as how the doll or puppet differs from the metaphysical doppelgänger over which the fictional character has little control; what lies behind our fascination with—and our fear of—images made in human likeness; why we are at one moment captivated, at another distraught by the miniature and gigantic doubles that we create; what impulses motivate characters in our fiction such as the Asiatic Professor in Angela Carter's "Lady Purple," Mary Shelley's Victor Frankenstein, or Atwood's Edible Woman to create and then destroy—or be destroyed by—images of themselves; and, finally, whether or not we must always relinquish power over these doubles, or rather disinvest them of that power granted by us, in order to gain control over our essential selves.

The pattern of disillusion and realization, experienced by the subject who loses power over the double in the process of gaining control over the self, can be established as a trend in the last two centuries. Miyoshi concludes that "the self divided is, as the Victorians had long ago anticipated, a condition of modern life, and it is only in this disintegrity or self-dissolution that we are free, paradoxically, to be a presence in the world, a meaning."[37] Inevitably, the fictional character, as well as the reader, must take control over the self by relinquishing power over the double and must be willing to endure both the disillusion and realization that this process brings about.

2

Creating/Erasing the Other:
The Double in Mary Shelley
and E. T. A. Hoffman, and the Automaton
in the Nineteenth Century

Freud: The Uncanny

In E. T. A. Hoffmann's short fiction, Mary Shelley's *Frankenstein*, and a number of other nineteenth-century works, the fictional character's struggle to create a figure both life-size and life-like (and even living) in his own image leads inevitably to a disintegrating other and a disintegrated self. Freud's 1919 essay "The 'Uncanny'" and the short story with which it deals, Hoffmann's "The Sand-man," provide an effective theoretical underpinning for an analysis of the loss and divided motivation with which the dichotomous fictional character struggles. Both "The Sand-man" (1816-17) and *Frankenstein* (1818) contain elements that Freud identifies as central to a sensation of Uncanniness: the double, the automaton, death, and the intrusion of the unfamiliar and undomesticated (what Freud terms the *unheimlich*) into the territory of the familiar and the tamed (the *heimlich*).

The first of these elements is the double. In "The 'Uncanny,'" Freud unravels the complicated scenario of doubling that unfolds within "The Sand-man." Freud's theory and Hoffmann's story play against each other as "a text and its hesitating shadow, and their double escapade."[1] Looking specifically at figures made in the image of their makers, who clearly function as doubled characters, I will analyze the various psychological implications and manifestations behind the creative/destructive impulse that produces the subject's double. The ambiguity of this dichotomous impulse echoes the "sentimental/Gothic split" in Romantic literature. Victor Frankenstein, for example, finds that "creation and rejection are . . . essentially the same act"; his relationship with his creature affirms "the fact that neither side is complete without the other, while their separation portends the destruction of one and the other's loss of meaning."[2]

The second element of uncanniness to be found in these works of fiction is the role of the automaton. Paul Coates suggests that Hoffmann is responsible for initiating the connection between the automaton and the doppelgänger, observing that "the emergence of the Double in literature is simultaneous with the invention of machines sophisticated enough to behave like humans." In an introductory essay to Hoffmann's *Best Tales*, E. F. Bleiler calls the automaton or robot one of Hoffmann's *idées fixes*. The stories "Automata" and "The Sand-man" reveal "Hoffmann's own strong feelings when he describes the horror he feels at the possibility of mistaking an automaton for a human being." Perhaps for the modern reader, well used to computerized and mechanized intelligence, Hoffmann's story may not carry the same emotional impact that it did for those earlier audiences, described by Jonathan Swift and Loren Eiseley, who flocked with great interest to marvel at the remarkable performances of the touring novelty automatons. Unfortunately, writes Bleiler, most of the late eighteenth-century and early nineteenth-century automata have been destroyed or are now inoperative: "During Hoffmann's lifetime, however . . . Vaucanson's mechanical duck . . . and his speaking head and similar marvels of mechanics were held to be almost miraculous"; Hoffmann's reactions were threefold: "admiration for their skill, horror at their inhumanness, and perhaps fear." Christian Bailly also devotes particular attention to Vaucanson as one of the masters of the automaton, who "had no lesser goal than the recreation of life." Seeking to uncover secrets of creation usually thought to be beyond the reach of mankind, the Promethean Vaucanson attempted to reproduce internal functions as well as physical gestures. He dreamed, for example, "of creating a mechanical figure that would demonstrate the circulation of the blood." Also writing of "animism and techno-transformation" is Valie Export, who notes the appearance of a trend similar to Hoffmann's *idée fixe* in Mary Shelley's *Frankenstein*: "It is of special historical importance in this connection to indicate that the image of the most popular artificial human, namely Frankenstein's monster, was created by a woman . . . at the beginning of the machine age and the industrial revolution."[3] Fearing the uncanny juxtaposition of animate and inanimate, Hoffmann and his characters—as

well as Victor Frankenstein and his family—experience horrified
disbelief when they encounter the automaton, who is also a double, the
"animated inanimate duplicate."[4]

Another element of the uncanny is the presence of death. Freud
focuses on the corpse as a source that can generate in the living uncanny
feelings "in the highest degree." He attributes fear of the dead to "the old
belief that the dead man becomes the enemy of his survivor" (Freud
241). The subject's tendency is to identify death not with the self but
with the other. However, once the other is acknowledged to be the
subject's double, the similarity between the subject/self and the
other/double brings their qualities into alignment. If the double can die,
then so can the self. Victor Frankenstein comes to this realization and is
forced to acknowledge that his attempt to create carries with it the
consequence of death. The inevitable product of his experimentation is a
firsthand and repeated acquaintance with death. His knowledge
endangers his entire family, and they must encounter along with him the
fall from innocence to experience and "the reality of death (which is
really the product of Frankenstein's knowledge)."[5]

Closely related to the presence of death is a final element of the
uncanny, the *unheimlich*. Cixous equates life and the "strange power of
death" with the *unheimlich*, observing that "there is nothing more
notorious and uncanny to our thought than mortality."[6] Death, disorder,
and disaster can be *unheimlich* while that which maintains a sense of
order is *heimlich*. In *Frankenstein*, for example, the monster looks in on
the De Lacey family and vicariously experiences domesticity (the
heimlich) as "a deliberately built defense against the disruptive norm of
disaster" (the *unheimlich*). Ironically, the De Laceys experience the
monster's kind gestures as the trespass of the uncanny, a disturbing
violation of their "idyllic landscape."[7]

Freud explores this aspect of the uncanny in the opening pages of his
essay, focusing on the etymological derivation of the term *heimlich* and
searching for the means by which it became synonymous in usage with
the word that should be opposite in meaning—*unheimlich*. He attributes
this convergence of meaning to ambivalence rather than to contradiction,
observing that "the word '*heimlich*' is not unambiguous, but belongs to
two sets of ideas, which, without being contradictory, are yet very
different: on the one hand it means what is familiar and agreeable, and on
the other, what is concealed and kept out of sight" (Freud 224–25).
Unheimlich, then, is the negation of the first definition but not of the
second. The second definition, though, is consistent with either term, for
both *heimlich* and *unheimlich* refer to something that is secret and hidden
from view. Thus it appears that "*Unheimlich* is in some way or other a

sub-species of *heimlich*" (Freud 226). Freud has further explicated this ambiguity by pointing out that the English word "canny," like *heimlich*, has also developed a shade of meaning identical to its opposite, "uncanny"—the term by which he translates the German *unheimlich*.[8]

Freud says "everything is *unheimlich* that ought to have remained secret and hidden but has come to light," and this intriguing concept provides the basis for his exploration of specific instances of uncanniness (Freud 225). In this definition, it becomes obvious how the home or the house is easily the seat of both sensations. Privacy and familiarity, what is never seen and what is always seen, reside side-by-side behind the closed or open door of a house. At home or in the house—these are the places where one should feel "free from fear . . . free from ghostly influences" (Freud 225).

Familiar, friendly, intimate, amicable, unreserved, tame—all are synonymous with *heimlich*. But from these nonthreatening adjectives a more sinister vision emerges: "From the idea of 'homelike,' 'belonging to the house,' the further idea is developed of something withdrawn from the eyes of strangers, something concealed, secret" (Freud 225). Thus the coincident meaning of both *heimlich* and *unheimlich* as "concealed, kept from sight, so that others do not get to know of or about it, withheld from others" is centered in the notion of privacy (Freud 223). When, however, the right to privacy in one's own home becomes not a privilege but a condition to be enforced, then the comforting connotations of *heimlich* transform to signify the unsettling *unheimlich*.

The subject's confrontation with the *unheimlich*, his admission of mortality, his creation of the automaton, and his conflict with the double—all elements of the uncanny—can lead the subject directly into the path of what Lacan calls "the adult quest for transcendence, lost time, lost paradises, lost plenitude, or any of the myriad forms the lack of object may take."[9] The desire for discovery and recognition motivates the search for a familiar other who will compensate for or explain the subject's lack of being. The self-awareness that occurs when such subjects confront—or are motivated to create—their second selves makes it possible to deal with this "lack of object."

Lacan: The Discourse of the Other

Two particularly helpful ways in which Lacan discusses the other are his description of the Mirror Stage and his view of the quest, sometimes pathological, for the self in the other. These theories illuminate the imperfect balance of opposites, doubles, doppelgängers, and others, the opposition between subject and object, and the subject's search for truth and fulfillment.

Lacan's concept of the Mirror Stage explains the child's discovery of one particular manifestation of the double: the Ideal-I whose image awaits him in the mirror. The *imago,* or specular image, that holds the child's gaze exhibits "the symbolic matrix in which the *I* is precipitated in a primordial form, before it is objectified in the dialectic of identification with the other and before language restores to it, in the universal, its function as subject."[10] In E. T. A. Hoffmann's tale of "The Golden Flower Pot," a child is mesmerized by the specular image, which gazes back at her from a hand-held medallion. The character Veronica gazes into "a little, round, bright-polished metallic mirror," finding not the subject, not her own reflection, but the image of the poet Anselmus, who "smiled on her in friendly fashion out of the mirror, like a living miniature portrait." Soon, however, this image is changed into a vision of Anselmus "himself alive and in person," sitting at a desk, writing. Simultaneously, Veronica perceives—and Anselmus writes—the other. When she finally achieves eye contact with him, the other is erased, for the vision is shattered, and she awakes, "as from a deep dream; and hastily concealed the little mirror."[11]

The effects of the mirror stage are, of course, central to Lacan's understanding of the subject and the subject's understanding of itself. Rather than reflecting pure visual matter, the mirror image for Lacan is a paradigmatic mechanism that allows the subject to replace fragmentation with unity and leads to the differentiation of subject/ego/others/things/ etc. What Lacan calls the "I" as opposed to the other/Other is the reflected image of itself with which the infant—and later the adult— identifies. He explains the continued significance of the image, which is initially so important to the child's perception of subject/object relations. Lacan portrays not the individual child gazing into one mirror but a pair—a man (the ego) and a desk (which has become his double or alter ego)—which stand sandwiched "between two parallel mirrors . . . reflected to infinity." The ego, being the vehicle of perception, is the privileged member of this unlikely pair; yet Lacan points out that the desk, in its stance between the double mirrors, will function as the observer "since in seeing one's image repeated in the same way, it too is seen by the eyes of another when it looks at itself, since without this other that is its image, it would not see itself, seeing itself."[12] The man, averting his eyes from his own returned gaze, could see the desk's image—but not his own—repeated to infinity. His own image he sees only once. Only by tilting one of the mirrors so that it were no longer parallel with, but at a slight angle to, the other could he see his own reflection more than once. Thus, this dualistic modification of the primordial gaze requires not only two mirrors but two subjects (or an object as well as a subject). Reading the other, in this case, is perceiving the other. The needed object could well be a second ego, rather than a desk. But Lacan chooses the desk to illustrate that, with regard to consciousness, the desk and the observer are no different when they are placed between mirrors, since the image of each is other for the observer: "The desk, like the ego, 'is dependent on the signifier,' for the word is responsible for the fact that it is not just a piece of wood."[13]

In discourse, then, the ego is no different from the desk; the significations of the desk are no less dignified than the ego's; grammatically, the desk can be either object or subject (like the ego). At the level of the imaginary, though, the desk can never be an ego. It is the ego that perceives the desk and bestows its meaning. The ego does not give itself meaning, but it does give the desk meaning. The desk, on the other hand, can do neither of these things. It can no more assign meaning to its observer than it can to itself. Thus, when it comes to reading the other, an ego is essential.

This ego is a questing, questioning entity. In "The Uncanny Rendered Canny," Meltzer identifies "the insistence upon curiosity" to be "the part of the uncanny which Freud chose to ignore," and examines Nathanael's "refusal to repress curiosity" as the source of his conflicts and his fate. She analyzes the story in terms of vision and the Lacanian Gaze, identifying the doubles in Hoffmann's story as "fragmentations of Nathanael" and the "various forms of scopic knowledge with which he is struggling."[14] Likewise, Coppelius and Coppola are more interested in the mystery of life than in destroying Nathanael. They "want to know, or have secrets about, how parts go together, that is, the mysteries of creation . . . how machines approximate living organisms . . . how can one make knowable and mechanical the inner [and unknowable] self."[15] Even Nathanael's father, an "experimentalist," is said to possess a "mind full of the deceptive striving after higher knowledge" ("Sand-Man" 191).

Nathanael, as manifested in his obsession with an elaborately constructed life-size and life-like wooden doll named Olimpia, and Frankenstein, as evidenced by his driven frenzy to re-create a living being, are both engaged in a pathological quest for the self in the other, a quest that in these two works manifests itself initially in the main characters' quests for knowledge. The monster's quest, for example, is a search for knowledge of self: "And what was I? Of my creation and creator I was absolutely ignorant."[16] Much like Oedipus, the monster feels "that his very definition depended on the discovery of his generation."[17]

Mary Shelley: *Frankenstein*

Concerning the quest for knowledge, Frankenstein claims that "it was the secrets of heaven and earth that I desired to learn; and whether it was the outward substance of things or the inner spirit of nature and the mysterious soul of man that occupied me, still my inquiries were directed to the metaphysical, or in its highest sense, the physical secrets of the world" (Shelley 37).

Frankenstein's quest becomes pathological when it results in the creation of a monster that is bound to his maker "by ties only dissolvable by the annihilation of one of [them]" (Shelley 95). The conflict between them is much like that described by Lacan as typical of two children whose competition for mastery "reveals not a conflict between two persons but a conflict within each subject, a conflict between two opposed and complementary attitudes."[18] The relationship between Frankenstein and his monster is an illustration of the Lacanian process of objectification and identification whose "symmetry makes it a closed system from which the subject could never escape without the mediation of the third term, the unconscious."[19] The monster embodies both the objectified second term and the mediating third term. Todorov, in his summary of the themes of the fantastic, the self, and the other, says:

> The *self* signifies the relative isolation of man in the world he constructs—the accent resting on that confrontation without an intermediary having to be named. The *other*, in contrast, refers precisely to that intermediary, and it is the third relation which is at the basis of the network. This opposition is asymmetrical: the *self* is present in the *other*, but not conversely.[20]

According to Todorov's network, Frankenstein's monster would again be the third term, the intermediary between *self* and *other*. To apply the schematic one step further, Frankenstein's isolation (which the *self* signifies) exists within the monster (which signifies both the constructed world and the *other*). The monster is a split figure that represents the monstrous, repressed, and unacknowledged part of Victor's divided personality but functions equally as an independent, created being, an "objective Monster."[21] The monster is thus Frankenstein's rather unsuccessful attempt to construct the missing object and a grotesque incarnation of the adult quest for transcendence. Frankenstein suffers the "disquieting consummation" of creating such a double, one who "absorbs the unrealized eventualities of our destiny which the imagination refuses to let go." Cixous equates the production of such a being or self with the "Lacanian 'imaginaire.'"[22]

Victor Frankenstein fails so miserably in his attempt to transcend reality and create life in his own image that even the monster accuses him of a flawed and grotesque result. While not fully understanding Victor's consuming quest, the monster is well aware of his own position: "God, in pity made man beautiful and alluring, after his own image; but my form is a filthy type of yours, more horrid even from the very resemblance. . . . I am solitary and abhorred" (Shelley 125). Because of his dubious gift of consciousness and his physical appearance, marred as it is by extraordinary size and unpleasing features, the monster looks "full into the face of the Vision of Horror" and sees his own; or, rather, upon seeing his own face, he glimpses the Vision of Horror.[23] He is terrified of the monstrous reflection he sees in the transparent pool, for it in no way mirrors the self-image he has formed. Jenijoy La Belle calls his terror "The Shock of Nonrecognition": "The monster is radically self-alienated. It initially responds to its own image . . . with horror. We must remember that this is *not* a man looking in a mirror—it is a synthetic creation by a man."[24]

What should be Victor's vision of self-awareness has been revealed instead to the artificially created monster. Grasping the distinction between his own form and the human forms he has seen, the monster defines himself as other, overcoming his incredulity to become "fully convinced that I was in reality the monster that I am" (Shelley 108). The monster, like his creator, has begun the fall from innocence. His sudden perception here indicates a sense of maturation and a growing awareness that closely resembles the process of Lacan's Mirror Stage. The recognition of otherness is quickly followed by self-recognition and, after that, a recognition of the ways of the world: "His sense of the way people will react to him modifies his self-conception—and not without good cause, since his destiny will be largely determined by that reaction. He has changed his consciousness of what he is in light of that impression all too accurately projected by the mirror."[25]

He determines almost immediately that there is only one subject position—and he is not in it. Such a privileged spot is reserved for those who share the appearance of the graceful, beautiful, delicate, and perfectly formed Safie, Felix, Agatha, and Mr. De Lacey. The monster has "sagacity enough to discover that the unnatural hideousness of my person was the chief object of horror with those who had formerly beheld me" (Shelley 126).

Frankenstein, on the other hand, never seems to fully grasp what makes his creature "in a very literal sense *monstrous*"—that he is the embodiment of a powerful Gothic element that is "consciously and unconsciously suppressed by the culture" and by Victor himself.[26] Thus the monster is an outcast in every sense, not just physically; he is the abhorrent subject of Frankenstein's abjection. He is what Cixous, in her analysis of Hoffmann's "Sand-man," calls "the offspring cast off by the self through critical solicitation . . . the ghostly figure of nonfulfillment and repression, and not the double as counterpart or reflection, but rather the doll that is neither dead nor alive. Expelled, but why?"[27] When Victor looks upon his handiwork, indeed he sees a Vision of Horror and strives to expel it from his own consciousness; but he fails to recognize that his own reflection is mirrored there: "It is Victor's tragedy to be closed, loveless, unaware of his selfishness (really of his *self*), and only partly aware of his responsibility for what has happened; it is the Monster's to be completely aware of the reasons for his suffering, including his own actions, and still unable to change either the causes of that suffering or his awareness of it."[28] The alleviation of their tragic situation depends upon a reconciliation that Victor is unable to effect. Both subject and object, creator and creature, are trapped within the closed system of Victor's making. This closed system is characteristic of the interior regression of the uncanniness. The private and interior qualities of uncanniness are emphasized by an epistolary mode of development, used by Shelley as well as Hoffmann. *Frankenstein* has been called a "regress of nested dreams," a "story-within-a-story (itself a story-within-a-story-within-a-story . . .)," and a "narrative china-box . . . [that] safely cocoons 'meaning' inside a double layer of stories."[29]

Overwhelmed by the enormity of his creation, Victor perceives the monster as "the shadow that can wax much larger than the person who casts it."[30] Frankenstein is engaged in the frustrating pursuit of this gigantic version of his own shadow, seeking to recover it while simultaneously avoiding if not his reflection in pools and mirrors then the act of self-reflection. Repressing the reality of this self-image allows the monster to identify the negative aspect of his reflection as the other, rather than the self, in the same uncanny way that the subject can align the fact of mortality with the other while denying it in the self. By ignoring his creation, Frankenstein achieves the same end that the monster does by ignoring his reflection. Victor and the monster are two distinct physical beings with remarkably similar personalities. However, it is the monster that must suffer the consequences of the void in which he was produced, making him more sympathetic and humane than Victor; as a subject, the creature is more real than his creator.

Unnaturally created, "imperfectly animated," the monster's tragedy is to be the unwitting incarnation of horror (Shelley xi). The unnatural process of creation by which the monster is produced has been discussed at length. William Veeder, for example, describes the monster's inception as "parthenogenetic," attributing its creation to Victor's "psychic bifurcation" and willful "procreative urge," and defining *parthenogenesis* as "more than creation from the self, it means creation of a self."[31] Not only does Victor attempt to reproduce himself without a partner, but he deliberately fails to create his offspring entirely in his own image. Victor explains that because "the minuteness of the parts formed a great hindrance" to the speed of his work, he would instead make a "being of a gigantic stature . . . about eight feet in height, and proportionably large" (Shelley 52). For no other reason than his own convenience, he makes his monster larger than life, a discrepancy that emphasizes the unnaturalness of his creature's birth. As the creature's self-awareness grows, he wonders about his birth and infancy, trying to imagine what unknown facts must fill the void of his past—that "blot" or "blind vacancy in which I distinguished nothing": "From my earliest remembrance I had been as I then was in height and proportion. I had never yet seen a being resembling me or who claimed any intercourse with me. What was I?" (Shelley 115–16).

Frankenstein, in his thoughtlessness, "has further increased the monstrousness of his creation by making a form that is both larger and more simple than a normal human being."[32] Guilty of ignoring the "conflicting demands . . . between large and small objects," he "should have better balanced the obligations of great and small, of parent and child, of creator and creature."[33] Unlike the idealized miniature, whose creation signifies the "erasure of disorder, of nature and history," Frankenstein's monster represents "the grotesque realism of the gigantic."[34]

Stewart's assessment of Gulliver's life in Brobdingnag accurately explains the reaction of the human community when witnessing the object of Frankenstein's creation: "The partial vision of the observer prohibits closure of the object. Our impulse is to create an environment for the miniature, but such an environment is impossible for the gigantic: instead the gigantic becomes our environment, swallowing us as nature or history swallows us."[35] The monster hopes by "gentle demeanour and conciliating words" to overcome the disgust that he is sure the De Laceys will feel; but even his kindest gesture is not enough to displace their fear of being swallowed by him (Shelley 109).

The creature becomes a monster because of the clumsiness with which his negligent creator bestowed "animation upon lifeless matter" (Shelley 51). Mellor attributes Frankenstein's negligence to his inability to "work and love at the same time."[36] Laboring in solitude, shunning the society of his friends and companions, Frankenstein overlooks the crucial fact that "disgust is a matter of perspective. . . . Grotesque or symmetrical, the body's place and privileges are regulated by a social discourse, a discourse which articulates the body's very status as the subjective."[37] Driven by a private demon, Victor fails to participate in the social discourse and leaves his creature—whom he immediately terms his "enemy"—to suffer "the fatal effects of this miserable deformity" (Shelley 60, 108). The monster is disenfranchised because of his gigantic stature, denied the privilege of social discourse, and alienated from communal existence.

Despite his ability to grasp social intricacies, the monster is forced to live outside the boundaries of culture. The central conflict between Victor and the monster is the articulation of this social alienation. The monster condemns Victor chiefly for alienating—for "irrevocably excluding"—him, and he requests a mate not to increase his strength and power but to rescue him from utter isolation (Shelley 95). His evil deeds spring from the misery of alienation and loneliness, and his violence stems from his futile struggle to participate in the world of human discourse. The monster's predicament exemplifies "the necessity and desperation" of the subject's quest to join this world. Levine says that the horror of the monster's estrangement "from both nature and social reality . . . is most forcefully and indirectly suggested by the fact that it has no name." Likewise, Coates says that by refusing to name his monster, Frankenstein "disowns it and its connection with his own psyche; hence the popular tradition that terms the creature itself 'Frankenstein' makes good its creator's lack of charity."[38]

As Victor's creation and the offspring of his peculiar education, the nameless monster is indeed a cultural product; yet his gross organicism overwhelms any other traits he might possess, making it impossible for him to rejoin the world, naturally or socially, from his place of alienation. It is the ambiguity of the monster's "postnatural and precultural" position that thwarts his efforts "to achieve recognition and to enter the signifying chain."[39] While the monster's most monstrous qualities may derive from nature, his creation derives from a motivation in Victor that is both *un*natural and cultural. Frankenstein's decision to create a monster had to originate out of more than "mere chance," says Levine: "The idea of Frankenstein could have emerged only from a culture that had imagined the perfectibility of humanity, or a French Revolution to bring about the perfection." Writing similarly of the century following the Revolution, Christian Bailly says that "clearly, the automaton was an intimate part of the society that created it, and like that society it was destined to undergo astonishing technical transformations and to endure changes in taste and fashion."[40]

As a culturally created imitation of human reality, the monster projects an image that "not only bears the tangible qualities of material reality but also serves as a representation, an image, of a reality which does not exist." This description of the role of the miniature in the signifying chain is also an accurate description of Frankenstein's creature, who shares properties of both the miniature and the gigantic worldview. Like the perfect miniature, Frankenstein's monster originates in imitation and enters "the chain of signification at a remove."[41] In nature, there is no original of the monster (other than his maker, in whose image he has been so poorly modeled), thus—like the miniature—he is a creature of imitation but not of duplication. The oversized monster is not the opposite but the inverse of such culturally created miniatures as the "valuable miniature" locket that contains Caroline Frankenstein's miniature portrait (Shelley 70).

A creature of extremes in a novel of extremes, the monster shares the exterior mass of the gigantic yet possesses the interior reality of a human consciousness and views the world from a refined, minutely philosophical (rather than grossly organic) perspective. The detail with which he reasons, however, makes him even more of an anomaly as he crashes through the undergrowth, gathering roots, nuts, and berries. He is an ungainly juxtaposition of culture and nature, his organs of digestion as well as those of speech being "harsh, but supple" (Shelley 109). The authentic miniature remains always and only cultural, the true gigantic always natural. Thus, no matter how much the misbegotten monster's creation may resemble a manifestation of either mode, he is stranded between the two: defined by the giganticism of his physical stature and denied the privilege of sharing with a sympathetic companion the precision of his psyche. United in his being are human sensibilities and monstrous realities.

Even Frankenstein, who assembled the creature with a view to making him "beautiful," cannot abide the lack of closure he feels upon beholding "the wretch . . . the demoniacal corpse to which I had so miserably given life" (Shelley 56, 57). Instead, he must acknowledge the failure of his fantasy to improve upon reality. Far from producing an ideal creature, Frankenstein has constructed one that is entirely unacceptable. The monster, created out of parts of real people, is a kind of fantasy—a restructuring "of the building blocks of accepted reality."[42] Frankenstein's withdrawal from his unsuccessful synthesis of fantasy and reality may be instinctive, and his ardent wish "to extinguish that life which I had so thoughtlessly bestowed" is not hard to understand. Yet, the monster's outrage at such injustice is more valid: "'You, my creator, abhor me; what hope can I gather from your fellow creatures, who owe me nothing? . . . You accuse me of murder, and yet you would, with a

satisfied conscience, destroy your own creature'" (Shelley 96).
Confronted by this solitary representative of his "new species,"
Frankenstein sees, not a "happy and excellent" nature but his second
self—a thwarted and despairing creature who "owes his being"
completely to his original (Shelley 52). In his Promethean attempt "to
make an equivalent and yet a better [reality]," Frankenstein proves that
"the ideal is the monstrous."[43]

E. T. A. Hoffman: The Sand-Man

Unlike Frankenstein, Hoffmann's Spalanzani creates a being whom he
is proud to display in public, the life-sized doll Olimpia with whom
Nathanael grows obsessed. Designed with such precision that her
appearance does not violate the body's privileged place in social
discourse, Olimpia is not shunned as Victor's monster is. Though her
artificial existence does come to a frightful end, she is never distressed
by the factor of self-awareness. If such power had been granted her, she
might soon have perceived the deficiency of her mental capacity;
physically, however, she is flawless. Thus her reception into society is a
temporary success, even though Spalanzani is eventually obliged to leave
town "in order to escape a criminal charge of having fraudulently
imposed an automaton upon human society" ("Sand-Man" 212).

Of the many doubled characters who permeate "The Sand-man,"
Nathanael's relationship to the conciliatory Olimpia is one of the most
significant. Though she is not of his making, he is bewitched by her in
much the same way that Victor Frankenstein is by his self-created
double. Whereas Victor is repelled by the monster's ugliness, Nathanael
is mesmerized by Olimpia's artificial beauty and "shows a thinly veiled
infantile tendency in his attraction to an overgrown toy."[44] This
superficial attraction, however, is soon subsumed by a more pervasive
apprehension of her power over his inner being. It is in Olimpia's
distorted face that Nathanael finally confronts the vision of horror.

Both Cixous and Meltzer maintain that Freud overlooks the profound
significance of the uncanny role played by Olimpia. Cixous, in her
analysis of Freud's treatment of "The Sand-man" feels that, along with
"diminishing the texture of the story," Freud also "minimizes the
uncertainty [a primary condition for uncanniness] revolving around
Olympia, thus pushing Olympia toward the group of the *Heimliche*." The
group of characters representing the *heimlich* includes Nathanael's fiancé
Clara, with whom Olimpia stands in juxtaposition as a double and as an

automaton. In fact, Olimpia's presence serves to expand the reader's comprehension of a number of characters besides Nathanael alone. Freud's "minimizing of Olympia," however, "leads to the focus on Nathaniel . . . even though Olympia is more than just a detached complex of Nathaniel."[45] Cixous contrasts the automaton ("Olympia, 'doll' adult, the object of Nathaniel's desire") with its inherent double ("Olympia, doll, the toy of little girls") and asks, "Why are not the dance, the song, the mechanisms, and the artificer brought back into the game or theorized upon by Freud? What are we expected to do with these puppets which have haunted the stages of German romanticism?" Cixous is not the only reader who has questioned why Olimpia is not "relegated to some more profound place" in Freud's critique.[46]

The automated doll Olimpia is listed by Meltzer as one of the story's uncanny elements, along with compelling curiosity and clarity of vision. Yet Olimpia's "highly uncanny quality . . . is rejected by Freud as the heart of the uncanny experience"; instead the uncanny is found "in the overtly bizarre connection between the Sandman and the eyes he seems to want to rob."[47] Meltzer, unlike Freud, situates the uncanny in Nathanael's realization that Olimpia is her own double, that she is at once self and other—the adult beauty and the child's (or perhaps the adult's) toy: "Is not the uncanny moment created when Nathanael becomes certain that Olympia is a doll, and when he simultaneously still sees her as the girl he loves?"[48]

As unlikely as this love for an automaton—no matter how finely designed—may seem, Nathanael completely forgets Clara's existence after spending several days peering through his spyglass at Olimpia. Already enchanted simply by the sight of her, he then spends the evening with her at Spalanzani's ball, and their romance begins in earnest. He comes to feel that only Olimpia understands him, and he discovers a "wondrous harmony which daily revealed itself between his own and his Olimpia's character" ("Sand-Man" 209). When his friend Siegmund tries to convince him that she is "soulless," "utterly devoid of life," and nothing more than an eerie piece of "wound-up clockwork," he resists such observations with his own pronouncement: "'You cold prosaic fellows may very well be afraid of her. It is only to its like that the poetically organized spirit unfolds itself'" ("Sand-Man" 208).

When Spalanzani comments on the "extraordinarily animated conversation" shared between the lovers, Nathanael is entirely oblivious to his sarcasm; and when "Nathanael ventured at length to hint very delicately at an alliance with Olimpia, the Professor smiled all over his face at once, and said he should allow his daughter to make a perfectly free choice" ("Sand-Man" 207, 209). His smile, of course, is occasioned by the tremendous success of his trickery with this one susceptible onlooker and suitor, even if with very few others. Needless to say, Olimpia is incapable of making a free choice, and Nathanael is unknowingly consigning his fate to Spalanzani and the insidious Coppola/Coppelius.

Strangely, Olimpia seems to be programmed to attract only Nathanael. She holds little appeal for any of his friends, she dances only with him, and he perceives that "upon me alone did her loving glances fall, and through my mind and thoughts alone did they radiate." He alone finds her profound, attributing her limited responses to intelligence, brilliance, and devotion, rather than to stupidity. Spalanzani himself "appeared to be greatly pleased at the intimacy" between them, although any intention he has of seducing Nathanael through the beautiful automaton is not revealed to the reader ("Sand-Man" 208, 209). Yet, the sequence of events that throws them together seems, somehow, fatefully predetermined. First of all, Nathanael is enrolled in Spalanzani's physics course. While Nathanael is away, his lodging house inexplicably burns down, and his friends, unbeknownst to him, move all of his belongings into an apartment that faces Spalanzani's. It is from this new dwelling that he is able to stare directly into Olimpia's room, and he resumes this activity with increased intensity after purchasing a small telescope from a mysterious peddler of spectacles and weather glasses named Coppola. This Coppola, whom he has met once before, reminds him uncannily of a long-ago character, the frightening Coppelius of his childhood. As Coppelius was something of his father's business associate, so Coppola is Spalanzani's partner of sorts. If Spalanzani has directed Coppola to sell his wares to Nathanael, no motivation for such entrapment is given; and Spalanzani, "that skillful mechanician and fabricator of automata," offers no explanation for his creation of Olimpia ("Sand-Man" 211).

Another character within the story, however, a certain professor of poetry and rhetoric, offers the suggestion that "the whole thing is an allegory, a continuous metaphor." The narrator of "The Sand-man" goes on to say that many "did not rest satisfied with this explanation; the history of this automaton had sunk deeply into their souls, and an absurd mistrust of human figures began to prevail" ("Sand-Man" 212). The doll Olimpia can be identified precisely as a metaphor or an extended analogy for human behavior, and the reactions to her existence suggest an explanation not only for the powerful impression and the unrest occasioned by her automated presence but also for the issue of why the double is sometimes a source of fear but at other times not. Meltzer, creating her own extended metaphor or allegory to explain Olimpia's being, describes her as a representation of "the machinery of psychoanalysis . . . the psychoanalytic machinery of destiny": "The irony is that psychoanalytic destiny becomes an inexorable machine of predictably moving parts, precluding all randomness—a machine of which the doll Olympia becomes the 'living' metaphor. . . . For there can be no arbitrariness in an automaton, its 'chance' behavior 'resolved into laws.'"[49] The uncanniness of this image puts Olimpia's role as fear-invoking automaton into the proper perspective.

That Olimpia is a machine makes her more fearful than an inanimate double would be. Her ability to dance and nod in acquiescence, however facile, aligns her more closely with her human audience than any stationary replica or mannequin. To Nathanael's psyche, she may be "a regressive substitute for the flesh-and-blood fiancée," but, in her elaborate construction, she is a progressive and impressive example of automated craftsmanship: "the automaton aroused an existential dread in Hoffmann's generation somewhat analogous to the fascination with thinking computers or androids in our own time. . . . The robots of [Hoffmann's] time, crude as they now seem, aroused doubts as to the primacy and uniqueness of human life and intelligence."[50] Representing more than the deterministic lack of will that is often captured in stringed puppets or marionettes, the automaton inspires questions such as Victor Frankenstein's "Whence . . . did the principle of life proceed?" and What causes "the change from life to death, and death to life"? (Shelley 50, 51):

> The automaton calls attention to the "dead machine" which the physical body in fact is, and it arouses new confusion as to what it is (perhaps electricity?) that enlivens it. . . . The actual automaton, like the computer, may be imbued with a cold, selfless spirit, mocking the human machine with its poorly incorporated and poorly controlled animating fluid.[51]

Frankenstein himself claims to be "animated by an almost supernatural enthusiasm" (Shelley 50), and it is this supernatural energy that he and Spalanzani seek to impart to their postnatural, precultural automatons. While Frankenstein—by projection (as much as by any mysterious transference of electricity)—animates his own object, Spalanzani's creation is animated by Nathanael's projection as well as by the hidden internal mechanisms inserted by the clockmaker. Nathanael, for example, when discussing his poetry with Olimpia, "fancied that she had expressed . . . the identical sentiments which he himself cherished deep down in his own heart, and even as if it was *his own heart's voice* speaking to him" ("Sand-Man" 209, emphasis added).

The automaton, once properly animated, has the ability to encroach—

whether invited or not—ever so slightly upon human territory. Trespassing in this way and inadvertently mocking the human machine are the wrongs, existential if not social, committed by Olimpia at the formal ball. Spalanzani's "cunning piece of knavery" is an even greater crime: "it was an imposture altogether unpardonable to have smuggled a wooden puppet . . . into intelligent tea-circles." Yet, the lawyers find it a difficult crime "to punish since it was directed at the public; and it had been so craftily contrived" ("Sand-Man" 211).

Sherry Turkle, in her discussion of Lacan's impact on contemporary culture, makes a similar observation regarding the issues of artificial intelligence, chance, laws, and free will. Her commentary on computers and computer metaphors is applicable as well to automatons and the metaphors occasioned by a walking, talking, life-sized doll:

> The growing presence of increasingly "intelligent" computers in everyday life has given the whole question of free will a new salience. Our culture is just now starting to meet the idea of "artificial intelligences" in the plans of industrialists, educators and toymakers. . . . Computer metaphors for thinking about people . . . are just now starting to make their way into the popular culture. A lot of people are reacting to intelligent machines and to machine images for thinking about people by asserting the opposite: that people can never be captured in code, in program. . . . [T]hey insist that people, unlike the machines, are not deterministic systems . . . that there is free will, an acting ego that slips through the net of science.[52]

The threat presented by the intelligent machine is what disturbs Olimpia's onlookers. Spalanzani has succeeded in capturing and encoding a number of social gestures, and despite the insults hurled Olimpia's way, her human betters are astonished to see their own behavior caught in the net of Spalanzani's science and to witness their own egoism mimicked by a mechanical doll. In Hoffmann's story, society is satirized as a series of predictable, automatized functions such as afternoon teas and dances, which are as uninspired as Olimpia herself. Nathanael, though enamored of Olimpia, is in conflict with the mechanistic social scene. He is wary, even fearful, of "this lifeless world of cuckoo clocks . . . this apparently smoothly running machinery."[53] This assertion of Nathanael's fear is in opposition to Freud's observation that while "The Sand-man" deals with early childhood fear, "the idea of a 'living doll' excites no fear at all" (Freud 233). Olimpia, the living doll, personifies (so to speak) the world of automata, clockmakers, eyemakers, and doubles by which Nathanael is haunted. He fears the likelihood that he too could become automated or dismembered, his vitality displaced by machinery.

This is a fear that Nathanael experiences twice in his life: initially when he fears as a child that he will be blinded and dismembered, and finally when he witnesses the blinding and dismemberment of his beloved Olimpia. The first occasion is his terrorization by the "Sandman"—his father's associate Coppelius, who treats the young Nathanael like an automaton. From this frightful occasion onward, Nathanael fears that he (like Frankenstein's monster) is the other, a piece of clockwork with no soul. This repressed nightmare of childhood recurs when Nathanael first encounters Coppola, the eyeglass salesman who reminds him of Coppelius. Nathanael's friend Lothair counsels him with an explanation that bears an uncanny resemblance to Freud's descriptions of the return of the repressed. Lothair describes a phantom self who exercises control over the soul: "If we have once voluntarily given ourselves up to this dark physical power, it often reproduces within us the strange forms which the outer world throws in our way, so that thus it is we ourselves who engender within ourselves the spirit which by some remarkable delusion we imagine to speak in that outer form" ("Sand-Man" 192).[54] This advice guides him to discern (perhaps mistakenly) that his instinctive fear of Coppola "proceeded only from himself, and Coppola was an honest mechanician and optician, and far from being Coppelius's dreaded double and ghost" ("Sand-Man" 203). But later, when Nathanael finds Coppola and Spalanzani fighting over Olimpia, the influence of the repressed nightmare is too powerful to resist. They are the outer forms by which the unsettling memory of Coppelius—be it dream, delusion, or history—is once again presented to him. Lodged in his memory is the fear he felt when the old Coppelius threatened to remove his eyes and "laid hold of me, so that my joints cracked . . . a sudden convulsive pain shot through all my nerves and bones; I knew nothing more" ("Sand-Man" 188).

The second instance of uncanny fear, which summons forth the threat of automation, occurs upon a chance visit to Olimpia. Overhearing an argument between Spalanzani and Coppola/Coppelius, Nathanael rushes in to confront the vision of horror that has haunted him since childhood. The frightening tale that the Sand-man might steal his eyes (or that Coppelius might steal Clara's eyes—an event narrated by Nathanael in one of his rather morbid poems) seems to have come true when he sees first Olimpia's pallid, empty face and then a pair of bloody eyes staring at him from the floor. "Impelled by some nameless dread," he struggles to prove that he is neither the wooden doll that Coppelius once toyed with nor the "inanimate puppet" that Olimpia is suddenly revealed to be. He sees Coppola throw the now blinded Olimpia over his shoulder and "laughing shrilly and horribly, [run] hastily down the stairs, the figure's ugly feet hanging down and banging and rattling like wood against the steps" ("Sand-Man" 210). Overwhelmed by the resemblance between his own frightful nightmare and Olimpia's cruel fate, his determination to assert his self-consciousness, even his consciousness, is undone once again. Experiencing the same dark, convulsive pain, he flies first into an insane rage but soon faints, not to reawaken for some time. As a child, he recovered from his swoon "as if out of the sleep of death" to find his mother bending over him; this time he wakes "as if he had been oppressed by a terrible nightmare" to the mental comfort provided by Clara ("Sand-Man" 188, 212).

The comfort she imparts is short-lived. Her soothing presence cannot relieve the threatening sense of alienation and instability that Nathanael experiences. He fears Clara, as he did Olimpia, because her lack of passion suggests to him the possibility of his own automation—as well as hers. As an "object-representation," a "narcissistic object," a "self-object," and an "unremitting" admirer of Nathanael's artistic self, Clara stands in juxtaposition to Nathanael's "self representation."[55] Like Olimpia, Clara is known as a simple girl who exhibits a nearly feelingless calm. Whereas Nathanael found Olimpia's monosyllabic responses inspiring, he finds Clara's more sensible, intelligent remarks to be quite commonplace. He resents her for being cold and unimaginative. He sees death in her eyes, for, like Olimpia, she sits "with her eyes fixed in a set stare" upon his face. He even calls her a "damned lifeless automaton!" Similar to the artificial beauty and perfection of Olimpia's form, Clara's figure is thought by some to be "almost too chastely modelled" ("Sand-Man" 200, 196). Perfection is appreciated no more in a living character than it is in an automaton.

From her debut until her destruction, Olimpia is criticized for being too nearly perfect. She dances with "perfectly rhythmical evenness," and Siegmund observes that "'her playing and singing have the disagreeably perfect, but insensitive timing of a singing machine, and her dancing is the same. . . . [S]he seemed to us to be only acting *like* a living creature, and as if there was some secret at the bottom of it all'" ("Sand-Man" 206, 208). After Olimpia's demise, it becomes more socially acceptable to "sing and dance a little out of time" and to "do something more than merely listen" ("Sand-Man" 212). To exhibit perfection is considered untrustworthy, insensitive, and inhuman.

In an earlier tale of the suspicion of perfection, Nathaniel Hawthorne's "Feathertop: A Moralized Legend," a character named Mother Rigby determines "to contrive as lifelike a scarecrow as ever was seen."[56] A cunning New England witch, she fashions the scarecrow's backbone from one of her broomsticks, thus imparting her magical skill to her creation. Deciding that her "fantastic contrivance" is capable of better things than standing "all summer in a corn-patch," she uses her necromantic arts to animate him, to "'make a man of [her] scarecrow, were it only for the joke's sake!'" She finds the scarecrow "better than any witch's puppet in the world" and assures it "that not one man in a hundred . . . was gifted with more real substance than itself" (Hawthorne 227, 232). Hawthorne's satire of society's parlors and tea parties is similar to that presented by Hoffmann in "The Sand-man." Like Spalanzani's Olimpia, Mother Rigby's Feathertop (as she christens her puppet) behaves "exceedingly like a human being" and has the vocabulary necessary for social success among those whose goal is complete artifice: "'Really! Indeed! Pray tell me! Is it possible! Upon my word! By no means! Oh! Ah! Hem!'" (Hawthorne 234). Instead of clockwork, however, Feathertop is animated by pipe tobacco. As Cinderella must remember to leave the ball by midnight, Feathertop must never let the fire in his pipe go out.

Like Olimpia, Feathertop is nearly too perfect, creating a distinct uneasiness in his human companions. Like "anything completely and consummately artificial, in human shape," he impresses his audience "as an unreality." He is an uncanny embodiment of the suspicion of perfection: "every motion and gesture . . . came in its proper place; nothing had been left rude or native in him; a well-digested conventionalism had incorporated itself thoroughly with his substance and transformed him into a work of art. Perhaps it was this peculiarity that invested him with a species of ghastliness and awe" (Hawthorne 242). Despite the uncanny awe he occasions, his "insinuating elegance" assures his place in high society until he catches a glimpse of himself in a mirror (Hawthorne 241). In the mirror, he sees a reflection not of the refined gentleman but of the patched-up scarecrow. For Feathertop—the "wretched simulacrum!"—the sight of his true self is a vision of horror, which obliterates entirely his will to live. No longer able to pose as human, he is "an Illusion [that] had seen and fully recognized itself." He debates his own right to existence and flings away the pipe that had sustained the illusion of his humanity (Hawthorne 244).[57]

Olimpia and Feathertop share the ability to pass as human. Shelley L. Frisch writes that "Freud considered it irrelevant to debate the illusion of Olimpia's humanity, because establishing whether she is in fact living or a mere automaton does not address the *effect* of the uncanny on Nathanael."[58] But Cixous asks the thought-provoking questions: "And what if the doll became a woman? What if she *were* alive? What if, in looking at her, we animated her?"[59] While it is true that the uncanny "is uniquely linked to the sentiments of the characters [e.g., Nathanael] and not to a material event defying reason [e.g., the creation of Olimpia]," the uncanny is dependent in great part upon fear—which is the sentiment experienced by Nathanael as his involvement with Olimpia deepens.[60] Thus Olimpia's uncanny and fearful effect on Nathanael is indeed directly related to the question of her humanity, just as Clara's impact on him is related to the issue of her *in*humanity. At the story's conclusion, Clara's character has been undermined by, and Nathanael has succumbed to, the threat of inhumanity embodied in Olimpia (whom, in fact, Nathanael *was able to animate*—by the projection of his own needs and fears, and *by looking at her*). The Sand-man reappears and "Nathanael behaves like an automaton . . . as if Coppelius were pulling his puppet strings." Looking through the telescope at Clara, Nathanael's final vision of horror comes into focus: Clara "is for Nathanael the doll Olympia whom he thought destroyed. But the multiplication does not end there: He fears as well that she is *his* double."[61]

Nathanael, who did not create Olimpia, does not consciously seek out and choose dichotomy to the extent that Victor Frankenstein does. But, his trance-like recognition of a monstrous dichotomy is similar to Victor's encounter with his self-created monster. Victor "reacts as one would to a nightmare: he rejects his creation, flees from it, and attempts to forget about it. Victor knows at once that the Monster is his own bad dream . . . and he knows that the content of the dream is personal, domestic and sexual."[62] This nightmarish awakening, what Lacan calls the "sublimation of reality," is much like Nathanael's reaction when his telescope reveals the similarities between Olimpia and Clara. Lacan explains that "the object [Olimpia] usually stands in the place of the double [Clara] with which the ego [Nathanael] first identifies and through which he can still confuse himself with the other."[63] For Frankenstein, the object and the double are perpetually combined in the form of the monster; but for Nathanael the two merge only gradually.

E. T. A. Hoffmann: Other Fiction

The Sentimental/Gothic dualities that inform Nathanael's perception of events are both "terrible and terribly familiar," that is, they are uncanny.[64] Working out of German romanticism and the fantastic, Hoffmann has created a contradictory, deterministic, dichotomous, *other* world, peopled by a persistently unusual and striking assortment of doppelgängers (such as Nathanael/Olimpia, Olimpia/Clara, and Clara/Nathanael). Fulfilling or frustrating in varying degrees the need to fill the void created by the missing object, these characters alternate between good and evil, brightness and darkness, fantasy and reality, stability and insanity, joy and melancholy. In addition to the tortured triangle of Clara, Nathanael, and Olimpia, numerous other characters from the tales of E. T. A. Hoffmann read, write, perceive, create, and then erase the other in a haunting variety of ways. Of particular interest are the predicaments of Deodatus Schwendy and George Haberland in "The Doubles"; Ferdinand and the Turk in "Automata"; and Professor Drosselmeier in "Nutcracker and The King of Mice." In each of these fictions, an other or a double is called into being and subsequently erased, absorbed, or otherwise done away with.

In Hoffmann's "The Doubles," the young traveler Deodatus Schwendy and the portrait painter George Haberland stand sandwiched between the parallel Lacanian mirrors. They suffer a reciprocal constriction of vision, and their egos cry out in protest. When Haberland's artist-friend Berthold expresses surprise at seeing George alive and describes to him the series of events that he thought had left George mortally wounded, George exclaims "with frenzied pain": "'Stop! You are stabbing my soul with glowing daggers! . . . [Y]es, brother Berthold it is very certain that I have a second ego, a doppelgänger, who pursues me, who wishes to do me out of my life and rob me of my Natalie.'"[65] In a similar fashion, when Natalie (admired by both members of the duo) refers to Schwendy as "'My George!'" the distraught Deodatus "cried in the madness of a mortal anguish and a fervent rapture, 'Mine—you are mine, Natalie! Believe in my ego. . . . [M]y ego lives. Natalie, just tell me if you believe in my ego, otherwise death will seize me right before your eyes. I am not called George, but I am still my own ego and none other'" ("Doubles" 305). Both men are overwhelmed by "a deeply ironical anger toward an unknown, remote arbitrary control under which one must strive to maintain one's own ego" ("Doubles" 275).

The tale's conclusion hinges on the convention of resolving the issue of the uncertain parentage and questionable legitimacy of the heir to the throne. As the truth of their mysterious childhoods and the mystical accounting for their identical appearances is revealed to them, the anger of the doppelgängers changes to horror and "sinister fear" ("Doubles" 313). Switched soon after birth, given new names, concealed and protected for political and personal reasons, each the cause of intrigue and confusion for the other—the young men do not meet happily. Haberland (discovered to be the young Earl or *Graf* Törny) rages, "'Ha, Fürst! Are you a doppelgänger come from Hell who has stolen my ego?'" Schwendy (revealed to be the sovereign prince, or *Fürst*) responds with equal ire, "'Why are you thrusting into my ego? . . . Let's see which one succeeds in getting rid of the doppelgänger—you shall bleed—bleed, if you are not a satanic illusion of Hell!'" ("Doubles" 313). The audience of courtiers and family members watches the confrontation with amazed uncertainty: "An oppressive uneasiness lay on the company; each searched his heart, wondering, 'Which one is the Fürst?'" ("Doubles" 311).

Or which one is the *first*, each ego asks. In their anger, Schwendy and Haberland strive to erase each other. The aggressive confrontation between them is a necessary step before each can form an image of his own ego and go his separate way. Lacan draws a connection between aggression and the formation of the human ego. He finds it to be an erotic and a self-alienating relation, which produces "the energy and the form on which this organization of the passions that he will call his ego is based."[66] Haberland and Schwendy, confused as they are by both strangers and friends (they can be distinguished only by a tiny hidden scar), see an image of the other that is too similar to the self. Not until they voice the emotions that will sever (or alienate) them from each other do they resume their distinct identities and proceed on to their separate callings: Schwendy as ruler, Haberland as artist.

In Hoffmann's "Automata," the distinction between self and other is clearly and vehemently expressed by Ferdinand's friend Lewis, who seeks to establish beyond any doubt that the Turk—that life-sized, life-like, speaking, multilingual, fortune-telling automaton—can in no way be identified with him or with any other human being. He expounds at length on the eerily inhuman nature of all man-machines, expressing his "repugnance to 'living puppets.'" He later declares that "'any human being's doing anything in association with those lifeless figures which counterfeit the appearance and movements of humanity has always, to me, something fearful, unnatural . . . about it'" ("Automata" 82, 95). It is their "staring, lifeless, glassy eyes" that impart the "horrible, eerie, shuddery feeling" that these creatures/creations evoke in him; and he traces his anathema to a waxwork exhibit that he was taken to as a child. From that time forward, he says, "'All figures of this sort . . . which can scarcely be said to counterfeit humanity so much as to travesty it—mere images of living death or inanimate life—are most distasteful to me'" ("Automata" 81).[67]

Despite Lewis's efforts to dissociate himself from the Turk and to convince Ferdinand to do the same, Ferdinand insists that they consult the Turk, and an incontestable connection presents itself: the Turk's apparent knowledge of Ferdinand's secret locket. Ferdinand, for his part, speaks favorably of a variety of automata. He does not sense them to be a threat to self, and he tells Ferdinand that the Turk is neither gruesome, ludicrous, nor repulsive. He advances the supposition—a stance finally adopted by Lewis as well—that the man-machine is actually no more than an elaborate disguise for a man, who is somehow able to hear the questions asked of the Turk and then formulate the puzzling and witty replies that have so mesmerized the crowd. The Turk has become well known primarily for "the spiritual power" that enables him "to read the very depths of the questioner's soul" ("Automata" 82). In the case of the Turk, reading the other is hearing or listening to him.

But even the open-minded and stout-hearted Ferdinand is unsettled by the "terrible prophecy" he hears ("Automata" 83). Not only does the Turk know of the secret locket, but he predicts for Ferdinand the eternal loss of the object of his desire. The Turk's role is similar to that of the Lacanian analyst, who replies to what he hears, returns something to the subject, and mediates the subject's recognition of his own drives. Jane Gallop describes the significance of both the reply and the return inherent in this process: "That reply sends back to the subject in inverted form (a reply being the inverse of the original statement) what he was saying . . . that he could never hear if he did not hear it returning from the analyst. . . . The analyst returns to the subject what the subject was saying so that the subject can recognize it and stop saying it."[68] Ferdinand inquires, "'Does this being which answers our questions acquire, by some process unknown to us, a psychic influence over us, and does it place itself in spiritual rapport with us?'" ("Automata" 92). And his question is not difficult to answer: Ferdinand has been placed in rapport with himself, with his own drive to comprehend the significance of his meeting with the mysterious woman whose portrait in miniature he carries in the secret locket, and with his desire to recapture the charm of that encounter. Of the reciprocal nature of sexual attraction, Lacan says that both partners must be more than "subjects of need, or objects of love. . . . [T]hey must stand for the cause of desire."[69] What truly drives Ferdinand is his desire to create desire in the unknown woman who created desire in him and recognized him, though he had never seen her before.

Gallop's comment, that "the subject must come to recognize his own drives, which are insisting, unbeknownst to him, in his discourse and his actions" accurately describes Ferdinand's state of mind.[70] Just as the locket, the objective correlative of his nostalgic desire, is unknown to all but himself, so the pervasive extent of the primary emotion (its insistence in his discourse and his actions) escapes even him. He feels that "every word relating to her uttered by any lips but mine would be a desecration of my secret" ("Automata" 86). The Turk's words inflict this pang of desecration, and Ferdinand says that his heart is broken by them. However, the most important question for him remains to discover the root of the Turk's knowledge or his source of information, for it is this access to the furthest reaches of Ferdinand's mind that convinces Ferdinand that he has encountered the other at the automaton exhibition—an other that he would prefer to erase.

Initially, Ferdinand is convinced that the Turk must have "powers at his command which compel our most secret thoughts with magic might" and a sense of second sight that allows him to behold "that germ of the future which is being formed within us in mysterious connection with the outer world" ("Automata" 83–84). This supernatural explanation seems so implausible, however, that he and Lewis seek to erase the power ascribed to the Turk by interviewing its inventor, Professor X—. They learn nothing about the clockwork of the mysterious automaton, and finally conclude that it is the professor himself who exercises some kind of telepathic connection with and power over Ferdinand's fate. Ferdinand is able to see the Turk only as automaton—or to use Lacan's earlier metaphor—as desk; he cannot accept it as ego. Thus, the Turk's otherness is erased through displacement. In conclusion, Lewis attributes the strange sequence of events to "the conflict of mysterious psychical relations (existing, perhaps, between several people) making their way out into everyday life . . . so that the deluded inner sense looks upon them as phenomena proceeding unconditionally from itself, and believes in them accordingly" ("Automata" 102).

Hoffmann's prose here calls to mind Lacan's description of the phallus—the *it* that "speaks in the Other, whether or not the subject hears it with his ear . . . by means of a logic anterior to any awakening of the signified" (the phallus, for Lacan, is the signifier whose function in the intrasubjective economy is to designate as a whole the effects of the signified). The other is thus "the very locus evoked by the recourse to speech in any relation [such as the "mysterious psychical relations" identified by Lewis] in which the Other intervenes."[71] Gallop clearly explains the Lacanian phallus as a linguistic concept:

> It is neither a real nor a fantasized organ but an attribute: a power to generate meaning. Language implies the ability to make meaning. But no speaking subject can, in reality, perform this generative act. And thus we grant this power to an ideal other . . . [who] is thus presumed to "know," that is, to speak and hear an unalienated language, which is the adequate expression of an integral self.[72]

This phallic other is at the center of discourse whereas the subject is unable to control language and can only "conform to that which comes from outside, from the Other." Whether in the form of Professor X— or the Turk, it is the other that Ferdinand fails to recognize, never fully comprehending what he hears nor grasping what it signifies. Ferdinand himself is the symbolically castrated subject who "can obtain no full satisfaction because the subject can never *know* what he wants because his 'wants' are alienated in language."[73]

A character who exercises a more refined control over the other is Professor Drosselmeier in "Nutcracker and the King of Mice." He creates, orchestrates, and erases not only his own other, but the other of his nephew (embodied in the Nutcracker) as well. He designs for his godchildren Maria and Fritz a miniature castle, complete in every detail, inside and out, including "very small but beautiful ladies and gentlemen. . . . A gentleman in an emerald green mantle came to a window, made signs, and then disappeared inside again; also, even Godpapa Drosselmeier himself (but scarcely taller than papa's thumb) came now and then, and stood at the castle door, then went in again" ("Nutcracker" 133). Fritz is soon disillusioned with the ingenious mechanism, demanding a closer alignment than is possible of the other with the self. He requests that the miniature Drosselmeier and the man in green come out onto the castle lawn. Drosselmeier explains the impossibility of this ("'The machinery must work as it's doing now; it can't be altered you know'"), and Fritz offers his assessment: "'Very well, then . . . I'll tell you what it is. If your little creatures in the castle there can only always do the same thing, they're not much worth, and I think precious little of them!'" ("Nutcracker" 134). Drosselmeier is annoyed of course, but actually Fritz shares his motivation for power and control. The boy's disillusion is caused not so much by the limitations of the toy palace as by his own lack of control over it—control that lies in Drosselmeier's hands. Fritz, on the other hand, prefers his non-mechanical toy soldiers precisely because he can maneuver them himself. His preference exemplifies a significant connection between the toy world and the struggle for control: "To toy with something is to manipulate it, to try it out within sets of contexts, none of which is determinative. . . . The desire to animate the toy is the desire not simply to know everything but also to experience everything simultaneously."[74]

Stewart investigates the motivations and artistic agendas of master automaton creators, giving particular attention to their creation of toys and to the toy's relationship to fiction, narration, and narrative time. The mechanical toy is thrilling and frightening "because it presents the possibility of a self-invoking fiction, a fiction which exists independent of human signifying processes"; for Maria, the animated toy world created by Drosselmeier is an interior space of privacy and fantasy.[75] The story, which is built around motifs of holiday sweets, glittering decoration, remarkable toys and figures such as the wooden Nutcracker, "is delicate and of miniature proportions." Although Maria is the only character to witness the battle between the Nutcracker and the King of Mice, that mythical world, even though it is one of warfare, does not "crash through" into her life. The sinister elements of the conflict are softened by "the diminutive size of the assailants, and the identity of the assailed as toys."[76]

The miniature likeness of himself in the clockwork palace is the signature Drosselmeier gives to his work, the kind of self-representation that Umberto Eco calls a partial double or a homomaterial replica. Drosselmeier places a signature on his verbal art as well, including in the story he tells to Maria a character—"'the court Clockmaker and Arcanist—whose name was the same as mine—Christian Elias Drosselmeier'" ("Nutcracker" 153). This is the self-invoking fiction that he has developed to complement his material creation. The interpolated "Story of the Hard Nut" becomes inextricably connected with the larger tale of the Nutcracker, and Fritz and Maria—as elements from one tale (the valiant Nutcracker doll, the seven mouse crowns) appear in another, crossing with ease the boundaries of the various fictions. The storybook Drosselmeier, double of the children's godfather, has a handsome nephew who is turned into a nutcracker at the story's end; the "real" Drosselmeier has a nephew who arrives to tell Maria of his unfortunate experiences as a handsome courtier mistakenly turned into an unattractive nutcracker. Thus the nephew and the nutcracker of the inner tale are absorbed by their others, the nephew and nutcracker of the outer tale; and when the storytelling is complete, one Drosselmeier is absorbed or erased by the other.

Lacan's Discourse of the Other proves an effective method of investigating the psychological implications and manifestations behind the creative impulse of a character such as Drosselmeier who re-creates reality and fashions a miniature in his own image. Drosselmeier, the gentle Maria, the impertinent but imaginative Fritz; Professor X— and his Turk, the puzzled Ferdinand and the introspective Lewis; the doppelgängers George Haberland and Deodatus Schwendy; the Sand-Man, Coppola, and Coppelius, Nathanael and Clara, Spalanzani and Olimpia—these are just a few of the many examples of doubles and others in the work of Hoffmann that can be profitably expanded upon and opened up with Lacanian analysis. There are numerous methods of creating or reading the other and as many motivations for destroying or erasing it. And, as Lacan points out, beginning with the initial fascination with the mirror image, the recognition of seeing and hearing, the identification of reading, and the alienation of erasing the body and the other are all necessary components of self-perception and ego-formation.

The Double in the Nineteenth Century

The preoccupation with re-creating and animating the human form, especially in miniature, is mirrored in any review of classic nineteenth-century works. Miyoshi, in a discussion of Gothicism, refers to "the sudden plethora of dual-personality stories" in the late nineteenth century, attributing the phenomenon in part to the popularity of *Dr. Jekyll and Mr. Hyde* and *The Picture of Dorian Gray*.[77] An overview of some prominent works from the canon of dual-personality fiction would include, in addition to the titles mentioned above, Conrad's *The Secret Sharer*, Dostoevsky's *The Double*, and Poe's "William Wilson." However, there are numerous other examples that more precisely illustrate the particular subset of this theme dealt with here: the created material object as double. In his poem "The Harlot's House," a work not as well known as *Dorian Gray*, Oscar Wilde writes of "strange mechanical grotesques" who dance "like wire-pulled automatons":

> Sometimes a clockwork puppet pressed
> A phantom lover to her breast,
> Sometimes they seemed to try and sing.
> Sometimes a horrible Marionette
> Came out, and smoked it's cigarette
> Upon the steps like a live thing.[78]

After watching "the ghostly dancers" for some time, the narrator concludes that "'The dead are dancing with the dead, / The dust is whirling with the dust.'" These automata cross the boundaries that distinguish animate and inanimate, living and dead, canny and uncanny.

The fiction of the period contains a number of works in which the double appears in a more conventional form, that of the child's doll. In Dickens's *Bleak House*, for example, Esther Summerson remembers from "when [she] was a very little girl indeed" her beautiful doll whom she considered to be the one and only confidant of her solitary childhood—always patient, expectant, and comforting. Suggesting a self-reflexive analogy, Esther says that she was cast upon "Dolly as the only friend with whom I felt at ease. . . . I knew . . . that I was to no one upon earth what Dolly was to me."[79] Esther's doll falls into the category of inanimate figures described by John Carey as intrinsic to the work of Dickens: "The effigy, the picture, the thing with human lineaments which watches, paralysed and dumb—this supplies a major imaginative level in Dickens' novels which interacts with the human beings just as importantly as the human beings react to each other."[80] Yet strangely enough when Esther leaves Windsor for Reading, embarking upon the next stage of her life, she leaves the doll behind, having buried it under a shade tree in the garden.

In *Our Mutual Friend*, the doll's dressmaker, Jenny Wren, is herself a doll-like character. In fact, Jenny's paralysis makes her puppet-like and more like a doll than a child: "The situation is complicated because Jenny, who makes the perfect little replicas [effigies of well-dressed society ladies], is herself a cripple, and hates healthy children."[81] In George Eliot's *Mill on the Floss*, Maggie Tulliver sees her doll more as a scapegoat than a companion, driving nails through its head when she is angry at her aunt (though she later removes them and treats the "wounds" that she has created). Hall and Ellis attribute Maggie's behavior to the fact that "smallness indulges children's love of feeling their superiority, their desire to boss something and to gain their desires along the lines of least resistance or to vent their reaction to the parental tyranny of anger."[82]

Dante Gabriel Rossetti's ballad "Sister Helen" and Hardy's *Return of the Native* illustrate the tendency to use the self-created miniature as a source of power and revenge. In these works, both based on the old superstition that melting the wax image of a person will bring about suffering and death, adults rather than children indulge their anger and their desires by creating and then erasing the other. Sister Helen accomplishes the slow, cruel death of her faithless lover by fashioning a plump waxen man in his image and then letting it burn away. In Hardy's novel, the character Susan Nunsuch plans to obliterate Eustacia Vye by this same method. Susan creates the doll in Eustacia's image, and even dresses the miniature effigy to resemble Eustacia, giving it a dress, a red ribbon, a black hairnet, and a pair of sandals. The dressed figure becomes, symbolically if not actually, a metonymic reference existing between object/part and object/whole in which the part is of the material of the original. These works explore the divergence that comes about when the double, even in the form of doll or effigy, becomes sinister, when it serves as the agent of its creator's will, or when it takes on a will of its own in opposition to its creator—an inanimate object becoming too much like an animate one.

Carlo Collodi: *Pinocchio*

Perhaps the quintessential example from the turn of the century is Carlo Collodi's *The Adventures of Pinocchio* (1883), a narrative that relies on the "image of the human being as a puppet created by a Master Puppeteer."[83] Pinocchio's behavior is uncanny in the Freudian sense because he straddles the border of inanimate and animate, having acquired a will and a willfulness of his own. Similar to Frankenstein's monster, Pinocchio is born with a consciousness and with an awareness of the physical dissimilarity between himself and his maker. Though the story is often perceived to be exclusively for children, *Pinocchio* translator Nicolas J. Perella says that such a view overlooks "the tale's underlying linguistic sophistication and narrative strategy, its various levels of irony and sociocultural innuendo, or its satirical thrusts against adult society."[84] Like the work of Hoffmann and Shelley, Collodi's narrative is one that describes the subject's growing self-awareness and the process of his ego formation, one that reveals "the most intimate of psychological springs (that is to say, the most archaic and secret doll)."[85]

Pinocchio is a man-made doll, a hand-carved puppet that undergoes a miraculous metamorphosis. Throughout the tale, Pinocchio longs to become what he calls "a proper boy" instead of being, as he also calls himself, "a puppet without any sense . . . and without a heart."[86] Pinocchio has gradually become aware of his own shortcomings, even though he initially feels insulted by the Talking Cricket, which says, "'I really feel sorry for you . . . [b]ecause you're a puppet and, what's worse, because you have a wooden head'" (Collodi 111). Pinocchio's maker, Geppetto, and even the reader, join the Cricket in pity for the wooden doll when he dozes off in front of the fire and his feet catch fire and turn to ashes. Poor Pinocchio sleeps right through this disaster "as though his feet belonged to someone else" (Collodi 121).

After yet another scrape, Pinocchio laments, "'If I had been a proper boy, the way so many others are . . . I wouldn't find myself here now. . . . Oh, if only I could be born over again!'" (Collodi 245). Not only does he want to be born a second time, he also wants to grow from a boy into a man. When his friend, the blue-haired Fairy,[87] suddenly changes from a girl to a woman, he asks her to share the secret, expressing his own wish "to grow a little too." The Fairy disappoints him by telling them that this is impossible, that puppets never grow: "'They are born as puppets, they live as puppets, and they die as puppets.'" Pinocchio can hardly bear this news; in despair he cries, "'Oh, I'm sick and tired of always being a puppet! . . . It's about time that I too became a man'" (Collodi 283). Though he is made of wood and behaves as a perpetual boy, he is also the first to point out to those more "proper" human folk who would try to take advantage of him, "'Can't you hear that I talk and reason the way you do?'" (Collodi 323).

After the series of mishaps and near disasters that constitute the bulk of Collodi's narrative, the picaro's wish is granted. As it turns out, Pinocchio's "most abject and humiliating adventures [lead] finally to his redemption."[88] Exhibiting good sense and heartfelt sensitivity at last, he passes the ultimate trial of self-sacrifice and is transformed into a well-behaved and self-possessed adolescent boy. This new Pinocchio is the doll made man. The willfulness he exhibits as a puppet is a necessary requirement for the long-awaited transformation, but it is also an inhibiting factor that stands between "the old Pinocchio of wood" and the handsome, "proper" boy who takes his place (Collodi 461).

The puppet's stubborn arrogance—even before he is fully formed—is well documented by the narrator of the text. When he is still no more than a voice locked within a piece of wood, Pinocchio slyly makes fun of his maker's yellow wig, calling out "'Bravo, Polendina!'" (which means something like "Corn-top"). As soon as the wood carver Geppetto creates the puppet's eyes, he senses that they are looking at him spitefully; next, he carves out the "endless" and "impudent" nose that refuses to stop growing; and even before the mouth is completed, the bold puppet starts laughing and sticking out his tongue at his creator (Collodi 91, 97–99). Next, the rambunctious Pinocchio uses his newly made arms and hands to pull off Geppetto's wig and place it on his own head. Concerning this incident, Perella observes that Pinocchio's mocking disrespect is one of the characteristics that establish an equivalence between the puppet and a "real" or "proper" child. Perella also attributes the apparently voluntary lengthening of the nose to Pinocchio's "aggressive self-assertion."[89]

Geppetto responds sadly to his creation's insolent behavior. With tears in his eyes, he says: "'Scamp of a child, you aren't even finished and you're already beginning to lack respect for your father! . . . And to think that I worked so hard to make him into a nice puppet!'" (Collodi 101, 105). The craftsman sees his animated handiwork as both child and artifact. Geppetto has made Pinocchio in his own image, but Pinocchio longs only to dissociate himself from his maker and to carve out his own domain of experience. To use Stewart's phrase, he is "the automaton [that] repeats and thereby displaces the position of its author."[90]

As the creation of the other by characters within the narrative can be analogous to the novelist's creation of characters, Collodi's creation of Geppetto is paralleled by Geppetto's creation of Pinocchio. Hoffmann's story "The Doubles" (see above) also offers a commentary on the relationship between puppet and puppeteer. It features a traditional traveling puppet show, in which the puppet "Punch" performs "in the customary Italian manner . . . saving himself from dangerous situations with skill, and always getting the upper hand over his enemies." When the show is nearly over, "the puppeteer, with a fearfully distorted expression, stuck his head up into the puppet stage and stared out at the audience with lifeless, glazed eyes." Punch and another puppet discuss this apparition or "monstrosity," finally interpreting it as a "synecdoche" for the whole human form. The more astute members of the audience soon notice "that this was not the kind of joking that amuses curious folk, but that it was the dark spirit of the irony which arises in the person whose soul is at war with itself." The "droll puppeteer," of course, turns out to be one of the doubles of the title ("Doubles" 286–87).

As Angela Carter has observed, the puppeteer is noted for vitalizing "inert stuff with the dynamics of his self" (Carter, "Lady Purple," 254). This is precisely what Geppetto accomplishes, with one notable exception: although he does give Pinocchio form, he does not give him life. The fact is that Pinocchio is not created of "inert stuff"; instead of simply carving Pinocchio from an inanimate chunk of wood, what Geppetto does is free him—by giving him human form—from the piece of wood in which his vital spirit is imprisoned. When the carpenter, Master Cherry, wants to turn this wood into a table leg, the spirit protests: "Don't hit me so hard!" "Ouch! you've hurt me!" "Stop! You're tickling my belly!" (Collodi 83, 85, 87). However, when Cherry turns the living bit of wood over to Geppetto, the trapped spirit hails him gratefully and no longer resists the modification of his shape. Quite fortuitously, Geppetto's plan for the wood will release, animate, and give form to the mouthy spirit captured within.

The coincidence is almost too good to be true, for Geppetto comes to Master Cherry because he has decided to make himself "a fine wooden puppet; but a wonderful puppet who can dance, and fence, and make daredevil leaps. I intend to travel around the world with this puppet so as to earn my crust of bread and a glass of wine" (Collodi 89). The magically possessed piece of wood is, of course, perfect for this purpose. Also significant is Geppetto's motivation for such a project. Perella observes that what Geppetto has in mind when he first conceives Pinocchio is the creation of an "exploitable boy-adult."[91] The old man wants "someone who is so lacking in will or opinions that his movements are regulated by someone else. . . . From out of his poverty and his patriarchal vision . . . Geppetto wanted—a son who would be a puppet in his service."[92] As described above, traveling puppet shows and exhibitions of mechanical dolls and toys were popular entertainment in the eighteenth century, and Geppetto's plan to earn a living in such a way is an enterprising one. The mechanical puppet described by Loren Eiseley in "The Bird and the Machine" is exactly the type of doll that Geppetto hopes to create.

Although Geppetto never gets the chance to tour with his little wooden daredevil, Pinocchio himself goes to visit a puppet show right in his own home town. On his way to school for the first time, he is distracted by the noise and excitement of a carnival band, and, "burning with curiosity," he sells his spelling book for the price of admission to the "GREAT PUPPET SHOW" (Collodi 139). Despite the fact that Pinocchio has ventured into the world only one or two times since his birth by Geppetto's hand, he is apparently familiar, even well known, to all of the performing puppets—Harlequin, Punchinello, and Signora Rosaura. In a scene of uncanny déjà vu, the puppets all recognize "their brother Pinocchio" and interrupt their act to give him a joyous welcome (Collodi 143). Claiming that Pinocchio is "atavistically attracted" to the puppet show, Perella refers to this section as Collodi's "most inventive treatment" of the "twin vision of man-as-puppet": "When the ever-straying Pinocchio is irresistibly and atavistically drawn to the puppet show, the marionettes on stage ignore their predetermined roles and produce what amounts to a revolt in order to greet him enthusiastically as their brother-in-wood."[93] However, their disruptive and affectionate reunion is squelched by the entrance of Fire-Eater, the manager of the traveling show. When the domineering puppeteer arrives unexpectedly, the puppets become instantly mute and cease breathing altogether. They tremble before their angry and authoritative master, and order is restored. They are quickly reminded to do his bidding only when he pulls their strings—not to choose their own movements or create their own show. While Geppetto is merely disappointed to learn that his puppet is not subject to him, Fire-Eater is furious. He cannot abide having his position as master puppeteer usurped by such manifestations of independence and self-sufficiency.

The wooden puppets are seen to have an existence of their own, a consciousness apart from and beyond the control of Geppetto and Fire-Eater. Somewhere outside the human realm in which they serve as manipulated showpieces—that "no-man's limbo" described by Carter—they have will, motivation, and experiences that are independent of human signification and language (Carter, "Lady Purple," 254). In their unruly display of camaraderie, they are like children, and, as Perella points out, "Our idea of maturity and a workable social order necessitates the repression of the child whose amoral vitality and primordiality represent a threat to that idea. Thus we classify children and puppets as ontologically and socially inferior or inchoate beings who do not possess the fullness of humanity."[94] It is this vitality and uncanny primordiality that make the mechanical toy, like the child, frightening and thrilling to the human observer. Perella's suggestion that Fire-Eater's role is to prevent unchecked fantasy is consistent with the connection that Stewart makes between the power of fantasy and the properties of the self-animating creation: "But once the toy becomes animated, it initiates another world, the world of the daydream. . . . [W]e have the mechanical toy speaking a repetition and closure that the everyday world finds impossible. The mechanical toy threatens an infinite pleasure; it does not tire or feel, it simply works or doesn't work."[95]

Geppetto the woodcarver invents Pinocchio, but it is the puppet himself who in turn invents his own double, the human child who shares his name and assumes his new and improved identity. Noting certain similarities between the invention of the double or the self-created other and the creation of fiction, Cixous writes that fiction is "an anticipation of nonrepresentation, a doll, a hybrid body composed of language and silence that, in the movement which turns it and which it turns, invents doubles, and death."[96] Pinocchio is the self-invoking character in the self-invoking fiction; however, as the doll made man, he finally becomes subject to the human signifying system that as a man-made doll he managed so successfully to transcend.

When Pinocchio looks into the mirror to discover the reflection of a proper boy, he wonders where the old Pinocchio of wood has "gone to hide." Spotting his doppelgänger propped against a chair, his limbs dangling lifelessly, he exclaims—not, as one might expect, with aversion to this particular vision of horror but "with a great deal of satisfaction": "'How funny I was when I was a puppet!'" (Collodi 461). Perella finds the radiant, newly emerged boy to be "priggish and anomalous"; he wonders "who is more the puppet: the wayward and at times irreverent wooden marionette or the handsome boy-adult who takes hold of the golden cord, never to let go of it again."[97] This boy, so willing to conform to societal expectations, is hardly the real Pinocchio—he of the ceaseless adventures who now rests discarded and inanimate. Apparently even Collodi was uneasy with the evolved Pinocchio's smugness in scorning his forerunner and prototype. But as such, the ending stands.

The automaton has displaced his maker and is in turn displaced by his own double. Geppetto's wish for a magical puppet is granted and then displaced by the puppet's fantasy of becoming real. These alternative visions of the self are each accomplished at the expense of the other. Created beyond the limitations of human existence, Pinocchio strives to make his way inside those very boundaries. Ironically, it is the fulfillment of this desire that makes his own displacement inevitable. He has finally achieved "the realization of the desire which in itself obliterates a limit." This ultimate accomplishment binds the affirmation of life with the assertion of death: "All that assures satisfaction appears to affirm the life forces. All of that has another face turned toward death."[98]

As he himself once skipped away from the stricken Geppetto, Pinocchio—having successfully authored his own double—is also left behind by the hardy being who has stepped into his position. The tangled puppet is now the one abandoned and derided by the creature of his own, once active imagination.

The creative impulse that yields the material double in any of its various forms—automaton, miniature, doll, puppet, robot, giant—is never free of conflict. Collodi's tale of the puppet and the proper boy, Shelley's narrative of the monster and its maker, and Hoffmann's stories of the suspicious subject and the unwelcome other illustrate the conflicted relationships brought about by the double's initial creation and its ultimate erasure. Even the artistically fashioned miniature may exhibit the double's tendency to seek revenge, an impulse fully realized by Frankenstein's monster.

In the following chapter, works by Yeats and Lawrence illustrate how the doll becomes sinister in late nineteenth- and early twentieth-century literature. The miniature double thwarts the fictional character's search for a narcissistic ideal, another manifestation of Lacan's quest for the self in the other (one that differs somewhat from Nathanael's and Frankenstein's Faustian pursuit of knowledge).

3

The Doll as Icon:
The Semiotics of the Subject in W. B. Yeats
and D. H. Lawrence

Yeats: "The Dolls"

In "The 'Uncanny,'" Freud lists, among those "things, persons, impressions, events and situations that are able to arouse in us a feeling of the uncanny in particularly forcible and definite form . . . waxwork figures, ingeniously constructed dolls and automata" (Freud 226). This particular group of figures is uncanny in nature precisely because it contains replicas of a very specific form—the human body. The unique appeal of dolls to the psyche goes beyond the uncanniness of their ingenious construction and their resemblance to the human body to include the fact that most dolls are miniatures, miniature idealized bodies.

Freud discusses dolls as a significant element of childhood life, describing how children frequently maintain that their dolls are alive or that they themselves can make the inanimate dolls come to life. Rather than fearing that their dolls will come to life, many children hope that this will happen. The source of uncanniness here is described as "an infantile wish or . . . belief." Freud observes a possible contradiction in this apparent absence of fear, noting that "perhaps it is only a complication, which may be helpful to us later on" (Freud 233). Indeed, he does return again to the issue of infantile fears, wishes, and so forth, but not to the uncanny feelings excited by the idea of a living doll. It is to these very complications and contradictions that I will turn my attention, using Yeats's poem "The Dolls" as an illustration of the contradictions

65

that become apparent when the living doll or the created miniaturized double of the subject stands in juxtaposition with its creator and the complications that arise due to its creation, its existence, and its maker's expectations (or, perhaps, its expectations of its maker).

Naomi Schor (like Hélène Cixous, earlier) comments on Freud's inadequate explication of the "the theme of the doll" in Hoffmann's "Sand-Man." Schor, writing of "the thrilling terror" of Duane Hanson's life-size sculptures, says that Freud overlooks the three-dimensionality of Olimpia and "displaces sculpture in favor of literature." Thus the doll, the three-dimensional figure, and the references to it are all repressed and detail is sublimated. Taking the notion of the uncanny one step further, Schor asks a question that Freud does not answer: Wherein lies the pleasure of the uncanny? Regarding Hanson's figures she suggests that it is "the infantile pleasure that comes from taking the doll apart and seeing how it is made, in other words, the pleasure of the critic."[1]

It is, then, the pleasure of the critic not only to take apart Yeats's poem but to do so by looking closely at the living dolls that inhabit the dollmaker's house and at the role they play in relation to the human beings who live there as well—the dollmaker, the dollmaker's wife, and their newborn child. Particularly useful in such an analysis are Schor's aesthetics of detail, Stewart's study of the miniature and the gigantic, and Umberto Eco's definition of the material icon. Eco seeks to establish that "the so-called iconic signs are *arbitrarily* coded . . . and may be subject to a multiple *articulation*, as are verbal signs" while opposing the assumptions that "the so-called iconic sign has the *same properties* as . . . is *similar* to . . . is *analogous* to . . . is *motivated* by its object."[2]

Eco deals with the issue of what properties of the denoted object the sign must possess in order to be considered iconic. The dolls in Yeats's poem may be considered iconic in that they possess "optic (visible)," "ontological (supposed)," and "conventionalized properties of the object."[3] Even by this definition, it is important to note, the dolls—the icons—have become the subject and their creator the object. What makes the dolls uncanny, in addition to this reversal of roles, is their property of animation, specifically their ability to speak (shared with the dollmaker and his wife) and their ability to cry (which they share with the child). Concerning such shared properties—and the reader's perception of them—Eco suggests "that in the iconic experience certain perceptual mechanisms function which are of the same type as the one involved in the perception of an actual object." He elaborates upon this proposition, however, by explaining "that iconic signs do not possess the 'same' physical properties as do their objects but they rely on the 'same' perceptual 'structure,' or on the same system of relations (one could say that they possess the same perceptual sense but not the same perceptual physical support)."[4]

"The Dolls," a poem about a dollmaker and the reaction of the dolls in his shop when a child is born to him and his wife, presents an unusual situation—one in which both the original *object* (to use Eco's term) and the icon do indeed require the same perceptual physical support. In fact, the dolls *demand* this similar mode of perception. The conflict of "The Dolls" is centered in the question of whether they are subject or object, and the poem contains what Freud has called "a particularly favorable condition for awakening uncanny feelings." He points out that "in their early games children do not distinguish at all sharply between living and inanimate objects, and that they are especially fond of treating their dolls like live people." But the adult apparently does not share this perception nor the pleasure derived from it. Quite the opposite, adults look for a clear delineation between the animate and the inanimate and become suspicious "when there is intellectual uncertainty whether an object is alive or not, and when an inanimate object becomes too much like an animate one" (Freud 233).

The dolls, who speak and see themselves as rivals to the newborn child, are perceived as uncanny because they are simultaneously inhuman and human, paradoxically striking the reader as inhuman to the very degree that they are animated (or "human"). Stewart describes this eerie sensation of the uncanny thus: "The dream of animation here is equally the terror caused by animation, the terror of the doll, for such movement would only cause the obliteration of the subject—the inhuman spectacle of a dream no longer in need of its dreamer."[5] The obliteration of the subject is clearly at stake in Yeats's poem, for we see dolls no longer in need of a dollmaker. Yet, while the dolls' animation is uncanny to the reader, it is the animation of the child that the dolls find threatening. They see themselves as subject and the child as object because their creation has preceded the child's arrival, and they are the ones who fear displacement.

The opening lines of the poem describe the dolls' outrage at what has come to pass:

> A Doll in the doll-maker's house
> Looks at the cradle and bawls:
> "That is an insult to us."
> But the oldest of all the dolls,
> Who had seen, being kept for show,
> Generations of his sort,
> Out-screams the whole shelf: "Although

There's not a man can report
Evil of this place,
The man and the woman bring
Hither, to our disgrace,
A noisy and filthy thing."[6]

Their territory has been invaded by a baby or—to invert the concept—a *living* doll. For the dolls, the word *living* is entirely negative in connotation; the baby is "noisy and filthy" because he is alive, crying, eating, drinking, urinating, defecating, requiring the mother's constant attention, distracting the father from his craft, and usurping the privileged position of the dolls.

Though the dolls have acquired the ability to "bawl" and "scream," thus sharing the baby's capacity for noise-making, they do not share the bodily needs and functions that make him seem "filthy" to them. Instead, their being is contained and exists within what Stewart calls "the seamless body of the doll," which is not only free from the requisite physiological processes but is also "erased of its sexuality." The erasure of sexuality is accompanied by a lack of power in the idealized miniature. The dolls do not function, yet they exist as ideal representations of the human body: "The body becomes an image, and all manifestations of will are transferred to the position of the observer, the voyeur. The body exists not in the domain of lived reality but in the domain of commodity relations."[7] Yeats's dolls are commodities; they are the source of livelihood for the dollmaker, a fact attested to by the oldest doll, who is "kept for show" and has seen many others sold. And it is true that these dolls live outside the domain of lived reality and outside of sexuality—the fear of power that they sense is the sexuality of the dollmaker and his wife. They proclaim the living, breathing baby an "insult" to their seamless bodies, and their annoyance is couched in the suspicion that the sexually created child of the man and the woman will outrank the dolls themselves—mere sexless re-creations that the dollmaker has built in his own image. The primary emotion that informs their outrage is fear, fear of sexual procreation.

In these self-created miniatures, the body does become an image, but the dolls in Yeats's poem maintain, rather than lose, the full expression of their own will. They inadvertently express the very fears from which their seamless bodies should free them, the fears from which the voyeur is freed when he looks upon the sexless body of the doll or the miniature or the child dressed as adult. But these outraged dolls have *become* the voyeurs; they are the observers, spying and eavesdropping on the husband, wife, and child. They are icons, not the body-made-object but the body-made-subject (or, more specifically, the object-made-subject by virtue of animation). Eco describes the significance of such semiotic transference in the designation of a sign as iconic. He says that "transformation seems to be, as yet, the best operational explanation of the impression of iconism." He emphasizes transformation over patterns of "similarity" and "analogy" (though in a passage peculiarly applicable to the conflict expressed in Yeats's poem, he calls analogy "a sort of native and mysterious parenthood between things or between images and portrayed things").[8]

Eco explains that, while the mirror image is intrinsic to identification, integration, and ego formation, it is not an icon itself. He distinguishes clearly between icons and specular reflections or mirror images, replicas or doubles, and empathic stimuli. He rules out the reflected mirror image as "pure visual matter" and says that a "double is not the icon of its model-object *except* in a very specific case: i.e. when an object is chosen as an ostensive sign in order to visually describe the character of every object of the same class."[9] Reminiscent of the Lacanian Gaze, is what Eco calls the "absolute icon":

> This virtual duplication of stimuli (which sometimes works as if there were a duplication of both my body as an object and my body as a subject, splitting and facing itself), this theft of an image, this unceasing temptation to believe I am someone else, makes man's experience with mirrors an absolutely unique one, on the threshold between perception and signification. And it is precisely from this experience of absolute iconism that the dream of a sign having the same characteristics arises.[10]

In fact, these descriptions seem to establish the place of the dolls as both double and icon. The dolls view the baby as representative—an ostensive sign—of what they object to in an entire class of beings; thus the dolls, particularly the one who initially "Looks at the cradle and bawls: / 'That is an insult to us,'" and the baby are doubles. On the other hand, the dollmaker has chosen the oldest doll for the iconic purpose of being "kept for show"—to visually describe every other doll, generation after generation, who passes from his workbench out of the shop. The very word "Generations" in the sixth line of the poem articulates the roles played and shared by the dolls and the child: they have all been fathered by the doll-maker; they all are products of his experience.[11]

The oldest doll then is both the double and the icon of its model-object, the baby. But it is the doll, not the baby, who possesses the idealized, model body that denies the possibility of death and transcends mortality. Viewing the doll as an object of desire illuminates the relationship between the physical generation of the dollmaker's newborn child and the generations of dolls he has crafted. Unlike these handcrafted objects of desire, the living baby is a creature of mutability, subject ultimately to death. The doll-maker's product is "the body-made-object . . . the body as potential commodity, *taking place* within the abstract and infinite cycle of exchange."[12] In Yeats's poem, the model body and the body of lived experience stand in juxtaposition. The dolls, as idealized commodities of exchange, are also subject to lived experience. This experience—their memory, their ability to comprehend the continuity of existence, their sense of passing time—is the source of both their power and their chagrin. They are "insulted" and "disgraced" because they are forced to confront the temporal nature of their animated existence.

They are disturbed not only by the realization that they stand to lose what the baby has to gain but also by the uncomfortable knowledge that they stand to lose exactly what he has to lose. His wailing presence serves as a reminder that they may not be transcendent, may not be immortal. As dolls they would be, but not as *living* dolls. Their idealized bodies deny the possibility of death, but their animated psyches reopen the possibility of mortality. Freud discusses the "infantile" motivation of overaccentuating "psychical reality in comparison with material reality" and describes the connection between "animism" and the uncanny effect that is "produced when the distinction between imagination and reality is effaced, as when something that we have hitherto regarded as imaginary appears before us in reality, or when a symbol takes over the full function of the thing it symbolizes" (Freud 244).

Not only does the dolls' ability to express anger efface the boundary between imagination and reality for the reader, but the elimination of this distinction is disconcerting to the dolls as well. They resist taking over the *full* function of the child (the thing they symbolize); they appropriate the privilege of expressing themselves while eschewing the less appealing physical properties of noise and filth—what Jane Gallop has called the "messy, carnal world of the nursery."[13] They choose psychical over material reality, even though their value (to the dollmaker, to his customers) resides in their idealized, material bodies.

The value of either the real or the ideal body is determined by social conventions that reflect a scale of measurement and a scale of values. Stewart says that the "body is culturally delimited" and the miniature body, in particular, is a culturally overcoded phenomenon.[14] The icon, on the other hand (both Eco and Riffaterre stress this point), portrays semantic knowledge and is semiotically overdetermined. Such overdetermination can be attributed to the conflict between cultural habits and iconic representation. The doll as icon transcends the limits imposed on its double, the human child. Even the child's mother accepts the harsh judgment of the dolls that the baby is a troublesome disgrace:

> Hearing him groan and stretch
> The doll-maker's wife is aware
> Her husband has heard the wretch,
> And crouched by the arm of his chair,
> She murmurs into his ear,
> Head upon shoulder leant:
> "My dear, my dear, O dear,
> It was an accident."

Implicit in the concluding line is the ultimate distinction between the child and dolls: the dolls are not, could not possibly be, created by accident. They are crafted painstakingly and deliberately. The icon, the body made subject, may be arbitrarily coded and subject to multiple articulation, but it is never an accident. And, as this poem aptly illustrates, the icon need not be motivated by its object. The dolls in Yeats's poem, the subjects, not only predate the existence of the child, the object, but maintain that their identity is distinct and separate.

When the critic pauses to take apart the doll as icon to see how it works, what comes to light is the ingenuity and the detail of the miniaturized ideal body. For Schor, "the modern fascination with the trivial, the playground of fetishism" is the forum for such investigation. Asserting "the detail's claim to aesthetic dignity and epistemological prestige," she says that "to focus on the detail . . . is to become aware . . . of its participation in a larger semantic network, bounded on one side by the *ornamental*, with its traditional connotations of effeminacy and decadence, and on the other by the *everyday* whose 'prosiness' is rooted in the domestic sphere of social life presided over by women."[15] In "The Dolls," Yeats accurately depicts both extremes of this semantic continuum, the dollmaker and the dolls representing the ornamental, the mother and child representing the everyday. Seeing the doll as icon provides a way to apprehend and understand the contradictions and complications that arise when the representatives of these two ends of the spectrum are granted the uncanny power to confront and be confronted by each other.

The dolls can also be viewed as an embodiment of what Julia Kristeva calls "the abject." This concept stems from the established meaning of the other as whatever exists as an opposite of someone or something else, or that which is excluded by something else; yet the abject describes a different entity than the object. Kristeva identifies the abject as having "only one quality of the object—that of being opposed to *I*."[16] However, in her approach to the concept of abjection, she focuses more on the quality of exclusion than on opposition, recognizing the abject as more similar to the subject than the object is. In fact, it is the undesired similarity between the subject and the abject that informs the subject's sense of abjection and motivates its forceful separation of itself from the abject.

Kristeva's notion of the abject is derived from an understanding of the other that is similar to the views held by Lacan. For example, Lacan has expanded his assertion that the unconscious is like a language by equating the unconscious of the subject with the discourse of the other. For both Lacan and Kristeva, the other, like language, "is always anterior to us and will always escape us, that which brought us into being as subjects in the first place but which always outruns our grasp."[17] Unconscious desire is both directed toward and received from the other. The abject, on the other hand, while it is related to and does proceed from the subject, is antithetical to desire. Not "an otherness ceaselessly fleeing in a systematic quest of desire," it is at once more deeply rooted in the subject and rejected by the subject. Rather than a ceaseless chase, it involves a ceaseless confrontation: "discourse will seem tenable only if it ceaselessly confront that otherness, a burden both repellent and repelled, a deep well of memory that is unapproachable and intimate: the abject."[18]

Kristeva describes the abject as a kind of "jettisoned object," standing apart from the subject yet distinct from the object. The abject is "radically excluded," the ego and the superego having combined forces to drive it away.[19] Seen in this light, the dollmaker of Yeats's poem is both ego (in relation to the child) and superego (in relation to the dolls). His role as dollmaker has merged temporarily with his role as father; and, much to the doll's dismay (and perhaps to the dollmaker's, as well), it is this second calling or responsibility that is given his immediate priority. Consequently, the dolls have been jettisoned, radically excluded.

The conflict between the dolls and their maker parallels the conflict between the abject and its master: The abject "lies outside, beyond the set, and does not seem to agree to the latter's [the superego's] rules of the game. And yet from its place of banishment, the abject does not cease challenging its master. . . . [I]t beseeches a discharge, a convulsion, a crying out." In the poem, one doll "bawls" while another "out-screams the whole shelf" in an angry and concerted effort to challenge the master and regain his undivided attention. Kristeva's analogy, "To each ego its object, to each superego its abject," is metaphorically drawn by Yeats— to each father his child, to each dollmaker his doll.[20]

Intrinsic to the concept of the abject is a well-defined sense of the improper/unclean, the loathing of "filth, waste, or dung," the turning away from "defilement, sewage, and muck." This is the loathing that the dolls have for the child, whom they perceive as filthy and disgraceful. They experience what Kristeva calls "the shame of compromise, of being in the middle of treachery. The fascinated start that leads me toward and separates me from them."[21] These ambivalent feelings and this ambiguous position mark vividly the uncomfortable situation in which the dolls feel bound and trapped. It is this very repugnance that inspires their clamor of disgust. Like Kristeva, who describes the repulsion that she felt as a child for the skin floating on the surface of the milk that her parents urged her to drink and the assertion of self that her refusal required, the dolls are in the "process of becoming an other at the expense of [their] own death." They "give birth to [themselves] amid the violence of sobs . . . without either wanting or being able to become integrated" into the "symbolic system" of the family unit; the "I"—the child of Kristeva's narrative, the outraged doll of the poem—"reacts . . . abreacts . . . abjects."[22]

For Kristeva, symbolic systems are normative positions and standardized value judgments, providing the means by which the subject learns to identify itself as distinct from other objects, such as the mother, within a sign system. The dictates of the symbolic order are always present, waiting to be encountered and recognized, a fact realized only gradually by the subject, whose earliest existence is rooted in another order—the semiotic. In contrast to the symbolic system, constantly challenging and being challenged by it, the semiotic order "refers to the actual organization, or disposition, within the body, of instinctual drives . . . as they affect language and its practice."[23] The dolls of Yeats's poem are similar to the resistant child of Kristeva's anecdote in their attempts to challenge the existing symbolic order, but paradoxically they also represent the order with which they are in conflict. The child's birth awakens them to a recognition of their own domain; their semiotic challenge to the symbolic is a confrontation not only with the dollmaker but, more significantly, with themselves. Each doll, desiring to partake of both orders simultaneously, is in conflict with itself, just as the two orders are in dialectical conflict with each other: "The semiotic is the 'other' of language which is nonetheless intimately entwined with it. . . . [I]t is bound up with the child's contact with the mother's body, whereas the symbolic . . . is associated with the Law of the father."[24] The child is the product of the mother, created by her (and by the father's) instinctual drives, whereas the dolls are the product of the law and order and judgment of the father as craftsman.

Kristeva shares with Lacan the idea that the father embodies the Law and the belief that language and experience can be ordered into two primary categories. For Lacan, these categories are the symbolic and the imaginary. The imaginary state, like Kristeva's semiotic order, is a condition in which the subject lacks any clear center of self; as the subject comes to perceive its own identity, determined by its relations of difference and similarity to the other subjects around it, the subject moves from the imaginary into the symbolic register, accepting the preexisting social codes and sexual roles that make up the various symbolic units (e.g., society, the family). Even though Yeats's dolls are the product of the craftsman's symbolic world, their existence—because of their ideal, material bodies—is one of the imaginary:

> The "imaginary," where loss and difference are unthinkable, where it seemed that the world was made for us and we for the world. There is no death in the imaginary, since the world's continuing existence depends upon my life just as much as my life depends upon it; it is only by entering the symbolic order that we confront the truth that we can die, since the world's existence does not in fact depend upon us. As long as we remain in an imaginary realm of being we misrecognize our own identities, seeing them as fixed and rounded, and misrecognize reality as something immutable.[25]

This summary of the imaginary realm accurately describes the life led by the dolls until the child's birth, when they suddenly comprehend that there are two modes of existence. Since they are not human (and thus not capable of ever being fully integrated into the symbolic system of the dollmaker's family), their self-perception has been accurate: their seamless bodies *are* fixed and rounded, and reality for them *is* immutable. However, when they venture to the border of the imaginary and question its juxtaposition to the symbolic, when the child's cry suggests that the world was made for more than them and that its continuing existence may not depend upon them—then their immutability is called into question and their death becomes a possibility.

The properties—"these body fluids, this defilement, this shit," to borrow Kristeva's list—that the dolls reject as signifiers of the baby's life (and his eventual death) are for the human child not symbols but indeed the requisite facts of existence: "Such wastes drop so that I might live."[26] Kristeva refines her discussion of the improper/unclean with the observation that "it is thus not lack of cleanliness or health that causes abjection but what disturbs identity, system, order. What does not respect borders, positions, rules." The newborn in Yeats's poem hovers at such a border; it is like the dolls in some ways but like their master, the dollmaker, in others. The dolls see the baby as "the in-between, the ambiguous, the composite."[27] They confront the child at a border between living and nonliving, a border that contains life and signification, a border of such mammoth symbolic and physically real proportions that it "has become an object." Kristeva examines the dilemmas of existence at this metaphorical border in terms of both birth and death. She describes the act of giving birth as a "strange form of split symbolization (threshold of language and instinctual drive, of the 'symbolic' and the 'semiotic')."[28] She describes the nonliving corpse for which all borders have been erased as "death infecting life. Abject. It is something rejected from which one does not part, from which one does not protect oneself as from an object. Imaginary *uncanniness* and real threat."[29]

Kristeva's definition of *abject* and the extent to which the subject is affected by abjection is related to Freud's notion of the Uncanny. Kristeva's denomination of the corpse as abject updates the belief that the dead and the living are enemies, and it offers a detailed explanation of why the corpse, the nonliving, must become the enemy of the living; it has crossed that all-important border and become a "thing that no longer matches and therefore no longer signifies anything." Having now become "the utmost of abjection," it remains an *other*. Yet—the question remains—an *other* in relation to what subject?[30]

Central to both theories is the confrontation of self and other. Such encounters are sometimes unexpected, sometimes unwilling, but at other times the "I" wills the meeting or involvement—or at least willingly embraces the confrontation with the other in one of its forms: object or abject. Kristeva writes from the ego's point of view: "I endure it [brutish suffering], for I imagine that such is the desire of the other. A massive and sudden emergence of uncanniness, which, familiar as it might have been in an opaque and forgotten life, now harries me as radically separate, loathsome."[31] Despite certain similarities, the uncanny and the abject are distinct sensations. As Kristeva points out, the state of abjection is characterized not by involuntary repetition and recognition but by a *lack* of repetition and a decided absence of familiarity. It is permeated by unfamiliarity: "Essentially different from 'uncanniness,' more violent, too, abjection is elaborated through a failure to recognize its kin; nothing is familiar, not even the shadow of a memory."[32]

Freud, however, insists on the significance of familiarity, recognition, and involuntary repetition in the subject's perception of the uncanny. The factor of involuntary repetition lends an uncanny atmosphere to events that would otherwise be perceived as mere chance or coincidence. Events that would otherwise be considered "innocent enough" are instead interpreted as "fateful and inescapable." In addition, involuntary repetition can recall "the sense of helplessness experienced in some dreamstates," the opaque, forgotten life described by Kristeva. Freud elaborates on these ideas, tracing them back to infantile psychology (he refers the reader to *Beyond the Pleasure Principle*) and to the "dominance in the unconscious mind of a 'compulsion to repeat' proceeding from the instinctual impulses." He draws the conclusion "that whatever reminds us of this inner 'compulsion to repeat' is perceived as uncanny" (Freud 237–38).

The dollmaker's creations are the product of this inner compulsion to repeat that motivates human beings to fashion objects in their own image. The dolls are uncanny as reminders of this compulsion and as inanimate bodies that have become too much like their animate originals. They are both uncannily like their creator and abjectly removed from his consciousness, artificial replicants that have somehow acquired the ability to express emotion. As uncanny doubles of the child, as icons, or as embodiments of the abject, their outcry is both captivating and distressing. In "The Dolls," they are the "me miserable treasure of the signifying act," as well as the subject or ego.[33] Their voices provide the "operating consciousness" of the poem, a role that is primary to the linguistic or semiotic conception of the subject. This operating consciousness simultaneously constitutes "the (transcendental) real object, and the ego (in so far as it is transcendent)."[34]

The dolls, designed by Yeats as the speaking subjects of the poem, perceive and express what the child is too young to know. They voice the parents' conflict, the anguish of the mother, the father's emotional distance from the event, and the distress that the child's birth has caused the family—the disruption of the symbolic order. The child exists as yet entirely in the semiotic realm, in relation to the mother, but the dolls, uncanny in their animation and iconic in their ideal form, traverse the semiotic/symbolic border, asserting their position as subject from a perspective of perfect outrage.

Outrage, horror, and loss characterize the abject. Nor is the abject restrained by the borders of self/other that define the subject's existence. When Kristeva specifies the characteristics of abjection, she emphasizes a sense of displacement, of searching for a space in which to feel certain of and secure in one's existence: "The one by whom the abject exists is thus a *deject* who places (himself), *separates* (himself), and therefore *strays* instead of getting his bearings, desiring, belonging, or refusing."[35]

The sense of loss and displacement experienced by the deject is a malaise dealt with in a number of modern fictions. In narratives such as "The Captain's Doll" by D. H. Lawrence, the characters who can be seen as Kristevan dejects thrust from themselves their idealized miniature mirror images—the abject in the form of the doll. These characters would readily posit, as Kristeva does, that "what is abject is not my correlative, which, providing me with someone or something else as support, would allow me to be more or less detached and autonomous."[36] Each doll is so like its subject that the correlation is inescapable; yet a closer look reveals that only by detaching themselves from the dolls do the characters gain the degree of autonomy necessary to live their own lives.

Lawrence: "The Captain's Doll"

"The Captain's Doll" is the story of Alexander Hepburn's search for a self and for a love relationship that is real—not ideal. He feels that he has suffered at the hands of the ideal—particularly others' literal and figurative idealizations of him, and he hopes instead to find a relational identity that is grounded in reality. In Lawrence's story, the ideal or model body of Hepburn is to be found in the form of a handmade doll, the creation of his lover, the Countess Johanna zu Rassentlow, who is called Hannele. He finds the doll so disturbingly like him that he is at once drawn to and repelled by it. Despite his fascination, in the end, his repulsion for the doll and what it represents dominates his behavior. Eradicating the doll's presence from their lives becomes a necessary step before he and Hannele can proceed to a shared life that is neither illusory nor imaginary. According to Stewart's theory, once the body becomes a image, all manifestations of will are shifted to the onlooker. The former self or subject becomes the observed object. This transferred point of view is particularly true in the case of the miniature: "The diminutive is a term of manipulation and control as much as it is a term of endearment." It is this transference or loss of will and control that so outrages and revolts Hepburn. His vital, physical presence has been transformed into "the seamless body of the doll."[37] Eco's notion of the partial replica and Michael Riffaterre's concept of dual signification also provide an understanding of Hepburn's struggle with himself and with his miniature double.

"The Captain's Doll" is in part a treatment of the gradually rising consciousness of both Hepburn and Hannele, as they struggle to distinguish the real from the ideal. In his essay "Psychoanalysis and the Unconscious," Lawrence explores, among other things, what is meant by the term "ideal" and whether or not the human personality is ideal in its origin. He grants that the developing human fetus "is an integral, individual consciousness, having its own single purpose and progression." However, "this consciousness obviously cannot be ideal, cannot be cerebral, since it precedes any vestige of cerebration." What is then a more important factor than consciousness is *will*, the will that governs the purpose and progression of development and that also "is the power which the unique self possesses to right itself from automatism."[38] In "The Captain's Doll" Lawrence illustrates these abstract concepts by opposing Hepburn's will with the idealized notions of him created first in his wife's mind (her romantic perception of him) and second by Hannele (her perfect re-creation of him in the figure of the doll). Hepburn himself says that he has been "insulted" by love and by the women in his life.[39]

He feels insulted by his wife, whose "denial of [his] living reality" is, according to F. R. Leavis, even more absurd than the doll, which represents for Hannele the "triumph of 'will' and 'idea' over reality."[40] The doll, having no will or consciousness of its own, is a material conception of the dollmaker's artistic consciousness (and later the doll itself becomes the subject of another artist's still-life painting). These configurations of Hepburn as doll affect both the consciousness and the unconscious of Hepburn as gentleman. He feels insulted and constricted by his small double, whose seamless body so resembles his own. Hepburn "is at a closed end; he is sewn up and going nowhere. Like the doll, his expression is characteristically blank . . . most of his actions are 'staged' and directed by others. Loving Hepburn, Hannele has literally made a puppet of him; and his wife . . . has implicitly done so."[41]

Finally "shocked out of his doll-like trance"[42] by his wife's accidental death, Hepburn reassesses his position and attempts to assert his will, his own unique self, against the artistic renderings of the doll and the still life. To him they are manifestations of the automatism and the "degradation from the spontaneous-vital reality into the mechanic-material reality [against which] the human soul must always struggle. . . . [W]hat tyranny is so hideous as that of an automatically ideal humanity?"[43] This question, which concludes Lawrence's essay, explains the force that Hepburn faces in "The Captain's Doll." Although the doll is lovely to behold, it is the tyranny of the doll that Hepburn resists. He feels that Hannele's icon of love is in fact a misrepresentation of him, a distortion of his true self. The enemy of human relationships in "The Captain's Doll" is "the trite dehumanizing conventions of the romantic tradition. And . . . far from being identified with women, these conventions victimize women as well as men."[44]

Indeed, Lawrence shows that both sexes are affected by patterns of dehumanization that tap into not only romantic love but any number of conventions. For example, religious and matrimonial issues, as well as romantic conventions, are at stake when Anna Brangwen in *The Rainbow* rebels against the tyranny she feels is portrayed in Tom's wood carvings, his idealized miniature of the Creation. He labors over it in "silent passion" and "infinite tenderness," but Anna does not care for it because she sees the artistic endeavor as the manifestation of Will's desire for "some form of mastery" in their marriage relationship. She objects to the disproportionate sizes of the primary figures: "She jeered at the Eve, saying, 'She is like a little marionette. Why is she so small? You've made Adam as big as God, and Eve like a doll. It is impudence to say that Woman was made out of Man's body when every man is born of woman. What impudence men have, what arrogance!'"[45] In response to this encounter, Will burns the Adam and Eve figures and with them the illusions of his early days of marriage. Likewise, after his wife's death, Hepburn attempts to realign his relationship with Hannele and to reestablish the terms on which it is grounded. Much of their conflict, too, stems from a question of proportion. When Hannele's friend Mitchka suggests that Hannele owes Hepburn a certain amount of respect because of his position in the army, Hannele exclaims, "'He isn't sacrosanct even then'"; he is not, after all, as large as God! (Lawrence 85).

When the story opens, Hepburn (whose wife at this time is still living) is a British officer, stationed in the same European town where Hannele and Mitchka (the Baroness Annamaria von Prielau-Carolath) reside as refugees after the first World War and work in their own small studio as seamstresses and dollmakers. The shop they run is a microcosm of the domain of *detail*, the private, domestic world of the miniature, with all of the aesthetic and epistemological connotations accorded it by critics such as Schor and Stewart. Lawrence describes the shop as a "studio where they made these dolls . . . and such-like objects of *feminine* art" (Lawrence 85, emphasis added). Schor indicates that the detail is bounded by the effeminacy of the ornamental and the prosiness of the everyday, the personal sphere of life presided over by women and often considered marginal beside the more authentic, collective social realm— the realm of the gigantic, which serves as "a metaphor for the abstract authority of the state and the collective, public, life."[46] The issue of commodity exchange within and between the worlds of the miniature and the gigantic is particularly applicable to the concerns of these dollmakers and their customers. When Mrs. Hepburn arrives in town to spend a vacation with Hepburn, she pays a visit to the shop where Hannele and Mitchka "make their bit of a livelihood" (Lawrence 102). Ostensibly looking for a souvenir to take back to England, the Captain's wife asks if she shall have to pay duty. No, explains Hannele, "'They don't charge duty on toys, and the embroideries *they don't notice*'" (Lawrence 87, emphasis added). Authority may be "invested in domains such as the marketplace," but, even as a place of exchange, the toy shop is apparently marginal.[47]

Mrs. Hepburn herself is well acquainted with the world of the miniature, the domestic, the ornamental. She dresses extravagantly, with careful attention to detail, and the story abounds with references to her finery—furs, feathers, rings, earrings, seed-pearls, lace handkerchiefs, white gloves, stylish hats, and the like. The narrator doesn't fail to note that her jewels tinkle "nervously," and Hannele's assessment of the Captain's wife is, "What a doll she would make herself! Heavens, what a wizened jewel!" (Lawrence 88, 108). The decorative nature of her appearance reflects, on a small scale, both the larger pattern of her life and what critic Eugene W. Dawson has described as "the tenuous and artificial contact" that she has with "'earthly' reality."[48] Much as she has made a decorative object of her body, she has furnished her house as a shrine to the ornamental. In fact, the Captain feels that her perception of the entire world around her is informed by this penchant for the souvenir and the collection. Stewart writes that objects of desire are classified into these two groups and that "under an exchange economy, the search for authentic experience and, correlatively, the search for the authentic object become critical." The significance of the souvenir is that it "offers a measurement for the normal and authenticates the experience of the viewer," while the collection presents a hermetic, autonomous world "which is both full and singular, which has banished repetition and achieved authority."[49]

Mrs. Hepburn's search for the objects of desire has been more successful than her search for authenticity. It is over her possessions that she has authority. Hepburn compares her existence—as an ornament surrounded by ornaments—to that of a bird in a cage filled with trinkets: "'But she loved the cage. She loved her clothes and her jewels . . . her house and her furniture and all that with a perfect frenzy'" (Lawrence 112). Dawson says that "Hepburn's attitude, at this point, toward his dead wife is a complex mixture of idealized, sentimental pity."[50] And Hannele feels that "there was something a little *automatic* in what he said" (Lawrence 110, emphasis added). He laments to her that his wife's "frenzy" of adoration for her favorite things was coupled with fear, "fear of everything—even all the things she surrounded herself with." Hannele, at a loss for a rejoinder, merely replies, "What other life could she have, except her *bibelots* and her furniture and her talk?" (Lawrence 113).

But Mrs. Hepburn's experience has not been confined entirely to the realm of the miniature. She well understands that beyond her world of *bibelots* lies a world of political power where value is determined on quite a different scale. Recounting her visit to the toy shop, she asks Hepburn, with condescension if not with malice, "Baroness, Countess, it sounds just a little ridiculous, when you're buying woollen embroideries from them. . . . After all, what is the good, what is the good of titles if you have to sell dolls and woollen embroideries'" (Lawrence 91). She observes that to trade on a valid title would constitute greater authority in the political world than running one's own small shop does.

Dawson describes Mrs. Hepburn's "iron will" and "calculating determination": she is "an independently wealthy and fashionable Irishwoman, near fifty; she herself is described as being doll-like. . . . But she is not by any means helpless in the affairs of the world, or in keeping her husband, as is seen by her vicious threats to deport Mitchka, whom she believes to be Hepburn's lover."[51] At the conclusion of the conversation mentioned here, Mrs. Hepburn says, in a tone that "conveyed a dire threat": "'I'm sure I am the last person in the world to bear malice'" (Lawrence 103). She then makes her parting request—that she might have the doll of her husband: "'But I'm sure she [Mitchka] will be so kind as to send it me. It is a little—er—indelicate, don't you think!'" Hannele expresses her opinion that the doll is no more indelicate "than a painted portrait," to which Mrs. Hepburn replies, "'Well, even a painted portrait I think I should like in my own possession'" (Lawrence 104). The doll in question—the captain's doll, Hannele's icon of love—is a life-like miniature replica of Hepburn, crafted by Hannele as a kind of tribute to him, "a perfect portrait of an officer of a Scottish regiment" (Lawrence 76). The doll, and the subsequent painting of it, are the *objets d'art* around which the story revolves, providing the focal point of the three central characters: Hannele, Hepburn, and Hepburn's wife.

From Hannele's point of view, the doll functions in the story as what Riffaterre calls a "dual sign." Every descriptive reference to the doll represents simultaneously her perception of the doll itself *and* her relation to the Captain. The two are metaphorical or metonymic interpretants that intersect or are linked at nodal points: "where two sequences of semantic or formal associations . . . [are] drawn along parallel paths by the sentence."[52] The doll made by Hannele is this type of parallel referent, developed in continual juxtaposition to the character of Hepburn. As the story begins, Hannele is holding the doll in a manner "not at all seemly" in order to put the finishing touches on his costume; sitting on her lap, "the poor little gentleman flourished head downwards with arms wildly tossed out" (Lawrence 75). Harris observes the duality operating in this opening description when she says that "this is the image of Hepburn 'loved' by his mistress Hannele."[53]

Hannele spends the evenings working on the doll and waiting for Hepburn: "why hadn't he come? She sighed rather exasperated. She was tired of her doll" (Lawrence 78). Hannele seems to comment on two sequences of events here, making no clear distinction between her weariness of the sewing project and her weariness of the strained romantic relationship that she shares with Captain Hepburn. The equivocal word in the passage is the final "doll"; it is the dual sign that "properly placed in one of these two sequences would have been just as much at home in the other."[54] More specifically, the word "doll" could just as well refer to her lover as to the puppet that she holds in her lap.

Even Mitchka's remarks, when Hannele proposes to display the doll in the studio, can be interpreted along these lines. Mitchka has already expressed her disapproval that Hannele visits the rooms of a man who has a wife and children back in England. But when the doll, "the wonderful little portrait," appears in the shop, she feels that Hannele's boldness knows no bounds. She says of the "masterpiece": "'A beautiful man, what! But no, that is *too* real. . . . [Y]ou won't leave him there?'" (Lawrence 85). In Mitchka's exclamation, the equivocal words are "man" and "him," potentially appropriate in reference to either the doll or the Captain. In explanation of the sign's capacity to denote two subjects simultaneously, Riffaterre says that the "potential appropriateness somewhere else, in another text, is a familiar concept. . . . [T]he difference here is that the other 'text' is very close at hand, the sequence is mixed with the one in which the equivocal word rightly belongs."[55] Similarly, Hepburn's comment when he first observes the doll created in his likeness seems to be as much about his own relation to Hannele as it is to her handiwork: "'You've got me,' he said at last, in his amused, melodious voice" (Lawrence 79).

In juxtaposition to Hannele's perceptions are Mrs. Hepburn's view of her husband and her feelings concerning the doll. Having seen the captain doll in the studio, she desperately desires to have it for herself. By appropriating the doll, she seeks to repossess her husband, hoping to accomplish the more difficult emotional task by way of the symbolic physical acquisition of Hepburn's miniature double. For her, as for Hannele, the doll and the Captain are dual signs. Her emotions toward the doll intersect with those which she feels for her husband. Yet, like Hepburn, she fears the power of the doll and the uncanniness of its resemblance to him. Her insistence that Mitchka and Hannele relinquish possession of the doll to her is a manifestation of this fear.

When Hannele and Mrs. Hepburn meet for tea, Mrs. Hepburn, adorned with her usual "medley of twinkling little chains and coloured jewels," rambles ceaselessly about her relationship with the Captain, causing

Hannele to feel that spouses should be left to each other, and "*no* stranger should ever be made a party to these terrible bits of connubial staging" (Lawrence 98, 105, emphasis Lawrence's). Hepburn feels a similar but more generalized dislike for being made audience to the "multifarious commotion" of others' personal narratives and confessions: "He could not get over his disgust . . . the moment they approached him to spread their feelings over him" (Lawrence 114). Certainly it is a "multifarious commotion" that Mrs. Hepburn stages at what Hannele calls their "little tea-party" (Lawrence 107). But after Mrs. Hepburn has spread her feelings sufficiently over Hannele, Hannele is left with more than a helpless disgust. She must come to terms with her own entanglement with the Hepburns and the probability that the vignettes and scenarios of Mrs. Hepburn's chatter are in fact accurate depictions of the Hepburns' married life. Hannele finds it difficult to reconcile Mrs. Hepburn's version of her husband to her own perception of the silent and passionate Captain whom she has loved. The vivid and disenchanting vision of Mrs. Hepburn's narrative is not lost on Hannele. She draws the conclusion, "A man never is quite such an abject specimen as his wife makes him look" (Lawrence 104).

One of the consequences of Mrs. Hepburn's revelations is that Hannele's eyes are opened to the negative qualities that permeate her love for Hepburn (as well as Hepburn's devotion to his wife). She becomes annoyed at her own obsession with him and feels revolted by the fear that she has been taken in by the elusive charm of someone who now seems to her rather awful, stupid, and vulgar: "Had she been dreaming, to be in love with him? . . . and so abjectly" (Lawrence 105–6). It is not surprising that emotions such as fear and obsession accompany Hannele's conviction that her love for Hepburn is tainted by postures of anxiety.

Mrs. Hepburn's incessant speech is hysteric, and she is overtaxed by her belief that Hepburn is romantically involved with Mitchka. Together, Mitchka, Hannele, and the doll embody the anxiety—the fear of her husband's unfaithfulness—from which she turns away. At the uncomfortable tea party, she uses language to ignore and seduce. She purges herself by conveying, however inappropriately, her opinions to Hannele (who is "almost indignant at being slighted so completely herself, in the little lady's suspicions" [Lawrence 101]). On the other hand, Hannele, even though she is filled with loathing at the new image of Hepburn presented to her by his wife, does not undergo a hysteric conversion. Instead, her revulsion is self-contained, taking the form of an introspective analysis of Captain Hepburn's effect, which is like a venomous injection, on her psyche and on her emotions; she refers to his charm as "the snake biting her heart" (Lawrence 107). She is the subject of abjection, a producer of the symbolic, and the doll, as cultural signifier, is her product.

Hannele's artistic creation externally manifests the way in which she has internalized the conflict surrounding her involvement with Hepburn. When he is absent—away on duty or occupied with his wife—he becomes entirely insignificant to her, nearly ceasing to exist, yet she senses that she is still functioning under his influence. Questions that she asks herself about the doll signify her misgivings about Hepburn: "Why had his doll been so important, if he was nothing? Why had she shown it to that funny little woman this afternoon?" She wavers uneasily on all these issues, fearing that Hepburn is "a nullus," that she is "entangled with an absolute nothing," that she has been risking her integrity and compromising herself for a "dead puppet." At such bleak moments, even glancing at the doll does not work to recall his existence to her, for it too seems "nothing but a barren puppet" that is bereft of all lifelikeness. She is sustained only by "a lurking suspicion that there might be something else" (Lawrence 90). But she does not assert her account of this troubling situation publicly or hysterically. Rather, she deals privately with the two conflicting views of her lover. On the one hand, he is vulgar and horrible; on the other, he is wonderful. She recalls his mystery, glamour, and sadness and is still captivated by the magic and illusion of their relationship. She resolves to fight "the vulgarity of disillusion" and insincerity (Lawrence 107).

Hepburn, as well as Hannele, eventually comes to realize and to loathe the vulgar aspect of both his marriage and his affair with Hannele. Lawrence portrays them both shuddering at the thought of ever again participating in a relationship so lacking in sincerity. They reach these conclusions separately; but they follow parallel trains of thought to get there and draw essentially the same conclusions. After Mrs. Hepburn reveals to Hannele the details of her marriage to the Captain, Hannele is forced to confront the true nature of her own relationship with Hepburn. After Hepburn's wife dies and he is able to objectively assess the history of their marriage, he also sees more clearly the role that he played in relation to Hannele.

Hepburn feels that even though he did not go down on his knees to Hannele as he did to his wife, Hannele still somehow condescended to him. With her, as well as in his marriage, he believes that he was victimized and damaged, a passive object rather than an active subject. It is beyond Hannele's comprehension, however, how she cast him in such a position, though she understands well enough how he did it to her. When he explains his theory that the doll embodies her condescension and that its creation has complicated their otherwise simple love, she is incredulous: "'Why shouldn't I make a doll of you? Does it do you any harm?'" He replies that indeed he does find it damaging, but he cannot find the words to tell her why (Lawrence 147). Actually, the answer is contained within Hannele's questions. He feels damaged by the doll's existence because, in his emotional remoteness, he *was* like the barren, dead puppet that lay lifeless in Hannele's lap during the long evenings. He cannot escape the correlation between himself and this miniature double Hannele has made in his image. He can be neither detached nor autonomous because the doll is too much like him, too similar to be the object that it should be. Hepburn is tortured by a need to separate himself from the doll, the abject.

The captain's doll is never animated as the dolls of Yeats's poem are, and it never actively attempts to usurp Hepburn's role as subject. As a passive materialization of the abject, it seems to maintain its position as an object much less ambiguously than they do. Still, Hepburn does not trust its apparent passivity. What he sees in the inanimate creation is Hannele's activity. Hannele, like Yeats's dollmaker, is a craftsman; and, like his dolls, hers are products of the symbolic order. Leavis says that Hannele's art—the creation of miniatures—"implies a *milieu* of sophisticated culture"; Stewart, too, aligns "the miniature world" with the "overcoded . . . cultural" world.[56]

Despite the striking similarity between Hannele's miniature and its model object, and the living quality that she has imparted to it, Hepburn senses the doll to be quite alien to his own identity. Though the doll itself displays neither violence nor anger, it evokes a nearly violent reaction in Hepburn, a disturbing confrontation with both the self and the other. He thinks of the doll as a usurper of his own autonomy, and he feels alienated from Hannele by its very existence, fearing the doll's ability to displace him in her affections. This is a complaint that he fails to register until halfway through the story, when it seems that the doll has ceased to be an object of his consideration. Having gone to England to look after his children and settle his wife's estate during the months immediately following her death, he has lost all contact with Hannele. But after a period of self-introspection, he determines not to spend the rest of his life alone and goes to Munich in search of her—even though to him she "did not exactly represent rosy love. Rather a hard destiny" (Lawrence 115). The few leads he has toward locating her prove fruitless, and he is idly wandering the streets of Munich one day when he happens to see the doll in the window of a little art shop.

His initial sensation at the sight of his doll is disgust, and he refuses to enter the shop. In his eyes, the doll stands for the self he has hoped to leave behind. No longer is he the detached lover, for he has decided that nothing "would have tempted him into the business of adoration any more. . . . [N]ever again. Never." Nor is he an army officer; noticing the type of army cap sported by the doll, he thinks, "But, thank goodness, his own cap now was a civilian tweed." Yet, what he notices first is not that their caps are different styles but that they wear them in the same manner, pulled rather low over the brow, not to mention their similar postures and expressions (each stands "with one hand in his pocket" and holds his "head rather forward, gazing/staring with fixed dark eyes"). Hepburn feels "spellbound" and "staggered" by the similarities, and frustrated in his attempt to distinguish clearly between himself and his double, "that wretched figure" that is both like him and not like him. Despite his initial distaste for the doll in the shop window, he cannot help seeing that it is indeed "himself in little" (Lawrence 116).

Having come to some acceptance of the connection between the two of them, he engages in an exercise of projection, lending to the doll his own current emotional state. He sees it as a "lonely little individual lounging there with one hand in its pocket, and nothing to do . . . stuck so incongruously in the world," and he ascribes to it an air of forlornness, "of isolation, or not-belonging." Hepburn, unable to locate either Hannele or Mitchka, is the one who feels like an isolated foreigner. With little else to do, he develops a strange affinity for the doll, going "every day for a week" to "look at himself in the shop window": "The oftener he saw it . . . the more he hated it. Yet it fascinated him, and he came again to look" (Lawrence 116).

He has the distinct sensation that the doll is misplaced. The world in which he sees it so incongruously stuck is the world of the miniature. Although the doll truly is a product and rightful inhabitant of the toy shop, it is not a handcrafted doll that the ex-captain sees standing "among the bric-a-brac and the bibelots." Confronted so unexpectedly and unmistakable with his double, Hepburn sees himself there: "And what a situation to be in!—lounging with his back against a little Japanese lacquer cabinet, with a few old pots on his right hand and a tiresome brass ink-tray on his left, while pieces of not-very-nice filet lace hung their length up and down the background. Poor little devil: it was like a deliberate satire" (Lawrence 116–17).

The satire that irks Hepburn is the miniaturization of his double and the relegation of the little officer to the world of ornament and fancy. His irresistible urge to witness the doll's confinement signifies his growing inclination to rescue himself from the captive existence of a decorative, idealized object. In fact, one of the motivating factors for his trip to Munich is that he has thrown off—along with the desire to adore—the temptation to be adored by the "fresh, impulsive girls ready to give all their hearts away": "One of those fresh young things would have adored him as if he were a god [or a doll]. And there was something *very* alluring about the thought" (Lawrence 115, 116). But he finds the possibility of a reunion with Hannele even more alluring than the adoration of his twenty-year-old admirers, and he is attracted to the hope of developing with Hannele a more mature affection than they shared in their earlier, miscarried liaison.

Hepburn is eventually reunited with Hannele as a result of his daily treks to the art shop. When he one day finds the doll missing from the window display, he enters the shop for the first time and confronts the girl at the counter concerning the sale of the doll, which he refers to as "that unknown soldier" (Lawrence 117). Now that the doll—"his not-so-secret sharer"—has disappeared, he is less reluctant to identify himself with it.[57] He cannot resist telling the girl that he knew the doll's creator and was himself the model on which it was based. "'It was me,'" he claims, asking the girl if she sees a resemblance. She does not answer his question, nor does she know who purchased the captain doll, but she does know for how much it was sold. Hepburn is anxious to learn the price, to see how he fared as a commodity. But he is not flattered by his evaluation on the consumer scale. "'So cheap,'" is his response when he hears that he was sold for "'five hundred marks'" (Lawrence 117–18).

Not long after this encounter, he finally discovers in the newspaper a clue as to the whereabouts of Hannele, who is now quite famous for her dolls. Scanning the "Chit-Chat column," he learns that the latest picture of an artist called Theodor Worpswede features "'an entertaining group of a doll, two sunflowers in a glass jar, and a poached egg on toast.'" The doll described by the columnist is none other than the Scottish officer, and the article goes on to reveal Hannele's address in Austria. Having lost his chance to buy the doll, Hepburn buys the still-life, even though he finds it "rather frightening." If he had found the doll to be incongruously situated among the knick-knacks in the art shop window, then surely this odd juxtaposition provides an even more disconcerting sensation of displacement. However, the reviewer praises the combination, offering a positive critique of the painting (Lawrence 118).

Packing up the picture, Hepburn leaves Munich for Austria. As mentioned in the gossip column, he finds that Hannele is now engaged to one Herr Regierungstrat, a disenfranchised Austrian official with a nostalgic plan to write a history of the old Austria. Hannele is attracted to his wit and charm, what she calls his "salty *hauteur*" and "chivalric abandon." She is convinced that he would "make her feel like a queen in exile" and "abandon himself to her!" Yet she hesitates to marry him, sensing somehow that it would be like marrying "the doomed captain of a doomed ship" (Lawrence 121). She would not choose as her fate to be the adored doll of a doomed captain, a captain's doll. Thus when her old captain, Alexander Hepburn, reenters her life, she is receptive to his attention, but cautiously, doubtfully.

They go together on an outing to a nearby glacier, and during their picnic lunch, Hepburn surprises her by pulling the picture, Worpswede's "Stillleben," from his knapsack. Her reaction is a series of astonishments. She first turns pale, then praises it, and finally tells Hepburn that she can only wonder why he bought it (Lawrence 134). He answers that he wanted to prevent anyone else from buying it, to keep track of it so that it could not become, as the doll has, the possession of someone else. (Much as his wife pronounced earlier, "even a painted portrait . . . I should like in my own possession" [104].) He hates the thought that the doll is on its own "in the world, in Germany somewhere" (Lawrence 151). He explains to Hannele how he discovered the doll in the shop window and tells her that he did not quite like the idea that she had sold it. She responds that she did not quite like the way he disappeared after his wife's death: "'I felt that you'd sold *me*,' she said, quiet and savage. . . . And all you can do is to come here with a picture to reproach me for having sold your doll. Ha! I'm glad I sold it. A foolish barren effigy it was too, a foolish staring thing'" (Lawrence 135, 137).

Lawrence establishes the psychological connection between the parallel referents, Hepburn and the doll, in the textual development of passages such as this description of the betrayal Hannele felt when Hepburn abandoned her for England. Hannele's decisions concerning the doll parallel the way in which she dealt with her emotions toward Hepburn at the time. The identity of the inanimate -created-double and the identity of its living model-object are inevitably linked both textually and psychologically in her perception of them as dual signs. Why keep the doll, why remain in love with Hepburn, when she could not believe in his love for her?

Hannele and Hepburn labor to arrive at a description of their relation that accurately reflects their shared past, their disparate views of it, and their potential for a shared future. Their confrontation persists throughout the remainder of the excursion, as they grapple for the language that will reorder and redescribe their experience. Though Hannele realizes that he is offended by her sale of the doll, she would prefer to let the issue rest than dwell on the disappointments of the past. Hepburn, however, props the "odious picture" against his knees and questions her relentlessly about how she could have even made the doll (let alone sold it) when they "were supposed to be in love with one another" (Lawrence 146).

Unable to comprehend his obsessive concern, she accuses him of coming all the way to Austria in search of petty revenge. However, it is not really revenge that Hepburn is after. It is just that before establishing a new relation with her, he must first conquer the threat presented by the creation and existence of his replicas—the doll she made in his image and the subsequent painting of it. For Hepburn, the emotional content of the painting and that of the doll are equivalent; their value to him is equal since both are idealizations of him or at least of someone he used to be.

In his discussion of copying one work of art after another, Eco brings up the question of idealization and replication: "The lust for authenticity is the ideological product of the art market's hidden persuaders; when the replica of a sculpture is absolutely perfect, to privilege the original is like giving more importance to the first numbered copy of a poem than to a normal pocket edition."[58] Hepburn fears being perceived as no more than the original subject on which Hannele's doll and Worpswede's painting were modeled. Although he privileges the doll and the painting equally, he wants to convince Hannele that he should be the privileged subject, not as the doll's original or the subject of a painting, but as an original, individual human consciousness. He wants to prove that he is more significant than either of the artistic reproductions, which, as replicas, are only visual entities, "strongly stylized pictorial entities, such as occur in handicrafts and primitive painting."[59]

Since the captain doll was created specifically to be the miniature "life picture" (Lawrence 88) of Alexander Hepburn, Hannele's motivation cannot be seen as truly iconic, according to Eco's definition that a double is an icon only when it visually describes every object of the same class. In the symbolic system of the consumer, the doll may well represent all Scottish captains, but to Hannele and to Hepburn (and to the reader) the doll represents Captain Hepburn, specifically. According to Eco's schema, the doll is what would be called "a partial replica." Once a duplicate is created, the double and the model-object become reciprocal, reversible roles; each is the other's double and they are equally original.

Eco concedes that the absolute replica is a rather utopian notion and suggests that, practically speaking, the double need reproduce all the properties of the model-object only "to a given extent." But even allowing for this margin of flexibility, he concludes that any duplication of the human body "produces only a given percent of the . . . properties of the model-object [and therefore] is not a double, but at best a partial replica." What *will* qualify as a double "are such craft products as are traditionally duplicated without appreciable differences, so that nobody will be tempted to consider the duplicate as an iconic reproduction of the original; the duplicate is as much original as is its model."[60] For example, if Hannele or some other artist had created a second doll in the image of the first, these two dolls could easily be true doubles, provided all the above conditions had been met (similar methods of production, no noticeable differences, etc.). As it is, the artist Theodor Worpswede has chosen an entirely different medium for his work, thus recreating in his still-life only a given percent of his model-object and producing an intentionally iconic reproduction of the original doll. Likewise, the reader is tempted to consider Hannele's doll an iconic reproduction (despite her intention to represent an individual rather than a class), for it shares many characteristics of Eco's iconic model, just as the still-life does.

For several reasons then, the doll is more accurately viewed as an icon or a partial replica, rather than as a double. For example, it does not require a microscope to detect the difference in size between the Captain and his doll, not to mention that the doll is not living—nor was it ever intended to be. Viewing the doll, in a material and external sense, as a *partial* replica provides a fitting parallel to the fact that Hepburn's mental, internalized perception of himself is also only *partial*. Dawson observes that Hepburn's fascination with the figure in the window "can be read basically as an unconscious attraction to . . . and revulsion from the 'I'-persona *image*—a partial awareness by the organismic self of the forebrain's artificial picture of self."[61] On one hand it seems clear enough to Hepburn that he and his doll are not, after all, similar enough to be doppelgängers; yet he must struggle to convince himself of the distinction between them, for he has internalized a fear of being reduced to the size and significance of the doll. He feels that it is not the doll but he himself who is subordinate in the signifying chain.

Stewart deals with the miniature as a very particular type of partial replica, one in which size is the most obvious, sometimes the only, dissimilarity between the model-object and the duplicate. She explains how our perception of the duplicate (whether it is perceived as double, icon, or otherwise) is governed by its size: "Even to speak of the miniature is to begin with imitation, with the second-handedness and distance of the model. The miniature comes into the chain of signification at a remove: there is no original miniature; there is only the thing in 'itself.'"[62] She recounts the historical tradition of the miniature Orkney Island chairs, which are like their model-objects in every way except size—a size difference that in turn affects their use value and quite possibly the way they are manufactured:

> The full-size chairs, handmade of local straw, were once a major furnishing of the peasant house, but because their manufacture is so labor-intensive and because their mode of production has become so esoteric, only the very

wealthy can now afford them. Hence the descendants of the peasants who once owned such pieces can afford only the miniature, or "toy," version. Use value is transformed into display value here.[63]

The popularity of these chairs and other small souvenirs, replicas, handicrafts, and "miniatures of traditional artifacts" is attributable to a certain charm that the real article can never convey: "Those qualities of the object which link it most closely to its function in native context are emptied and replaced by both display value and the symbolic system of the consumer."[64] The captain's doll is the type of artifact or object described here by Stewart. The primary quality linking it to its native context is the officer's outfit that it wears. Clearly, the function of this apparel has been reduced to the level of decorative display; furthermore, the original uniform of which it is an imitation has also been "emptied" of its native value. The value of the uniform to Hepburn, who has resigned his commission and taken up the civilian life of an amateur astronomer and writer, is symbolic—at best—of a profession with which Hepburn no longer associates himself. Thus the doll is an object not once but twice removed from the original subject that it purports to represent (and in the still-life that comes to serve as a substitute for the doll, this remove is carried one step further).

Hepburn's goal is to transform his display value, as love object, doll, and painting, back into use value. This is why he insists so adamantly that marriage must be based on a promise of honor and obedience rather than on a sensation of being in love. Though Hannele harbors a secret hope that he will go down on his knees to her, this is, in fact, a posture that he has unequivocally renounced. He is no longer interested in displays of adoration, which he values but little. Instead, love must be active—to love, to cherish. His new emphasis is on action: "'I have many things to do,'" he insists (Lawrence 151). He wants to replace any miniature or toy versions of himself with the genuine being.

One of the fears Hepburn expresses to Hannele is that "'the most loving and adoring woman to-day could . . . make a doll of her husband—as you made of me.'" In exasperation, she exclaims: "'Oh, that eternal doll! What makes it stick so in your mind?'" In answer to her question, he finally gives a full expression of his apprehension: "'It wasn't malicious. It was flattering, if you like. But it just sticks in me like a thorn'" (Lawrence 151). He explains the similarity he sees between Hannele's doll and his wife's silly perceptions of him. To his wife, he was no more than a doll, despite her hero-worship of him. Although she chooses not to, Hannele could well attest to the conclusions Hepburn draws here about his wife's view of him, for certainly Hepburn never appeared less dignified to Hannele than he did in the conversation she shared with Mrs. Hepburn. But Hannele herself is not one particularly given to hero-worship. Dawson says that "Hannele's creation of the mannikin, and the attitude toward her lover implied in this doll-making, suggests the artificiality and superficiality of the relationship."[65] What seems more accurate, however, is that the doll-making indicated her attempt to control not even Hepburn so much as an entire situation that seemed otherwise unmanageable; as a miniature, the doll represented for Hannele "a mental world of proportion, control, and balance."[66] Her ability to act on a larger scale was preempted by her position and by Hepburn's priorities. Her love for him was under constraint, but it was neither artificial nor superficial. The only constraint operating during their excursion to the mountains is whether or not she can come to terms with Hepburn's plan for a marriage based on something other than love—and whether or not she can forgive the fact that before now he "never really *undertook* to love" her properly (Lawrence 149, emphasis Lawrence's).

It is significant that the altercation over the doll takes place atop the glacier, whose "intolerable steep slopes" strike Hepburn as "almost obscene . . . unthinkably huge and massive" (Lawrence 129, 130). Hepburn's odd plan of bringing the picture along to display during the excursion results in the juxtaposition of the two perceptual modes outlined by Stewart: the miniature and the gigantic. The still-life, with its peculiar assortment of doll, flowers, and poached egg on toast, represents—even more than the three-dimensional doll—the "closure, interiority, the domestic, and the overly cultural" characteristic of the miniature. The glacier, on the other hand, as a manifestation of the gigantic, "represents infinity, exteriority, the public, and the overly natural."[67] Hepburn's antidote to his unpleasant experiences as a miniature is to assert himself against the gigantic, to confront the icy glacier and prove that it is no more powerful, no larger than he. He aligns himself with the glacier in the hope of severing his identity completely from that of the doll. Identifying with nature is a purifying gesture for him because it removes him from the cultural realm of the miniature. He chooses the natural rather than the cultural mode of manipulating the physical world and apprehending experience.

Lawrence's description of the glacier relies upon a "gigantic reading of the landscape."[68] The glacier is perceived as a being so large that it can be known only partially. Every part of it, from any perspective, is seen as a greatly magnified body part or described in terms of some bodily function taking place at great magnitude. It has become a great, sweaty, monstrous beast of prey, with a huge tongue and fangs of ice that bite the earth's flesh. Lawrence refers again and again to the huge paws of this ice monster, which breathes through gills, gives off a birth cry, and has a sloping back, lolling before Hepburn like a gigantic body of flesh and ice. The effect of this description is to project an abstraction of the human body upon the natural and public world. In this mode of projection, the landscape becomes an enormous body that fills Hepburn with terror and Hannele with ecstasy.

The emotions that they experience suggest the sense of transcendence that is characteristic of the gigantic. As well as terror, fear, and ecstasy, their experience on the glacier leaves them "pondering, rather thrilled." Hannele asks Hepburn how he found the climb, and he responds, "'Marvellous. And awful, to my mind'" (Lawrence 144). In any number of forms or embodiments (for example, the abstractions of institutions, the abstractions of technology and corporate power, the anonymity of corporate architecture, the pseudopersonalism of advertising, or the natural domination of an environmental factor such as the great ice bear described by Lawrence), the gigantic occurs "in a transcendent space . . . above the body."[69]

If the environment is to become a huge body, then the human beings who inhabit that environment and occupy "the crowded space below the giant" are necessarily miniaturized.[70] Just as the human hand provides a landscape for a miniature such as the captain's doll, so too does the gigantic ice body provide a background against which the mountain climbers and sightseers become miniatures. When Hepburn and Hannele make their first stop, halfway up the hill, they see the other tourists, "quite tiny . . . little as stones" (Lawrence 133). They can be seen moving through the landscape, through the gigantic body of the foothills. While the doll is exemplary of the human body's relation to the miniature, the body's "most fundamental relation to the gigantic is articulated in our relation to landscape."[71]

Hepburn resists being enveloped or surrounded by the gigantic. He resents standing in the shadow of the glacier, just as he resented standing in the doll's shadow. For him the glacier's challenge is a serious confrontation, and he holds in contempt the tourists who treat the excursion as a holiday activity. He does not want to see his conflict with nature reduced to the status of a tourists' nature walk, a mere imitation of real adventure. Any suggestion of artificiality, such as the Tyrolean costumes of the Austrians, is too reminiscent of his doll, posed among the trinkets of the window display, a scenario of which he does not want to be reminded. Hepburn cannot comprehend why the tourists would choose to accentuate the insignificant, toylike aspects of themselves. He wants to eradicate the memory of his own displacement into the realm of insignificance, replacing it with a more authentic experience. He is vehement in his contempt of those who take the imposing mountains lightly; he wants them to be trapped in the gigantic as he once was in the miniature. Hepburn "associates the sentimental idealism of the mountain-cult with the unrealities of ideal 'love'"—and with the unrealistic, sentimental idealization of the doll.[72]

Hepburn becomes as obsessed with conquering the glacier as he was in Munich with his daily visits to see the doll. He accuses not only the tourists but the mountains themselves of affectation, and after his burst of rage against them, Hannele exclaims that he must be suffering from madness and megalomania. Like Anna Brangwen, who points out her husband's megalomania in making man as big as God, Hannele calmly urges Hepburn to maintain a more realistic perspective concerning his stature: "'You must be a little mad,' she said superbly, 'to talk like that about the mountains. They are so much bigger than you.'" But he insists, "'They are not bigger than me. They are less than me'" (Lawrence 137, 138).

Despite his claims, he does not necessarily feel equal to the task of scaling the mountains. He declares several times that he hates the mountains, fears the glacier, and detests the entire expedition; "'I am no mountain-topper,'" he admits (Lawrence 131). His physical fear of the steep and treacherous ice is synonymous with the psychological threat presented by his replicas, the doll and the picture. If he can overcome his hatred and fear of the gigantic, then he can also in some measure deal with the threat of the miniature. Hannele sees Hepburn's tortured climb up and down the glacier as a ridiculous exhibition of bravado, but once he has descended he feels satisfied with his efforts. He has proven something to himself by confronting his natural fear, and he is pleased with himself for having gone beyond it. He told Hannele that he wanted revenge against the doll "in small measure" (Lawrence 147); but against the glacier he has gained it in large, even gigantic, measure. As a step toward finally obliterating the image of both the doll and the rather ludicrous version of himself presented in the still-life, Hepburn's battle proves successful. At the end of the day Hannele not only concedes to burn Worpswede's odious rendition of the figure but also implies that she will consider his proposal of marriage. In denying Hannele's ideal picture of him, Hepburn "escapes . . . egoistic, self-reflexive isolation." Instead he embraces a "desirable otherness," allowing him to enter into a relation with Hannele that is much more substantial than the superficial notions of "togetherness" that he shared with Mrs. Hepburn.[73]

One other element of the gigantic that runs like a motif through "The Captain's Doll" is Hepburn's preoccupation with the stars. The sky represents to him the same exterior and overly natural world that the glacier does. It is infinite, not bound by the threat of closure. He first chose the loft apartment, next door to Hannele's attic room, because "he had wanted to be high up, because of his stars." When Hannele encounters him, standing at the telescope in his makeshift observatory, she imagines "some tom-cat staring round with wide night eyes" or "some leaden figure on the roof . . . fixed and motionless" (Lawrence 92). In this star-gazing posture, he reminds her of a large cat, and later, when he stares in awe at the glacier, she is reminded of that greatest and most inanimate of cats, the sphinx: "And she . . . saw the queer, blank, sphinx-look with which he gazed out beyond himself. His eyes were black and set, and he seemed so motionless, as if he were eternal facing these upper facts" (Lawrence 132).

His tendency to displace the minute (the doll, the earth) with the "upper facts" (the glacier, the sky) is clearly seen when he contrasts the vastness of his own hobby of astronomy to his wife's narrow life of detail and ornament: "Instead of looking inside the cage, as I did at my bird, or at her—I look right out—into freedom—into freedom" (Lawrence 113). He appropriates for himself the limitless exteriority of the heavens, while his wife's existence is limited to the interiority of parlors, shops, and tearooms. Her interest in life is sustained by a succession of petty flirtations and jealousies from which he stands aloof. Her life is earth-bound, as is her death. In contrast to the life-giving, restorative value he finds in star gazing, his wife suffers from spells of vertigo and dies by falling from a third-story window. Hepburn explains the phobia that led to his wife's death in terms of her perception of the gigantic. It seems that she feared, when looking up into the space above the body in which the gigantic is located, that she would fall downward into it: "She used to say she couldn't really look at the moon, it made her feel as if she would fall down a dreadful height. She never dared do more than glance at it. She always had the feeling, I suppose, of the awful space beneath her" (Lawrence 110).

After Mrs. Hepburn's death, Hannele determines not to be jealous of Hepburn's affinity for the moon. But when she is likely to be directly affected by the issue, her point of view is somewhat altered. On the day of the glacier climb, Hepburn reveals to her his plan to go to Africa and then write a book on his favorite topic, the moon. This time she responds quite differently, not with jealousy but with caution and derision. Wondering what role he intends for the wife who he hopes will accompany him, she asks if this woman will "do all the honouring and obeying and housekeeping incidentally, while you ride about in the day and stare at the moon in the night" (Lawrence 152). She does not see how his plan for their revised life together can be any less imaginary than the old way if he would consign his wife to the domain of the miniature (the everyday prosiness of housekeeping) while reserving for his own design the realm of the gigantic (the open landscape and the solar system).

Regardless of how Hannele interprets his hobby, Hepburn has tried to maintain a position in which the stars function less as a manifestation of the gigantic than as a factor that governs his perception of the relative importance of the people and events in his life. Early in his relationship to Hannele, when she asks what is significant to him, he answers, "Nothing in time or space matters to me" (Lawrence 84). The most important thing is the present moment and her presence in the room with him. He is not threatened or overwhelmed by time and space, by the past or the future. He does not see the night sky as a force to contend with (as he sees the glacier), nor does he feel dwarfed by it. Instead it is a constant by which he locates himself in time and space.

The shadows of miniature and gigantic having been erased, what remains is Hepburn the individual, the consciousness he has struggled to assert—contained neither within the body of the doll nor within the icy heart of the glacier. "The site of the body" is the origin, the conclusion, and the "'still center' or constant measure, of our articulation of the miniature and the gigantic."[74] This theme is suggested early in the text when the narrator says that beside Mrs. Hepburn, who "was looking extraordinarily like one of Hannele's dolls . . . Hannele looked almost huge" (Lawrence 95). In fact, Hannele is not huge; rather, her body is the constant measure, the standard balance between the two modes of exaggeration. Lawrence makes this clear when Hepburn rows across the lake to Hannele's villa and finds her swimming with a group of friends: "Her legs were large and flashing white and looked rich . . . magnificent" (Lawrence 124, 125). This is the human body, neither doll-like nor mammoth, the body that functions "as the instrument of lived experience, a place of mediation . . . the direct relation between the body and the world it acts upon."[75]

Finally, Hannele and Hepburn see each other in a fully human context. Dawson says that "Hepburn has had enough 'human' or idealized contact with people . . . and . . . is seeking a new, organically rooted basis for human contact."[76] The image of Hannele swimming through the water and then speaking to Hepburn from the dock in her robe and slippers is not one of perfection. She is surprised to see him, not expecting him until the following day, and is rather at a loss for words. In this awkward moment, their contact is not idealized—it is organic. They meet on a natural footing that initiates their "new, organically rooted" relation.

Months before, when Hannele and Mrs. Hepburn met for tea, Mrs. Hepburn divulged that Hepburn never "thought of another woman as being flesh and blood, after he knew me. . . . [T]hey were just people, callers—that kind of thing . . . no more to him than, let me say, a pot of carnations or a beautiful old piece of *punto di Milano*" (Lawrence 99). If this were ever the case, as the voluble Mrs. Hepburn believed, it certainly is true no longer. Hannele has clearly materialized into more than an inanimate piece of pottery or handiwork for Hepburn. He too has become flesh and blood for her, evolving from the days when she perceived him as an incomprehensible gargoyle with "a strange, lurking, changeless-seeming grin," or as a mask "carved half grotesquely in some glossy stone," or as one "of those Chinese carved soapstone apes" with their "fixed sadness" (Lawrence 81, 82).[77] Fixed and changeless, remote and distant, lifeless and barren—these were once her adjectives for him, the characteristics that—along with the uncanny physical resemblance to him—she captured in his doll. But he is no longer "a continual blank silence in front of her" or a perfectly realized miniature over which onlookers murmur and hold their breath (Lawrence 83).

Hepburn has developed a discourse with which to confront otherness, in order that he and Hannele can clearly distinguish self from other without the need to objectify or idealize. They accomplish an evolution from a symbolic to a semiotic apprehension of experience—not a return to the semiotic register of birth where the subject is undifferentiated from the object, but a transition to "higher" or "radical" semiotic comprehension, a register akin to Yeats's notion of "radical innocence."[78] They reapproach the instinctual, semiotic border with full symbolic knowledge of the laws of language, order, and self-awareness. Having successfully challenged the cultural, and for Hepburn the psychological, significance of the doll, they can now rely on a more organic, considered understanding of the structure of their relationship—an understanding that is semiotic at the root.

4

Contemporary Narratives of Abjection and Imperfection: The Body of the Doll in Landolfi, O'Brien, and Atwood

In the preceding chapter, the doll is viewed as both material icon and perfect miniature, both uncanny double and loathed abject, both the dual sign and the semiotic subject's symbolic counterpart. As Yeats's poem "The Dolls" and Lawrence's story "The Captain's Doll" clearly suggest, what remains crucial from any perspective of the literary automaton is the privilege accorded the subject and the potential for perfection, a potential never quite as evident in the subject as in the object, or double. Such seamless and permanent perfection takes the form of the doll's resistance to aging and its freedom from what Kristeva calls the "defilement" or "sewage" by which human life is sustained.[1] However, a number of modern and contemporary authors have created worlds in which the doll as well as the human is threatened by the inherent imperfection of lived reality.

Lacan describes a number of these imperfect elements, warning that "the total form of the body by which the subject anticipates . . . the maturation of his power" is little more than a tenuous mirage. Hinting at a world of miniature and gigantic figures, Lacan suggests that the exterior body form appears to the subject "in a contrasting size . . . that fixes it and in a symmetry that inverts it, in contrast with the turbulent movements that the subject feels are animating him." Symbolizing "the mental permanence of the *I*" while simultaneously prefiguring the subject's "alienating destination," this "*Gestalt*" of the body "is still pregnant with the correspondences that unite the *I* with the statue in which man projects himself, with the phantoms that dominate him, or

98

with the automaton in which, in an ambiguous relation, the world of his own making tends to find completion."[2]

Jane Gallop writes of the body's insubordination to these worlds of our own making and its resistance "to man-made meaning." Ultimately, it is death that "undercuts the will": "Death is a key part of the bodily enigma, perhaps the most violent sign that we live in a nonsensical body which limits the powers of our will and consciousness." Laura Mulvey, on the same topic, says, "Woman's beauty is like a *memento mori*, suggesting by its very perfection the inevitability of human decay."[3] Likewise, Mary Shelley allows Victor Frankenstein to discover how "bodies deprived of life, which, from being the seat of beauty and strength, had become food for the worm":

> My attention was fixed upon every object the most insupportable to the delicacy of human feelings. I saw how the fine form of man was degraded and wasted; I beheld the corruption of death succeed to the blooming cheek of life; I saw how the worm inherited the wonders of the eye and brain. I paused, examining and analysing all the minutiae of causation, as exemplified in the change from life to death, and death to life. (Shelley 50–51)

Although Frankenstein hopes to create a perfect race of beings, it is, after all, imperfection—not perfection—that signifies humanity and that is, "paradoxically, a guarantee of survival."[4] Lacan, writing of the relation between the human body and social practices, includes the following example of the human tendency toward imperfection and destruction: "One only has to listen to children aged between two and five playing, alone or together, to know that the pulling off of the head and the ripping open of the belly are themes that occur spontaneously to their imagination, and that this is corroborated by the experience of the doll torn to pieces."[5] Needless to say, the doll described here is not immortal nor does it inhabit a world protected by symbolic borders.

Italian writer Tommaso Landolfi's short story "Gogol's Wife" features a doll that, rather than reject the bodily functions called "filthy" by the dolls in Yeats's poem, seeks to enter this world and assume these functions as evidence of her humanity and experience. In her animated state, she is granted a speaking voice for one purpose only, the expression of these bodily needs and requirements. She is "the automaton in which . . . the world of [the subject's] own making tends to find completion" (see Lacan, above). Edna O'Brien's short story "The Doll" focuses on a doll that ages while living in the house of an undertaker. Surrounded by the motifs of death, it must daily witness the cost of life, the price of semiotic existence so greatly feared in Yeats's "The Dolls."

When first received as a Christmas present, the doll was used by her young owner to symbolize the Virgin Mary; but, trapped in the funeral parlor, it is no longer protected by the sacred, symbolic borders of the Nativity scene. It becomes the statue in which O'Brien's narrator projects herself.

Margaret Atwood's "The Resplendent Quetzal" also treats the often ambiguous distinctions between sacred and secular, symbolic and semiotic. In this story a woman mourns the loss of her stillborn child by taking from a Nativity scene the plaster doll representing the Christ Child and throwing it into an ancient sacrificial well. For her, unlike the crouching dollmaker's wife, it is the accident of death, not that of birth, that has caused an unbreachable rift in her marriage. In the doll, she confronts the phantoms that dominate her.

In each of these stories, the subject is overcome by the powers of horror and abjection. Landolfi's Gogol character, O'Brien's narrator, and Sarah—the cynical and wounded woman in Atwood's story—all cope with these emotions by projecting them onto the dolls that figure in their lives: the blow-up wife, the cherished princess, and the plaster baby. Though each of these dolls may have its moments of ostensible perfection, they are all in fact flawed and subject to the same ravages of time and experience that afflict their respective owners—quite unlike the captain's doll, which stands on flawless display in the storefront window and poses for its own portrait. They are vulnerable not only to time but also to the wishes and desires of those who, however inappropriately or briefly, possess them. Thus, they each become the subject of abjection or the mirror image of their owners' personal distress.

To narrate "Gogol's Wife," Landolfi creates a persona, Foma Paskalovitch, who has assumed the task of writing a definitive biography of Nikolai Vassilevitch Gogol and with facetious honesty relates "the whole complicated affair of Nikolai Vassilevitch's wife." He explains right from the beginning that the tale to follow may well contain information to "offend the sensibilities of all sorts of base, hypocritical people, and . . . honest people too."[6] He adopts a tone of reverent curiosity toward the subject of his biographical research, attributing anything he cannot understand about the Master to the capriciousness of great minds:

> Is it given to us to know, not only what intimate needs, but even what higher and wider ends may have been served by those very deeds of a lofty genius which perchance may appear to us vile? No indeed, for we understand so little of these privileged natures. "It is true," a great man once said, "that I also have to pee, but for quite different reasons." (Landolfi 2)

On this note then, Landolfi, or rather Paskalovitch, launches into a detailed "description of the most noteworthy peculiarities" of the anatomy and physiology of Gogol's wife (Landolfi 5–6). It soon becomes evident not only that Gogol might urinate for reasons quite different from those of the common man but also that his wife's excretory needs serve a function far removed from those of the ordinary woman.

"Gogol's so-called wife," the narrator explains, "was not a woman. Nor was she any sort of human being, nor any sort of living creature at all, whether animal or vegetable. . . . She was quite simply a balloon . . . an ordinary dummy made of thick rubber" (Landolfi 2–3). Her physical appearance, it turns out, is determined by "nothing else but the will of Nikolai Vassilevitch himself [who] would inflate her to a greater or lesser degree," changing her shape, physical attributes, and such characteristics as hair color and clothing to create the type of woman he desired or fancied at any given moment. By way of these manipulations, Gogol was usually able to obtain "more or less" a version of womanhood that suited him, although "in rare cases, the form he obtained perfectly incarnated his desire" (Landolfi 4). But, far from perfect, the rubber doll, which is named Caracas, is as vulnerable and fallible as any human being—just as willful and just as determined.

Paskalovitch, who is Gogol's close friend as well as his biographer, is often a house guest of the odd couple, Gogol and his wife, and as such he witnesses the gradual evolution of her identity and personality. Her varied physical identities provoke him initially to question "who she really was, or whether it would be proper to speak of a single 'person'" (Landolfi 3). But he is soon forced to admit that, more than just an object, she is indeed a "unitary personality" (Landolfi 9). Paskalovitch notices that in her behavior Caracas shows evidence of "independence" and "autonomy." And Gogol himself observes "that she was acquiring a personality of her own, indecipherable perhaps, but still distinct from his, and one which slipped through his fingers" (Landolfi 8).

Caracas makes an effort to assert her own will by speaking out one evening to Gogol in the presence of Paskalovitch, while the two men are discussing literature. On this memorable occasion, Paskalovitch becomes the single eye-witness (aside from Gogol) to the one and only time Caracas has ever been known to speak. Paskalovitch has already described the perplexity and indignation expressed by other visitors to the house, friends and biographers, who complained of never seeing the Master's wife or hearing her speak aloud. For himself, he has seen her often enough, in her many shapes and forms, but always sitting mutely. He does know, however, "that she could talk, but Gogol had never explained to me the circumstances under which this happened" (Landolfi 6). Paskalovitch is, then, surprised to hear the usually silent Caracas interrupt, "with a husky and submissive voice, like Venus on the nuptial couch . . . 'I want to go poo poo'" (Landolfi 7). Her comment is designed to call attention to the fact that she is subject to the same physiological processes as her husband and his friends and thus to prove that her body is not just an image or an object but is rather a "body of lived experience," a manifestation of her existence in "the domain of lived reality."[7] In anger and embarrassment, Gogol responds to the need she has expressed by pulling out her stopper and deflating her until she slides to the floor "*in utter abjection.*" He then explains to his guest, "As a matter of fact she does not have such needs" (Landolfi 7, emphasis added).

That Caracas becomes the subject of abjection is due to a culmination of ill feeling on the part of her husband. He is not pleased with Caracas' proud acquisition of a distinct personality. Paskalovitch takes note of the crucial transition of power. His initial impression that Gogol determines the parameters of his wife's being gives way to the certainty that Caracas has become "no longer his slave but his tyrant. And here yawns the abyss . . . the 'Jaws of Tartarus'" (Landolfi 4). These "Jaws" are none other than the abyss—or as Kristeva says, the deep well—of abjection. The attempt by Paskalovitch to understand the relation Gogol shares with the various incarnations of Caracas leads to speculation on his part that can be profitably compared to Kristeva's identification of the roles traded off by subject and abject:

> Perhaps it was no more and no less than the creative afflatus of Nikolai Vassilevitch himself. But no, it would have been too singular and strange if he had been so much divided off from himself, so much averse to himself. Because whoever she was, Caracas was a disturbing presence and even—it is better to be quite clear—a hostile one. (Landolfi 9)

In Kristevan terms, Gogol is the superego, Caracas the abject. He is the rejecting master against whom the thwarted abject rails. Not only does each manifestation or embodiment of Caracas somehow resemble its predecessors, but each one also bears a resemblance—the undesired similarity of abjection—to Gogol the creator, the subject from whom they all proceed. Caracas is the otherness deeply rooted in, yet rejected by, her husband. Viewing Caracas as the subject of Gogol's abjection renders his growing aversion to her and her disturbing hostility toward him less mysterious to the reader than it appears to Paskalovitch.

Regarding the assertion that his wife has no bodily needs, it seems that

Gogol may be mistaken. True to what Kristeva says of the abject's behavior, Caracas lives outside of the rules that Gogol has set for the game of their life together, refusing to agree to or even to acknowledge them. Gogol has designed for her a secluded parlor in a remote and windowless room of the house, decorating it with Oriental silks, cushions, and recliners. But rather than relishing the pampered life of this private and artificial boudoir, Caracas demonstrates that her body is subject to change, transformation, and death. Unlike the dolls in Yeats's poem, she neither fears nor lives outside of her sexuality, nor is she inclined merely to languish in her sequestered bower. She learns to masturbate, "giving herself up to solitary pleasures, which he [Gogol] had expressly forbidden" (Landolfi 11), and he also suspects that she has been unfaithful to him, a fear that seems to be confirmed when she somehow contracts syphilis and passes it on to him. She even conceives and bears a child: "Not a flesh and blood baby, of course, but more something in the line of a rubber doll or a model" (Landolfi 16). The conclusive evidence that Caracas is fully participating in the human condition is the fact of her mortality, the signs of which Gogol observes with frank astonishment: "'Believe it or not, *she's aging!*'" (Landolfi 11, emphasis Landolfi's).

Surely in the life-sized, inflatable companion, Gogol had hoped to find the perfect wife whose appearance he could whimsically determine and whose lack of will assured a life peacefully free from conflict and conjugal turmoil. Caracas has been created whole; Paskalovitch calls her "well built and proportioned in every part. She had every smallest attribute of her sex properly disposed in the proper location. Particularly worthy of attention were her genital organs . . . formed by means of ingenious folds in the rubber. Nothing was forgotten" (Landolfi 5). Yet it seems that Gogol's secret preference was for what Gallop, in her reading of Freud, calls the "really castrated" or "phallomorphic" woman, the one in whom the ingenious folds of the genitalia have been reduced to only the clitoris, that phallic miniature: "As such she is the guarantee against man's castration anxiety. She has no desires that don't complement his, so she can mirror him, provide him with a representation of himself which calms his fears and phobias about (his own potential) otherness and difference, about some 'other view' which might not support his narcissistic overinvestment in his penis."[8]

In fact, speaking to Paskalovitch of their nights in bed together, Gogol says of Caracas that "no companion could be quieter or less importunate than she." To later find that she does indeed have desires that don't mirror his, that "what lay at the heart of Caracas . . . was the spirit of syphilis," and that she could go so far as to bear a child that may or may not be his is for him an outrage beyond endurance (Landolfi 8, 9). He must undergo long and painful treatments for the illness, which continues to infect his wife and becomes the constant specter of the very phobias he had intended to calm. The image of disease here suggests more than just the venereal affliction from which they both now suffer; it represents the otherness and difference against which there is no guarantee, the larger, pervasive condition of human existence, the physicality of a body that deteriorates even as it sustains life.

The amazingly crafted Caracas, it turns out, is no more free from these gnawing processes than Gogol himself, the aging master craftsman; nor can he do anything to side-step the reality of her mortality: "Gogol deluded himself for some time that, by blowing his wife up and down and furnishing her with the most widely divergent aspects, he could obtain a woman immune from the contagion, but he was forced to desist when no results were forthcoming" (Landolfi 10). None of his machinations, however well devised, will yield up the perfect woman of his dreams, the complementary other of his unconscious desire. Despite her ingenious construction, she bears the distinguishing marks and needs of any other human being, and none of Gogol's old tricks of modifying her superficial characteristics can alter this truth. She, like the lofty genius evoked at the outset of the story, must, after all, urinate, defecate, fight infection, and age along with the rest.

Throughout the story are recurrent hints that Gogol himself is the creator of this miraculous yet flawed piece of handiwork. For example, the craftsman's identity is always kept a secret, and Paskalovitch laments Gogol's adamant refusal to share the talented creator's name. Also, as seen above, Paskalovitch wonders if the similarities that appeared consistently in each rendition of Caracas can be attributed to the creative "afflatus" or impulses of Gogol, the inspired master-manipulator. Hoping only for a well-groomed, obedient reflection of himself, Gogol, like Frankenstein, has instead created a companion whom he cannot abide; and like Frankenstein's monster, Gogol's becomes a martyr, sacrificed on her own funeral pyre. Gogol handles the unpredicted complications of his feelings for his creation with the ambiguous mixture of love, hate, and desire that is characteristic of intimacy with the abject. The narrator reports that Gogol's "distaste for his wife became stronger, though his love for her did not show any signs of diminishing. Toward the end, aversion and attachment struggled so fiercely with each other in his heart that he became quite stricken, almost broken up." Finally Gogol's agitation and disdain reach "an unprecedented intensity," growing to such proportions that "one could feel in him a real repugnance, a repugnance which had, I suppose, now reached the limits of the endurable" (Landolfi 10, 11, 12).

In response to the disdain that Alexander Hepburn feels toward the captain doll, Hannele promises to burn the painting of it, thereby obliterating the only remaining evidence of the doll's existence. Gogol destroys his rubber doll/wife in a similar fashion. He takes her life by inflating her mercilessly and then, once her surface has shattered, tossing all the remaining bits and pieces into the burning fireplace. He carries out this execution "like one possessed," shouting: "'She's going to burst! Unhappy Caracas, most pitiable of God's creatures! But die she must!'" Next he gathers her offspring in his arms and likewise stuffs the rubber child all at once into the fire until nothing is left of the two of them "but a heap of silent ashes" (Landolfi 13, 15). Kristeva says of the abject that "the ashes of oblivion now serve as a screen and reflect aversion, repugnance. . . . [T]he sought-after turns into the banished, fascination into shame."[9]

The image of fire and ashes draws, once again, the parallel between the artist's written work, the product of his creative mind, and the intricately designed doll, his ultimate material creation. Paskalovitch recounts what Gogol muttered to the ravaged body of Caracas: "'My dearest! My beloved! My best! . . . She too must end up in the fire.'" With tongue-in-cheek, he also explains that Gogol, who had once destroyed his manuscripts in a similar fashion, has "like all Russians . . . a passion for throwing important things in the fire" (Landolfi 14). He calls the earlier burning of the manuscripts—which was a well-known act not only of Landolfi's fictitious Gogol but of the real-life author as well—the "famous 'pyre of vanities'" (Landolfi 11). Caracas, baby, and written work alike are the victims of Gogol's vanity.[10]

In addition to modeling his fictional Gogol on the author himself, Landolfi also attributes some of the real author's characteristics to the doll Caracas. Like Gogol at the end of his life, Caracas, shortly before her murder by inflation and fire, "whether aged or not, had turned into a bitter creature, querulous, hypocritical and subject to religious excess" (Landolfi 11). In drawing such correlations between the real-life Gogol and both fictional characters—Gogol and Caracas—Landolfi also succeeds in emphasizing the parallels between the two fictional characters. Caracas, far from playing the role of passive complement to Gogol, is as stubborn and assertive as he is. As he grows older, he too is given to the "strangest impulses . . . the most senseless fears." He has syphilis, so does she; he is dying, so is she; the product of his labor has been thrown into the fire, so must hers be. She has grown to be so much like him, so much his double, that he can no longer tolerate her presence in the house—or even her existence. She is neither his antagonist nor his ideal opposite; rather she is the imperfect and excluded other. Not only is she alienated from Gogol in her own mysterious way, but Paskalovitch confides that "neither Gogol nor I ever succeeded in formulating a remotely tenable hypothesis as to her true nature" (Landolfi 9). She is the experimental object of his creative impulses; but, more than the object of art or desire, she is the feared and fearful abject, standing just a bit too near for comfort to the angry and hostile subject. Like the dollmaker's creations in Yeats's "The Dolls," she takes an active and animated role in the subject-object-abject dance, making her opinions known by actions if not by words; and the only solution Gogol sees is to vanquish her as he feels she has tried to vanquish him. The narrator, in his effort to quell any rumors that Gogol "ill-treated or even beat his wife, as well as other like absurdities," succeeds in documenting not only the utterly absurd but the destructively abject nature of the writer's relationship with the ill-fated inflatable Caracas, whose flawed existence failed to satisfy his yearning for an irreproachably perfect creation (Landolfi 16).

In another short story, Edna O'Brien's "The Doll," the featured figure is a passive one—much like Alexander Hepburn's double, who stands by as inanimate witness, seemingly unaware of the tension and confusion its existence creates. Like "Gogol's Wife," this story is about a doll that grows old. This one, however, lives not as a wife but as a sainted tribute to the past in the house of an undertaker, surrounded by the motifs of death. Caracas is cremated, after Gogol inflates her to death on the night of their twenty-fifth wedding anniversary, while the doll in O'Brien's story is enshrined in a kind of glass coffin, wearing her burial shroud. Unlike the lusty Caracas, this doll is a virgin whose bridal-like gown turns to mold during the stagnate years of her incarceration. In O'Brien's narrative of abjection, the narrator and the doll stand in an uneasy juxtaposition that is exemplary of Freud's notion of the Uncanny. The question of the doll's subjectivity leads to an awakening of uncanny feelings. Freud's description of children—like O'Brien's narrator—maintaining that their dolls are alive or that they themselves can make the inanimate dolls come to life is particularly applicable to the opening pages of O'Brien's story (see Freud 233). In conjunction with Freud's "Uncanny," Kristeva's concepts of abjection, dejection, and displacement illuminate the narrator's crisis in "The Doll."

The narrator of "The Doll" is a woman who as a child received a doll each year for Christmas. The behavior of this unnamed child is like that of the children observed by Freud in "The 'Uncanny'" who treat their dolls as living people, making no distinction between the living and the inanimate. For example, not only do her dolls have names and living quarters but each has "special conversations allotted to them, special endearments, and if necessary special chastisements" as well.[11] Her favorite is "the living representation of a princess . . . a sizable one," and her description of it as "uncanny" is consistent in every detail with the characteristics named by Freud as specific to the sensation of uncanniness. In fact, O'Brien uses this term when she describes the doll's apparent animation: "She was *uncanny*. We all agreed that she was almost lifelike and that with coaxing she might speak. . . . [T]he gaze in her eyes [was] so fetching that we often thought she was not an inanimate creature, that she had a soul and a sense of us. Conversations with her were the most intense and the most incriminating of all" (O'Brien 49, emphasis added).

After several of her classmates see the splendid doll, lying in state in its silver box, it becomes "the cynosure of all," and the children beg that it be used to represent the Virgin Mary in the Nativity scene that is being assembled for the school's Christmas pageant. The child has mixed feelings about volunteering her doll for the event. When the doll must be stored in a schoolroom cabinet, the girl is "grieved at being parted from her," yet she is pleased by her doll's popularity and success. At the program, the doll outshines the faltering pupils; they are subject to the human failing of forgetting their lines while the inanimate doll is protected by the composure of the ideal. Standing calmly amidst the other Nativity figures, the lovely doll "was the star of the occasion and . . . saved the play" (O'Brien 50–51).

Representing the Virgin Mary, in her "flowing blue cloak with a sheath of net over it and a little diamante clasp" (O'Brien 50), the lovely doll is like the finely finished figures described by Stewart in her comparison of the modern dollhouse to the crèche of the Middle Ages:

> The Neapolitan crèches displayed figures made of wood or terra cotta, with finely finished faces and hands, silk clothing, and silver and pearl ornaments. . . . In the Sicilian crèche tradition . . . there seems to be an important movement toward locating the sacred within the secular landscape. At the heart of such crèches are the abstract mythologized figures of the Nativity, but as one moves out from that location, the landscape becomes more familiar.[12]

The doll in O'Brien's story is unusual in its sacred role because it was initially created to be a child's toy or an object of decorative display— not to represent one of the mythologized Nativity figures. Its placement at "the heart" of the Nativity provides an interesting example of the juxtaposition of secular and sacred, an inversion of the movement described by Stewart. Here the secular is located within the sacred landscape.

In "The Doll," this inversion signifies the displacement of abjection. The doll, the secular representative standing in for the sacred, exemplifies what Kristeva calls the purified abject. She says that the history of religious catharsis is likewise a history of purifying the abject and that the artistic experience is rooted in the abject: "Seen from that standpoint, the artistic experience, which is rooted in the abject it utters and by the same token purifies, appears as the essential component of religiosity."[13] Posing as the Virgin Mary, the finely crafted doll is both an art object and a religious symbol.

In exchange for the doll's privileged treatment, however, the girl is dejected and separated. She is the one who "*strays* instead of getting [her] bearings, desiring, belonging, or refusing."[14] She suffers loss and displacement at every level—in her family, in her school, and in her village. She is the only one of her sisters, for example, to receive one of these miraculous dolls each year, for the dolls do not come from their parents but from an eccentric friend of the family who has whimsically chosen the narrator as her favorite. The child is victimized by her own good fortune because her older sisters "of course were jealous and riled against the unfairness," even though like the narrator they are "smitten" with the lifelike princess doll (O'Brien 48–49).

At school, too, the girl is outcast. She remembers that the teacher "harbored a dislike for me" and, rather inexplicably, "referred to me as 'It.'" Perversely, the teacher, who like everyone else is enamored of the doll, objectifies the child. The doll and the child change places—the doll becoming a subject, the child an object. After the Christmas pageant, the strangely tyrannical teacher refuses to return the child's doll, a loss that makes the girl feel "berserk" (O'Brien 51). After requesting the doll's return several times to no avail, the child must resign herself to the teacher's unkindness. When she finally leaves the narrow life of the village for boarding school in the city, she hopes to forget the school teacher, to "be free of her forever, and . . . forget the doll, forget most of what happened, or at least remember it without a quiver." She believes that she can leave behind her anguish over her stolen doppelgänger, the lost doll. Having decided to leave home and develop a new identity, she is once more separated from her environment, the third level at which she is displaced. She says to herself, "I am on the run from them. I have fled. I live in a city. I am cosmopolitan" (O'Brien 52).

Along with the memory of the treasured doll, she also seeks to abandon her old self—the shy, intimidated, village schoolgirl. But just as she is not truly reconciled to losing the doll, she cannot escape her fearful self simply by changing locations. As a subject of displacement and abjection, she is unable to realize the potential energy and excitement that the nearly animated doll once signified to her. The impulse and its object are now separated, but her flight to the city is not necessarily unsuccessful. Kristeva says that the deject "is on a journey, during the night, the end of which keeps receding. He has a sense of the danger, of the loss that the pseudo-object attracting him represents for him, but he cannot help taking the risk at the very moment he sets himself apart. And the more he strays, the more he is saved." The narrator's escape to city life is her receding journey, and the princess doll is the pseudo-object that represents loss to her, both literally and figuratively. As she strays into her search for a meaningful existence, what saves her is self-awareness. The deject, according to Kristeva, "is not at all unaware of" her dejections, whether she wishes to know them or not.[15]

Feeling "far from those I am with, and far from those I have left," the narrator is the stray, the figure without bearings (O'Brien 52). She is without a sense of belonging in her new situation as much as she was in the old. Yet, she is, to use Kristeva's description of the deject, "situationist in a sense, and not without laughter—since laughing is a way of placing or displacing abjection."[16] The dinners and parties hosted by the narrator of O'Brien's story are filled with this sort of laughter and "feats like dancing, or jesting, or singing, inventing a sort of private theater." Musing on the course that her adult life has taken and the wary detachment of her new friends, she observes how their talk takes the form of a pleasant, drifting, wandering hallucination—a conversational style that she says "was not something I cultivated. It developed of its own accord, like a spore that breathes in the darkness" (O'Brien 52).

She does not share with these new acquaintances the intense and special conversations that she once shared with her doll. Instead, their desultory chatter resembles the distracted and detached speech of what Kristeva calls the blank subject, the nonobject, "he through whom the abject exists." This subject moves about in a daze of fear, "that has cut off his impulses from their objects . . . a fluid haze, an elusive clamminess . . . [that] permeates all words of the language with nonexistence, and with a hallucinatory ghostly glimmer."[17] The language of abjection does not retain the property of naming and describing experience. If language itself has been permeated by nonexistence, then it is no surprise that the subjects who utter such a language stray in their search for significance and meaningful existence. This eerie mode of communication is missing a crucial quality, the capacity to confront otherness and tap into the wellspring of memory and history.

The narrator realizes that her discourse and that of her friends does not address the self and does not confront otherness. No allowance is made for intimacy. Issues of identity and personal history have no place in their lively meandering conversations. Similarly, the narrator of Atwood's *Surfacing* thinks: "My friends' pasts are vague to me and to each other also, any one of us could have amnesia for years and the others wouldn't notice."[18] Their innermost thoughts remain submerged in the deep well of memory, camouflaged by the laughter that conceals abjection: "None of us ever says where we come from or what haunts us. Perhaps we are bewildered or ashamed" (O'Brien 52). She herself, for example, is still haunted and bewildered by the unforgotten princess doll, which is for her the repelled and neglected other, the absent body that now maintains an existence entirely separate from hers, stuck away somewhere among the school teacher's belongings (much like the captain's doll, whose separate existence out in the world somewhere causes Hepburn so much distress). What she is ashamed of is the jealousy that this miniature representation of her own fate evoked in her childhood acquaintances, and she has consigned this emotion to the unapproachable regions of her consciousness.

The narrator has repressed not just her memory of the doll but many other memories as well, and she waits to find a discourse with which to confront their otherness and free herself of their power. She describes her recollections as if they are a series of Russian Matreshka dolls. Each self that one has been and each person that one has known grows smaller and smaller, gradually being replaced and then encased by its successive identity. The metaphor of decorative nesting dolls or boxes more aptly captures the reality of lived experience than does her memory of the Christmas dolls, whose ideal bodies seemed each year to be bigger and better than the last. But in real life, "the years go by and everything and everyone gets replaced. Those we knew, though absent, are yet merged inextricably into new folk, so that each person is to us a sum of many others and the effect is of opening box after box in which the original is forever hidden" (O'Brien 52).

When the narrator returns home for a relative's funeral, she is forced to confront her own intimate history, the selves tucked one inside the other, each one further removed than the last from her present-day self. The familial responsibility of making the funeral arrangements falls to her, and she must visit the village undertaker, named Denis, who is the son of the once-hated teacher. When she goes to pay her aunt's final debt, the dead body that she sees in Denis's care is not that of her aunt—it is her own. Her mission turns out to be much greater than she had expected. She encounters the metaphorical interment of a small part of herself, her own abandoned double, with whom she comes face-to-face at last; and what is "fixed up," paid off, fully dealt with at this final reckoning is her lingering emotional aversion to its existence. When she spies the confiscated doll in the overstuffed "china cabinet along with cups and ornaments," she is shocked to see that it has defied the immutability of its idealized body by aging. It now resembles that most extreme and abhorrent form of the abject, the corpse: "If dolls can age, it certainly had. Gray and moldy, the dress and cloak are as a shroud, and I thought, If I was to pick her up she would disintegrate" (O'Brien 51–53). The doll has retained her distinctive status for old times' sake but lost her initial luster and all the stimulating attributes that had made her seem like a living subject. She has become a "nullus," a dead and barren puppet."[19]

When Denis sees that she has noticed the artifact, he tells her how much his mother, who has since died, admired the doll ("'God, my mother was fond of her'"), and he boasts that he does not let his children play with it ("thereby implying that she was a sacred object, a treasured souvenir"). But the very thought of how both she and her doll were misused by the older woman gives the narrator a chill. Even from an adult perspective, she feels certain that the woman "kept the doll out of perversity, out of pique and jealousy. In some way she had divined that I would have a life far away from them and adventures such as she herself would never taste." This envy of her opportunity to leave the constricted village life informs the son's behavior toward her as well as the mother's. She senses that Denis is filled with curious notions of what her life is now like, and she knows that the reality of her experiences must differ widely from his expectations. Their encounter ends awkwardly because, she says, "I could not stay, and I could not reminisce, and I could not pretend to be the fast kiss-easy woman he imagined me to be" (O'Brien 53).

After her visit to the undertaker's, the narrator feels reduced to wretchedness. The sight of the captive, shrouded, corpse-like doll gives her the sudden "conviction of not having yet lived," of dying the same slow death that the doll has. Stewart says that, as a mirror of the world, the miniature "is the antithesis of the 'self-reflecting' mirror, for the mirror's image exists only at the moment the subject projects it." The miniature, on the other hand, "projects an eternalized future-past" and "consoles in its status as an 'always there.'"[20] For O'Brien's narrator, however, the image of the doll fails to give any consolation. Instead of projecting the past and the future of "always there," it represents the narrator's past and future, times that are *never* there. Like a living subject, it has responded to the passage of time and has existed in the reality of the present. Rather than feeling consoled by her miniature self-image, the narrator mourns the doll's loss of vibrancy and fears that such potential may be forever unrealized in her own life as well. Far from the days when her favorite doll was "the cynosure of all," the narrator has become cynical and wary of the contradictions of life. More like a mortal than an idealized object, the doll comes to represent only her abjection: "A sickness had come over me, a sort of nausea for having cared so much about the doll, for having let them maltreat me, and now for no longer caring at all" (O'Brien 53).

She overcomes the sensation of nausea by admiring the "singular and wondrous" stars, which symbolize to her some hope against the "cruelty and stupidity of the world." They seem to her "a link, an enticement to the great heavens. . . . [O]ne day I would reach them and be absorbed into their glory" (O'Brien 53–54). The element of euphoria in her vision is analogous to Captain Hepburn's preoccupation with astronomy and to the correlation between the sublime and the abject identified by Kristeva: the sublime "expands us, overstrains us, and causes us to be both *here*, as dejects, and *there*, as others and sparkling."[21] Kristeva's here/there formula of abjection/sublimation can be used to explain the narrator's dichotomous stance. Standing on the sidewalk (i.e., here), she is a deject, made nauseous and frustrated by her memories and by the world's abjection. Looking to the sky (i.e., there), the anguish caused by her brief, distasteful reunion with the doll and the teacher (in the form of the undertaker) is alleviated. The unpalatable otherness of the doll is sublimated by the sparkling otherness of the stars. They restore her perspective, just as Hepburn's is restored by the calm and constant measure of the heavenly bodies.

Kristeva says that "the abject is edged with the sublime" and describes this relation in an imagistic passage that approaches the visionary. For her the abject, as a non-object, is closely related to the sublime: "For the sublime has no object either. When the starry sky, a vista of open seas or a stained glass window shedding purple beams fascinate me, there is a cluster of meaning, of colors, of words, of caresses, there are light touches, scents, sighs, cadences that arise, shroud me, carry me away, and sweep me beyond the things that I see, hear, or think."[22] She then finds herself removed from the location of the "I" to what she calls a secondary universe. In this secondary universe, delight sublimates loss. It is appropriate that the subject of abjection turn to an experience of transport as an alternative to the complexity of lived reality, for Kristeva emphasizes that the deject is more concerned with questions of place than with questions of being: "'*Where* am I?' instead of '*Who* am I?'"[23] In accordance with this priority, the narrator, at the conclusion of "The Doll," thinks only of leaving the small oppressive town for somewhere else: "Tomorrow I shall be gone. . . . I had not lost the desire to escape or the strenuous habit of hoping" (O'Brien 54).[24]

Having endured an unnerving confrontation with the abject, she seeks to escape from the "here" of her childhood home into the "secondary universe" of the stars or the "there" of the city. Kristeva says that the sublime "expands memory boundlessly," but for the narrator, it is the surfacing of old and unpleasant memories that triggers her escape into the sublime. She expresses the need of the abject, the tireless straying "in order to be" by which she is saved.[25] Even though she realizes her own lack of groundedness, she is still compelled, in the true mode of the deject, to "constantly question [her] solidity."[26] A positive result of this questioning is that the abject may become the sublime and the "deep well of memory" that contains the shunned and hidden history of abjection may be transformed into the "raptures of bottomless memory" where the sublime object is finally dissolved.[27] Thus, O'Brien's narrator, having relinquished her hold over the abjected doll, is herself finally liberated from its uncanny power.

The doll, however, is left behind, on her own in the glass case. Her future—to grow even older, to atrophy beyond all hope, to disintegrate as indeed the narrator felt she would if touched—is no longer the concern of her owner. The doll's life has been divided into three distinct stages: she begins her existence as a prized Christmas gift, a finely dressed sleeping princess; next, rather than being united with a handsome prince, she is chosen to be the virgin mother of the Christ Child; and finally, well beyond those days of glory, she becomes the captive patron saint of Denis's funeral parlor. The binding motif of these roles is the sacred one. Now trapped in a place of death, the doll is no longer protected by the sacred, symbolic borders of the Nativity scene. If the one shining hour during which she symbolized the Virgin Mary was the highlight of her young owner's childhood, it was the apex of the doll's life as well.

In "Psychoanalysis and the Unconscious," D. H. Lawrence looks at the function of the iconic Madonna. Observing the archetypal bond between Madonna and Child, he explains various ways by which the relational identity is formed. In his discussion of consciousness, he looks particularly at relationships such as "The Child and His Mother" and "The Lover and the Beloved." His explanations prefigure the pattern developed by Kristeva—that the subject moves from semiotic to symbolic understanding, coming gradually to recognize itself as distinct from others. Lawrence describes this process as the acquisition of "objective knowledge, as distinct from objective emotion." Objective emotion governs during the "first mode" of consciousness (somewhat like Kristeva's semiotic realm) in which "there is perfect surpassing of all sense of division between the self and the beloved." Objective knowledge, on the other hand, is acquired when the child or lover comprehends that the other is "that which I myself am not." For

Lawrence, "the very discovery of the features of the beloved contains the full realization of the irreparable or unsurpassable, gulf," a realization that signals the "second mode" of consciousness (somewhat like Kristeva's symbolic realm). There is an element of "self-amplification" in this discovery and also "the knowledge of the *limits* of the self."[28]

Lawrence illustrates this process of differentiation between subject and other with a general description of Madonna and Child in the pictures of Leonardo, Botticelli, and Filippo Lippi:

> It is the Mother who crosses her hand on her breast, in supreme acquiescence, recipient; it is the Child who gazes, with a kind of *objective*, strangely discerning, deep apprehension of her, startling to northern eyes. It is a gaze by no means of innocence, but of profound, pre-visual discerning. So plainly is the child looking across the gulf and *fixing* the gulf by very intentness of pre-visual apprehension, that . . . [i]t seems almost a cruel objectivity.[29]

Kristeva also refers to several renderings of the Madonna and Child as exemplary of the subject/object relation. In her essay "Motherhood According to Giovanni Bellini," she writes of the various "idealist ideologies" that have been developed in regard to motherhood, focusing specifically on pictorial art from "Byzantine iconography to Renaissance humanism." Like Lawrence, Kristeva situates the origin of the self/other conflict in the womb, and her description of the "purpose and progression" of the fetus is similar to Lawrence's: "Cells fuse, split, and proliferate; volumes grow, tissues stretch, and body fluids change rhythm, speeding up or slowing down. Within the body, growing as a graft, indomitable, there is an other. And no one is present, within that simultaneously dual and alien space, to signify what is going on." She says that motherhood is apparently impelled by a "nonsymbolic causality" and an instinctual drive that transcend "the social, symbolic bond" and the laws of social coherence. This primal regression (i.e., regression from the second mode of consciousness back to the first, from objective knowledge back to objective emotion) is readjusted and in fact often turned "into melancholy as soon as the child becomes an object, a gift to others, neither self nor part of the self, an object destined to be a subject, an other."[30]

Kristeva's essay provides a detailed analysis of the theme of motherhood in the Virgins and Madonnas painted by Bellini and Leonardo Da Vinci. It is interesting, for example, to compare her study of the maternal hands in one of Bellini's works to Lawrence's comments above. Kristeva provides an interpretation not on an objectifying gaze or a uniting touch but rather on a touch that severs:

> Painted with austere and graphic precision . . . they bear witness to a maternal appropriation of the child. There is a crushing hug, a tussle between a possessive mother and her child, who tries in vain to loosen her grip. . . . There is a shiver of anguish and fear in the child's hand, which grips the mother's thumb. . . . Is this an archaic memory of maternal seduction, a recollection of the hand whose precocious, already sexual caresses are more threatening than comforting?[31]

The posture of mother and child is the subject of Margaret Atwood's short story "The Resplendent Quetzal." In this story, both the main character, Sarah, and her husband, Edward, envision her as a Madonna, a figure tortured by birth on the one hand and smugly content on the other. The resplendent quetzal of the title refers to the child of this pained and haughty Madonna. The quetzal is a bird found in Mexican cloud forests that Sarah would like to see during the vacation tour of Mexico which she and Edward, who is a grade-school teacher, are taking. Bird watching is Edward's passionate hobby, and she has been thumbing through his handbook, *The Birds of Mexico*. He explains to her simply that "Quetzal Bird meant Feather Bird," but to himself he thinks, "The Aztecs thought hummingbirds were the souls of dead warriors, but why not all birds, why just warriors? Or perhaps they were the souls of the unborn, as some believed. 'A jewel, a precious feather,' they called an unborn baby, according to *The Daily Life of the Aztecs. Quetzal*, that was *feather*."[32] He does not share with Sarah the myth of the unborn souls, for ever since their first child was stillborn, the topic—or even the slightest reference to the event—has become taboo between them. They carry their griefs separately, Edward trying desperately and Sarah disdainfully to guess or ignore the other's moods and reactions.[33]

On this vacation to Mexico, Sarah is uncomfortably reminded of her pregnancy and the stillborn child when she spies an absurdly unlikely Nativity grouping in one of the tasteless restaurants that Edward insists will supply them with a bit of "local colour." Here the confrontation between the sacred and the secular becomes almost shockingly, ludicrously complicated. In this pastiche, it is not just a matter of one well-mannered doll (who, in O'Brien's story, did in fact even look the part) standing in as understudy for the Virgin Mary. On the contrary, this religious landscape is populated by at least as many secular representatives as sacred ones. The boundaries between the two worlds have been all but erased, with abstract mythologized figures and cartoon characters worshipping side-by-side at the very heart of the crèche:

> On the bar beside the television set there was a crèche, with three painted plaster Wise Men, one on an elephant, the others on camels. The first Wise

Man was missing his head. Inside the stable a stunted Joseph and Mary adored an enormous Christ Child which was more than half as big as the elephant. Sarah wondered how the Mary could possible have squeezed out this colossus; it made her uncomfortable to think about it. Beside the crèche was a Santa Claus haloed with flashing lights, and beside that a radio in the shape of Fred Flintstone, which was playing American popular songs, all of them ancient. (Atwood 152)

Sarah clearly sees herself as the stunted Mary, though in her own case the "colossal" aftereffect of the birth is the resultant emotional anxiety rather than physical distress. Atwood's juxtaposition of the stunted Mary and the enormous Christ Child is reminiscent of the portrayal in Marilyn French's novel *The Women's Room* of a tiny Barbie doll acting as mother to a huge baby doll. Much like Sarah, the character Adele struggles with issues of inadequacy and proportion. A tired wife and mother, Adele overhears her daughter Linda playing dolls. The child takes on first the voice of the mother doll, then the voice of the whining baby doll. The scenario Linda creates with her dolls is a parody in miniature of Adele's own life, and of course the dialogue of Linda's drama is drawn from her own conversations with her mother and those she has overheard. The symbolism is obvious—that the mother feels overwhelmed by the children, whose energy and presence seem to loom so much larger than her own.[34]

Sarah finds it uncomfortable just thinking about the enormous doll. The way in which she was drained emotionally by her pregnancy and the way in which she felt betrayed by Edward are the memories that make eating dinner in the squalid restaurant "even more depressing than it should have been, especially the crèche. It was painful, like a cripple trying to walk" (Atwood 152).

Sarah is not the only Atwood character to react negatively to the disconcerting presence of a doll. The narrator of *Cat's Eye*, a girl named Elaine, recalls her first "girl-shaped" doll. It was a "Barbara Ann Scott doll," modeled after the famous figure skater whose pictures Elaine has admired in the newspaper:

The doll of her has little leatherette skates and a fur-trimmed costume . . . but it looks nothing at all like the real Barbara Ann Scott. According to the pictures she's muscular, with big thighs, but the doll is a slender stick. Barbara is a woman, the doll is a girl. It has the worrying power of effigies, a lifeless life that fills me with creeping horror. I put it back into its cardboard box and tuck the tissue paper around it, over the face. I say I'm doing this to keep it safe, but in fact I don't want it watching me.[35]

Years later, as a teenager, she is reminded of this doll when a local girl is raped and murdered. Elaine has long dismissed the warnings of "bad men in the ravine" as a "scarecrow story, put up by mothers"; now, however, she acknowledges that "it appears they exist, despite me": "This murdered girl troubles me. . . . She stirs up something, like dead leaves. I think of a doll I had once, with white fur on the border of her skirt. I remember being afraid of this doll. I haven't thought of that in years."[36] In both cases—for Elaine and for Sarah—the dolls are reminiscent of death and a certain loss of hope and optimism. In "The Resplendent Quetzal," while Edward harbors a secret hope that they may one day have another child, Sarah has promised herself that she "would never take that risk, go through all that work again. . . . She wasn't going to try again. It was too much for anyone to expect of her" (Atwood 157). She cannot contemplate ever again enduring the self/other conflict of carrying the "indomitable graft" only to lose it in the end.[37]

The story's focal point is an ancient sacrificial well, a pre-Columbian ruin whose imposing presence governs the private thoughts of both Edward and Sarah. Edward, for example, imagines "picking Sarah up and hurling her over the edge, down into the sacrificial well. Anything to shatter that imperturbable expression, bland and pale and plump and smug, like a Flemish Madonna's. . . . But it wouldn't work: as she fell she would glance at him, not with fear but with maternal irritation" (Atwood 148). Thus to Edward, Sarah is not a distressed but a supercilious Madonna. He also senses vaguely that Sarah would be inappropriate as a sacrificial victim. For one thing, he feels it would not be quite right to toss her in the well fully clothed. And for another, she's no longer a virgin, though he recalls in wonder the days when he had "treated her body . . . as something holy, a white-and-gold chalice, to be touched with care and tenderness," and she had not been, as she now was, derisive of his reverence. Any vestige of this worshipful attitude is now, she feels, directed toward his favorite birds rather than toward her; and she shares his use of holy imagery when thinking that "Edward thumbed through his Peterson's Field Guide as if it were the Bible or the bird were the Holy Grail" (Atwood 149, 146). In fact, for Edward, the Holy Grail is the resplendent quetzal, green and red and iridescent blue— the unborn baby, the precious feather of his fantasies, and the one and only bird that Sarah has any interest in seeing (despite Edward's expressed doubtfulness that one will appear since they will not actually be near any cloud forests).

For Sarah, the doll in the restaurant becomes the rather unlikely Grail for which she has been searching. Because of its absurd placement, the doll here does not appear to hold the promise of the ideal miniature. The doll—the entire display, even—seems as grotesque as it does miniaturized. The combination of these elements may obscure but does not prevent the body of the doll from assuming its revelatory function: "These forms of projection of the body—the grotesque, the miniature, and the microcosm—reveal the paradoxical status of the body as both mode and object of knowing, and of the self constituted outside its physical being by its image."[38]

Atwood's novel *Surfacing* deals also with the body as an object of knowing and with an ill-fated pregnancy. Although the narrator of this novel does not seek to replace the lost child with a doll, she does feel, whenever discussing her pregnancy, that "the words were coming out of me like the mechanical words from a talking doll, the kind with the pull tape at the back; the whole speech was unwinding, everything in order, a spool."[39] Seeking, among other things, a reconciliation that will replace this false mode of knowing with a reconstitution of the self within the physical body, she visits the town in which she grew up. Signifying the order for which she searches is a miniature world of consistency and control, a barometer that she remembers from childhood: "A wooden house with two doors and a man and a woman who lived inside. When it was going to be fair the woman . . . would emerge. . . . [W]hen it was going to rain she would go in and the man would come out." As a child, she thought of these dolls as controlling the weather "instead of merely responding to it."[40] What she longs for now is to replace the confusing world of events in her own life with the orderly, predictable existence of the miniature woman in her long skirt and tidy apron. While she does not desire to control anything as gigantic as the weather, she would like to be in control of, rather than passively reacting to, the experiences of her troubling past. Like Sarah, she evades and modifies the truth of her own lived reality.

While Sarah identifies herself with the troubled Madonna, mother of the grotesque and overwhelming doll, Edward imagines the Sarah who would be the mother of a resplendent bird-child. He envisions her kneeling before him, the high priest, in preparation for her sacrifice. Though the real-life Sarah has come to terms with her own "comely" body ("You would never use that word for a thin woman" [145]), Edward, in his own way, modifies reality; he sees Sarah as an image, not as a physically constituted self. In his vision, "he thought of her body, which he made slimmer and more taut, with an abstract desire which was as unrelated as he could make it to Sarah herself" (Atwood 149). Mentally he adorns her naked body for the task of entering the well— with gold bracelets, feathers, long flowing hair, and "blood drawn with thorns from his own tongue and penis," but he feels that even in the proper attire she might not be a fit sacrifice. Why would she be chosen if the object of the exercise were to ensure fertility? At the conclusion of his fantasy, the high priest is "supposed to give her the message to take to the god. But he couldn't think of anything he wanted to ask for" (Atwood 150). Of course, the obvious request would be for a child of their own, a second baby who would be perfectly formed as the first one was but also alive and well, unlike the stillborn infant whose cord was fatally twisted. Edward does not understand that the reason that there continues to be no child—no jewel, no precious feather—born to them is Sarah's determination to avoid conception and the oral contraceptives that she takes daily to guarantee her infertility.

Sarah is obsessed with the idea of perfection. To her, the cruelest blow of the child's death is the fact that the newborn appeared to be without flaw yet still did not live: "A perfect child, the doctor said; a freak accident, one of those things that happen" (Atwood 149–50). She also had a flawless pregnancy, taking every precaution, following an impeccable diet and regimen of exercise: "Yet she had been disturbed by the thought that the child would be born with something wrong, it would be mongoloid or a cripple, or a hydrocephalic. . . . But the child had been perfect." What Sarah cannot now abide is that despite appearances something could have gone so drastically wrong with the pregnancy, that despite her best efforts she produced an imperfect child: "What had she done wrong? She hadn't done anything wrong, that was the trouble" (Atwood 157). The experience of pregnancy has revealed to Sarah what D. H. Lawrence refers to above as the knowledge of the *limits* of the self, a revelation of separation and imperfection that even now she has not fully come to terms with.

Edward finds Sarah's obsession with perfection to be one of her most bothersome traits, and it touches their life together in areas of much less significance than the loss of the child. He finds her concern for propriety annoying, and he thinks, with some derision, that "she was concerned for appearances, always" (Atwood 148). He laments that "even when she was wrong, she always managed, somehow, to be right. If only just once she would admit . . . what? That she could make mistakes. This was what really disturbed him: her assumption of infallibility" (Atwood 155, ellipses Atwood's). Such a posture derives, of course, from a desire to appear in control at all times, to be invulnerable to "freak accidents," to present a respectable front regardless of the circumstances, to mask the uncanny with the familiar.

If Sarah is the prim and perfect Madonna, rudely yanked from the sacred landscape, denied her firstborn, and cast into the world, then Edward is a player from the secular landscape, the court jester with no pretense to infallibility and little or no self-respect, "pouring out his own enthusiasm, gesturing, posturing, acting." Seeing himself this way, through the eyes of his sixth-grade students, he imagines that "they liked him because he danced for them, a funny puppet, inexhaustible and a little absurd. No wonder Sarah despised him. . . . It was always there, that gentle, patronizing mockery" (Atwood 150). She exercises control over him by insulting him and taking advantage of his passive nature (sending him, for example, on wild-goose [or quetzal] chases in hopeless pursuit of rare birds she claims to have spotted) and by responding vacuously to his serious comments and absolutely refusing to share her feelings with him. Though it is quite impossible to force her to engage in meaningful conversation with him, he could easily refuse to run after the imaginary birds, but he does not. He pretends to believe her because he is afraid to confront her with "the many lies that propped things up," afraid that "all the pretenses would come crashing down." He is as dependent as she is on the games they play to keep the relationship afloat, and one of these games is the constant assumption that she is perfect, that nothing is ever her fault—though actually he thinks of her as devious and stupid and resents her self-righteous perception of him as a "total idiot" (Atwood 48).

Despite Edward's dislike of Sarah's stance of perfection, when he sees her in a moment of tearful vulnerability at the story's conclusion, he is disconcerted. He remembers that she did not cry when the child died, and to encounter her now, apparently "crying, behind her hands, soundlessly and without moving," catches him completely off guard: "The ordinary Sarah, with all her perversity, was something he could cope with, he'd invented ways of coping. But he was unprepared for this. She had always been the one in control." Unused to consoling her, Edward, "trying to disguise his desperation" can only cajole: "'This isn't like you' . . . pleading, as if that was a final argument which would snap her out of it, bring back the old calm Sarah." For once she does not respond with patronizing indulgence or disdain, but to herself she thinks, "It is like me" (Atwood 158–59).

Entirely unaware of what has undone her, Edward cannot know how closely related these few tears are to those she never shed at the baby's death. The mood of the vacation—the Mexican village, the shabby restaurant, the wretched Nativity display, the misplaced baby doll, the mysterious yet repulsive well, which looks to Sarah more like a swamp than a sacred orifice—has inspired her to dredge up and act upon (if not actually confront or share with her husband) some of the long-buried feelings regarding her pregnancy. Sitting in the shade near the well, she overhears the guide of another tour group explain that "'archaeologists have dived down into the well. They have dredged up more than fifty skeletons, and they have found that some of them were not virgins at all but men. Also, most of them were children. So as you can see, that is the end of the popular legend'" (Atwood 156). With the myth of the erotically attired sacrificial virgins shattered, Sarah feels free to proceed with a purification ritual of her own.

Much to the reader's surprise, she withdraws from her purse the plaster Christ Child that, the narrator now reveals, she had stolen from the crèche the night before. Even Sarah is surprised at herself: "It was inconceivable to her that she had done such a thing, but there it was, she really had. She hadn't really planned it beforehand. . . . She'd just suddenly reached out her hand, past the Wise Men and through the door of the stable, picked the child up and put it into her purse." Remembering how enormous the doll had looked in the sacred yet vulgar setting of the motley Nativity, she now perceives it differently: "Separated from the dwarfish Virgin and Joseph, it didn't look quite so absurd." She also notices that, like her own child, this one looks perfect. Actually it has one tiny imperfection: "A perfect child, except for the chip out of the back, luckily where it would not be noticed. Someone must have dropped it on the floor" (Atwood 156–57). In this case, the flaw is not a fatal one, for the doll is only an inanimate replica of a baby, and the superficial appearance of perfection is quite enough. She has picked up this artificial child as a substitute for the one she lost:

> "*Lost*," people called it. They spoke of her as having lost the child, as though it was wandering around looking for her, crying plaintively, as though she had neglected it or misplaced it somewhere. But where? What limbo had it gone to, what watery paradise? Sometimes she felt as if there had been some mistake, the child had not been born yet. She could still feel it moving, ever so slightly, holding on to her from the inside. (Atwood 158)

Sarah associates the baby with water, fearing before its birth that it might be "hydrocephalic with a huge liquid head," imagining its continued existence in a "watery paradise" (Atwood 157, 158). This imagery, as well as the archaeologists' revelation, prepares the reader for the inevitable connection between the "lost" child and the well.

In "Five Poems For Dolls," Atwood writes that "all dolls come / from the land of the unborn, / the almost-born." She describes these dolls as the souls of "lost children," who have died or gone away.[41] Sarah's baby is like these lost children, who were never quite born. In her sensation that the child has not yet been born, Sarah is the subject "still pregnant with the correspondences that unite the *I* with the statue," the self with the other, the living human body with the artificial body of the doll or automaton.[42]

The guide continues with his narrative of the ancient customs, speaking as if the ritual were still observed: "'They do not do these things [sacrificing the children] to be cruel. . . . They believe these people will take a message to the rain god, and live forever in his paradise at the bottom of the well.'" One member of the group, a lady carrying what Sarah has observed to be a tastelessly decorated straw handbag, mutters to her companion "'Some paradise,'" but Sarah herself takes the guide's final observation more seriously, wondering indignantly at the disrespect of these graceless onlookers, sporting the big hats and sunglasses of the incorrigible tourist (Atwood 156). Only a short time before, Sarah had impertinently, if privately, shared the sentiments of the women's prattle, displaying no interest in the educational brochures provided for her by Edward ("'I'll see the same thing in any case, won't I?' she said. 'I mean, knowing all those facts doesn't change the actual statue or whatever'") and resisting "his attempts to explain things to her by her usual passive method of pretending not to hear" (Atwood 148–49). Before arriving at the village, she had even imagined that the well would be "smaller, more like a wishing well" (Atwood 144). Now, however, having witnessed its imposing depth, she realizes that its significance goes far beyond that of a wishing well, and she is suddenly imbued with a mysterious and serious purpose that far transcends throwing coins into a fountain: she "placed the baby on the rock beside her . . . stood up . . . picked up the child and walked slowly towards the well, until she was standing at the very brink." Suddenly the narrative shifts to Edward's perspective. He sees her standing "at the well's edge, her arms raised above her head." He fears that she is preparing to jump in, "but she merely drew back her right arm and threw something into the well" (Atwood 158).

The reader knows, as Edward does not, that the hurtled object is the plaster Christ Child, sent to save his and Sarah's misplaced child from the limbo in which it hangs. Sarah, like the natives, has not performed this ritual out of cruelty. She has sent the messenger to the watery paradise at the bottom of the well, perhaps as a reenactment of her own child's death, a reenactment over which she has full control instead of herself being the victim of surprise and shock. As Kristeva points out, "The corpse . . . upsets even more violently the one who confronts it as fragile and fallacious chance."[43] So Sarah seeks to dispel once and for all the anguish caused her by the physician's hurtful remark that the death of her child was "a freak accident, just one of those things." In Edward's fantasy he had not known what to ask the gods for, but Sarah has certainly sent the doll with a message for the liquid god of the ancient well. Whether she has prayed for fertility or infertility, however, remains unclear to the reader. Her deliberate sacrifice of the sacred doll seems designed to purge from her heart the haunting memory of the unsuccessful pregnancy. For as Lacan points out, "the phantoms that dominate" are lodged in the three-dimensional body, in the ambiguous automaton.[44] Separating herself from this representation of the abject and overcoming her fear of the past could mean either change or stasis, adopting a new position or resolving afresh to maintain her current one, gaining the courage to conceive again, despite the hard truth that a perfect child is not guaranteed, or denying herself forever the possibility of sighting the resplendent quetzal.

Sadly, the latter conclusion seems more likely, considering that when Edward reaches her—in that tense moment when he perceives her grief but cannot fathom an appropriate response—she fails to share with him a glimpse of her true self. Her tears are the sign of human fallibility that he has longed to see, but she wipes them away before uncovering her face:

> Sarah took her hands away from her face, and as she did so Edward felt cold fear. Surely what he would see would be the face of someone else, someone entirely different, a woman he had never seen before in his life. Or there would be no face at all. But (and this was almost worse) it was only Sarah, looking much as she always did. (Atwood 159)

Despite the stalemate of their relationship, Sarah has changed. Like Gogol and Caracas, she has looked into the abyss of abjection, the frighteningly deep sacrificial well, the land of oblivion. The plaster baby, which doubles as her own, represents the otherness that she has unsuccessfully strained to root from her unconscious. Kristeva says that the abject from which the subject "does not cease separating is for [her], in short, *a land of oblivion* that is constantly remembered."[45] Cowering behind the seamless and proper surface that Sarah presents to the world is this flawed other who cannot separate herself from the abject, cannot stop remembering. She is continually haunted by the ghost of her own child because it is not only the object but the abject of her desire. That Sarah feels threatened is understandable. Kristeva emphasizes that "abjection is above all ambiguity. Because, while releasing a hold, it does not radically cut off the subject from what threatens it—on the contrary, abjection acknowledges it to be in perpetual danger."[46]

Maintaining a facade of self-possessed calm is so important to Sarah because she fears the ambiguity of abjection and the threat of primal regression, the loss of symbolic coherence and objective knowledge. Concealing her emotions, especially from Edward, has become second nature to her, and the memory of the stillborn child has become a repository for all the repressed emotions she would rather not feel and the concealed failings she would rather not acknowledge. In fact, Kristeva points out that the melancholy of such primal regression is likely to set in soon after birth, when the child becomes "a gift to others, neither self nor part of the self, an object destined to be a subject, an other."[47] Sarah's grief is compounded precisely because her child was *not* destined to be an object, a subject, or a self in its own right; not until her moment of vision at the sacrificial well is she able to present the baby's surrogate as a gift to the unknown Mexican god. This gesture seals her acceptance that the stillborn child is no longer part of herself, and finally she can feel with certainty that it has indeed been born. The figure that she casts into the water is a distinct other—neither self (i.e., Sarah's own body, which Edward initially fears she is preparing to sacrifice) nor part of self. She has thrown in that which she herself is not—the other. The doll serves as substitute both for herself and for her "lost" child.

Kristeva describes the birth of a child and the rejection of the abject in terms of uncanny similarity. She attributes this similarity to the pre-objectal relationship between mother and child, explaining that it "is a composite of judgment and affect, of condemnation and yearning, of signs and drives. Abjection preserves what existed in the archaism of pre-objectal relationship, in the immemorial violence with which a body becomes separated from another body in order to be."[48] The merged imagery of these two events seems especially appropriate to a story like Atwood's "Resplendent Quetzal," which treats the mother's fear of giving birth to death rather than life. Kristeva calls the corpse "the most sickening of wastes . . . the utmost of abjection," and what Sarah cannot forgive Edward is that he left her alone with a corpse.[49] He realizes that Sarah blames him: "He still didn't know why. Perhaps it was because he'd gone out for cigarettes, not expecting it to be born so soon. He wasn't there when she was told; she'd had to take the news alone" (Atwood 155). Edward has deduced this on his own, without conferring with Sarah, but he is correct. She feels that her life was infected by death and that he was not there as he should have been to keep it at bay. Shortly before performing the sacrifice of the stolen doll, Sarah recalls of the real child that "there was nothing and no one to blame, except, obscurely, Edward; and he couldn't be blamed for the child's death, just for not being there. . . . This, she realized, was what she resented most about him. He had left her alone with the corpse, a corpse for which there was no explanation" (Atwood 157).

Gallop, in explanation of a book cover, describes a photograph of a child being born: a doctor's gloved hand grasps the infant's newly emerging head, a monitoring device rests on the abdomen of the mother—whose face is not visible, and two attendants swathed in masks and shower caps stand nearby. "I like the entanglement, the difficulty in sorting out one body from another. . . . Of course, that *uncanny* little head is surrounded by body for but a brief pause in an irrepressible progress. Things will soon be sorted out into their proper categories: mother, baby, doctor, nurse."[50] The unlikely grouping in the Mexican bar—a headless wiseman, an elephant-sized baby, a stunted father and dwarfish mother, a St. Nicholas night-light—strangely mirrors and parodies the solemnity of the entangled group depicted by Gallop. Sarah's petty theft is motivated by an instinctive urge to "sort things out," to categorize the doll as a miniature, inanimate replication of humanity. The problem, if this image is applied to the nativity of her own child, is that when all was sorted out, not only was Edward missing but so was the baby. For her, there was only the doctor with his harsh report; and the uncanniness that pervaded her experience was the emergence of death in the place of life. Gallop says that "thinking that truly passes through the body only occurs in brief intervals, soon to be reabsorbed by the powerful narratives of mind over matter."[51] But Sarah has continued to think through her body ever since that unhappy day in the hospital.

Before encountering the pictorial narrative presented by the peculiar juxtaposition of miniature figures, she has not been able to transform the disappointing birth experience into a narrative of any kind. This explains why, to Edward's dismay, "she'd never gone back to university either and she wouldn't get a job. She sat at home, tidying the apartment, looking over his shoulder, towards the door, out the window, as if she was waiting for something" (Atwood 150). What she waits and looks for is the "lost" child. In the most paralyzing sense of the word, all Sarah can do is think through her body and wait powerlessly for her mind to reabsorb the matter of the afterbirth. In setting forth her "poetics" and "thematics" of the body, Gallop decries "talk about the 'body itself,' as if it were transparently there in a text, as if there were such a thing as a 'body itself,' unmediated by text."[52] In fact the body of Sarah's transparent ghost-child does seem to pervade the watery text of the story—though not until Sarah lifts the doll from the manger is it perceived as palpable, a body itself. In the doll, matter has triumphed over mind, but it triumphs as an object of knowing.

That Atwood's story is one of the palpable body is made clear, as it is in Landolfi's story, with an opening anecdote concerning the bodily reality of urination. In search of one of Sarah's mystery birds, Edward follows a small path that "smelled of piss, and he could see by the decomposing Kleenexes further along that this was one of the places people went when they couldn't make it back to the washroom behind the ticket counter" (Atwood 147). Since the narrative is designed so that, despite their differing locations (Edward in the woods, Sarah by the well), their thoughts and sensory perceptions, and the images that they use, run parallel, it seems only natural that a few pages later Sarah should overhear a couple of offending tourists preparing to make good Edward's assumption:

> "Nature is very definitely calling," said the woman with the handbag. "I couldn't get in before, there was such a lineup."
>
> "Take a Kleenex," the other woman said. "There's no paper. Not only that, you just about have to wade in. There's water all over the floor."
>
> "Maybe I'll just duck into the bushes," the first woman said. (Atwood 153)

The Kleenex, flimsier than a sheet of writing paper yet strong enough to absorb the bodily triumph of matter over mind, is ever present in the useful capacity of tidying up after the body and restoring order when the wastes that signify abjection cross one of those boundaries that separate interior from exterior, viability from decay:

> These body fluids, this defilement, this shit are what life withstands, hardly and with difficulty, on the part of death. There, I am at the border of my condition as a living being. My body extricates itself, as being alive, from that border. Such wastes drop so that I might live, until from loss to loss, nothing remains in me and my entire body falls beyond the limit. . . . [D]ung signifies the other side of the border, the place where I am not and which permits me to be.[53]

Another narrative of the palpable body is Atwood's *Edible Woman*. In this novel, the character Marian extricates herself from the ambiguous border described here by Kristeva and permits herself "to be." Her first step in embracing self-consciousness is to acknowledge the existence of defilement and waste without feeling threatened by them:

> In a spirit approaching gay rebellion Marian neglected to erase her bath-tub ring.
>
> What she needed was something that avoided words, she didn't want to get tangled up in a discussion. Some way she could know what was real: a test, simple and direct as litmus-paper.[54]

In preparation for ending a suffocating relationship, Marian performs a ritual of self-reclamation. The test she devises is one of the physical body; as she begins her reality check, "her image was taking shape." Her plan is to bake a sponge cake (she decides that "sponge" is more fitting than "angel-food"), and she works in the kitchen, "concentrating all her attention on the movement of her hands" (Atwood, *The Edible Woman*, 274–75). She is mesmerized by her body as she re-creates it. Only by such intense concentration on her own physical being can she make reparation for the months of feeling absorbed, gnawed, and swallowed up by someone else.

She cuts the finished cake into the shape of a woman, then clothes the "blank white body" with icing and decorations:

Now the woman looked like an elegant antique china figurine. . . .

Her creation gazed up at her, its face doll-like and vacant except for the small silver glitter of intelligence in each green eye. While making it she had been almost gleeful, but now, contemplating it, she was pensive. All that work had gone into the lady and now what would happen to her?

"You look delicious," she told her. "Very appetizing. And that's what will happen to you; that's what you get for being food." At the thought of food her stomach contracted. She felt a certain pity for her creature but she was powerless now to do anything about it. Her fate had been decided. (Atwood, *The Edible Woman*, 277–78)

She regrets also having no birthday candles; for, although it is not her birthday, the cake—herself in miniature—represents her rebirth as a self-contained personality. She has recovered from the passive role of "edible woman" that her creation must now assume. When her fiancé arrives, she ceremoniously serves the cake, offering up her edible doppelgänger with the pronouncement, "'You've been trying to assimilate me. But I've made you a substitute, something you'll like much better. This is what you really wanted all along, isn't it? I'll get you a fork,' she added somewhat prosaically" (Atwood, *The Edible Woman*, 279). Peter declines a piece, and Marian fears that as a symbol the figure has failed.

Yet, the cake's significance goes further than the confrontation with Peter. Admiring her "enigmatic, mocking, succulent" double, Marian helps herself to the feet of the woman-shaped cake, thus breaking a long fast. She has become consumer rather than consumed. Her roommate walks in as she starts on the thighs and exclaims in horror, "'Marian! . . . You're rejecting your femininity!'" But, having regained her stride, Marian is not to be stopped: "'Nonsense,' she said. 'It's only a cake.' She plunged her fork into the carcass, neatly severing the body from the head" (Atwood, *Edible Woman*, 279–80). Having consigned her fear to the body of the doll, she confronts and conquers it, and the narrative shifts from third to first person, signifying the restoration of her identity: "Now that I was thinking of myself in the first person singular again I found my own situation much more interesting" (Atwood, *The Edible Woman*, 284).

The role of the cake-lady baked by Marian is similar to that of the baby doll Sarah has kidnapped. Both are designated to travel beyond the border that protects life from death, and both "fall beyond the limit" of waste and defilement in order that the subject whom each represents might sustain her "condition as a living being" (see Kristeva, above). Marian and Sarah are enabled to live, as Kristeva puts it, "from loss to loss." In fact, Marian gains perspective of her loss even as she eats the first few bites of cake: "Already the part of her not occupied with eating was having a wave of nostalgia for Peter, as though for a style that had gone out of fashion" (Atwood, *The Edible Woman*, 279).

At the conclusion of "The Resplendent Quetzal," as Sarah uncovers her vaguely tearful face and regains her composure, she takes a Kleenex out of her purse and wipes her nose. She has determined to live, despite her loss. Her body has not yet fallen beyond the limit, into the sacrificial well. In fact, from the outset Sarah determined that "you would never get her to jump into a muddy hole like that" (Atwood 144). However, the doll's body has indeed fallen beyond the limit. Seamless though it is, and free from waste and defilement ("It's diaper was cast as part of it" [Atwood 157]), it has suddenly become a participant in the drama of human existence. No longer passively displaying the symbolic drama of Christ's Nativity, it is now actually partaking in the seamy and unseemly activity by which life is both sustained and lost. Like the stillborn child, who from the very first was consigned to the other side of the border, the doll is now consigned to the muddy hole and sinks to the murky bottom of the mythic well, the place where Sarah is not, the place that permits her to be somewhere else.

Whatever may be in store for Edward and Sarah together, her act is ultimately one of affirmation, of overcoming the opposition of mind and body with which she has lived since the stillbirth. Gallop describes the positive outcome of repairing the mind-body split: "Locating thinking in a desiring body is also, in another vocabulary, locating thinking in a subject in history. To read for and affirm confusion, contradiction is to insist on thinking in the body in history. Those confusions mark the sites where thinking is literally knotted to the subject's historical and material place."[55] The tour guide's narrative provides Sarah with a text by which to understand her own history, to affirm the various contradictions of her loss, and to locate her body in the confusing yet material present; the body of the doll is the objective correlative of this revelation.

All three stories treated in this chapter, "Gogol's Wife," "The Doll," and "The Resplendent Quetzal," knot the desiring body with the thinking subject. Each subject grapples with the materiality and the imperfection of the mortal body, and each suffers the frustrating realization that even the objective and artificially created body is often neither perfect nor immortal—is instead abject and flawed, the double being no nearer ideal than the original. Describing Lacan's use of the mirror image, Gallop explains how it is that the "play of mirrors" may yield something other than a perfect double or a reflection identical to the subject:

> Lacan in fact situates opposites, rivalry, and aggressivity in identification; the adversary is simply one version of the alter ego. He terms the type of relation between the self and its mirror image (either as adversary or as identity) "imaginary." "The imaginary" . . . is the realm where intersubjective structures are covered over by mirroring. Lacan's writings contain an implicit ethical imperative to break the mirror, to disrupt the imaginary in order to reach "the symbolic."[56]

Thus, Caracas is simply one version of Gogol's alter ego, and when she strives to think through her body, Gogol must do the same whether or not he is prepared for such a challenge. When he can no longer tolerate the image of himself he sees reflected in the glass of Caracas, he breaks the mirror by inflating her beyond endurance. When Sarah tosses into the well the doll that represents both her own sense of abjection—her own adversarial alter ego—and her baby's double, she succeeds in breaking the surface of the imaginary realm and shattering the structures that have concealed from her mind the history of her own body. Though O'Brien's narrator does not literally break the glass case that contains her moldy double, she does affirm her own confusion and insist on thinking in her own body rather than vicariously through the body of her alter ego, the lost and sainted doll. Lacan's symbolic register is one of "radical intersubjectivity," one in which the subject confronts the power of its own abjection and comes face to face with the mirror image of its own imperfection.[57]

5

Heimlich/Unheimlich:
Interiority, Perfection, and the Uncanny
in Katherine Mansfield and Angela Carter

Katherine Mansfield: Within the Doll's House

In two short stories, "The Doll's House" and "Prelude," Katherine Mansfield treats the element of the uncanny that is related to the familiarity and privacy of the home—what Freud calls *Heimlich* or *Unheimlich*. The qualities of interiority and perfection govern the doll's house in Mansfield's fiction, and the *heimlich / unheimlich* manifestation of the uncanny pervades the country home in "Prelude."

The interior of the house is the domain of uncanniness. The *heimlich*, the security of those four walls called "home," contains not only whatever is appropriately homely or homey but also the potentially *unheimlich*—the unhomelike. Animals, for example, are tamed to live as members of the human household. Thus the wild (the *unheimlich*) is safely situated within the domestic (the *heimlich*). Similarly, concepts, like death, which are distressing to human beings are "domesticated" or interpreted in ways that make their mystery more comfortable to live with. By such paths of civility, elements of exteriority find their way inside. Stewart says that this "movement inward" is true of dollhouses as well as the full sized versions in which human families dwell:

A house within a house, the dollhouse not only presents the house's articulation of the tension between inner and outer spheres, of exteriority and interiority—it also represents the tension between two modes of interiority. Occupying a space within an enclosed space, the dollhouse's aptest analogy is the locket or the secret recesses of the heart: center within center, within

within within. The dollhouse is a materialized secret; what we look for is the dollhouse within the dollhouse and its promise of an infinitely profound interiority.[1]

These concepts are vividly played out in Mansfield's story "The Doll's House." Like the dolls given to the narrator of O'Brien's "The Doll," the dollhouse in this story is presented as a gift, bestowed upon the Burnell children by an elderly friend of the family. The dollhouse always presents the most typical of all miniature worlds, and its most striking characteristics are the smallness, the perfection, and the secretiveness of its interior landscape. "But perfect, perfect little house!" the narrator exclaims.[2] And when the house is first pried open, this same omniscient voice says, "That is the way for a house to open. Why don't all houses open like that?"

> The whole house-front swung back, and—there you were, gazing at one and the same moment into the drawing-room and dining-room, the kitchen and two bedrooms. . . . How much more exciting than peering through the slit of a door into a mean little hall with a hatstand and two umbrellas! That is—isn't it?—what you long to know about a house when you put your hand on the knocker. (Mansfield 319)

The desire expressed here is for the *unheimlich*. The narrator's interpolated question identifies an uncanny curiosity to become acquainted with the inaccessible recesses of another's dwelling, those areas that are both private and familiar only to the residents.

"The Doll's House" opens with the secrets of the miniature house revealed to the reader and to the Burnell children—Isabel, Lottie, and Kezia. With its interior open to the viewer, the house displays not only the recesses of its heart but also a vision of perfection, a self-enclosed, miniature world of proportion, control, and balance. Emotions of "profound aloneness" accompany the visual confrontation with such a world: "Once the miniature world is self-enclosed, as in the case of the dollhouse, we can only stand outside, looking in, experiencing a type of tragic distance." This experience of isolation is captured in the work of the artist Fasanella, "who paints views of apartment buildings and tenements as if their structures could be sliced open and we could simultaneously examine all the interiors they enclose . . . [presenting] an arrangement of simultaneous and unconnected dramas, which, as in viewing the dollhouse, we can attend to only one scene at a time."[3]

In their innocence, Isabel, Lottie, and Kezia do not suffer the loneliness of the giant unable to communicate its existence to the inhabitants of the miniature realm (Stewart mentions Frankenstein and

King Kong in this respect); nor do they envy the unattainable perfection of the miniature world. However, the excitement they experience is not unrelated to these more sophisticated and tragic expressions of emotion: "'O-oh!' The Burnell children sounded as though they were in *despair*. It was too marvellous; it was too much for them" (Mansfield 319, emphasis added). They are enchanted by the small furniture, the stove complete with oven door, the table set with tiny plates, the wallpaper, the carpeting, and the miniature gold-framed pictures.

The only thing they perceive to be amiss are the small people within the house: "The father and mother dolls, who sprawled very stiff as though they had fainted in the drawing-room, and their two little children asleep upstairs, were really too big for the doll's house. They didn't look as though they belonged" (Mansfield 319). The stiffness of the father and mother dolls suggests a sense of tension between the girls' parents, who do not figure in "The Doll's House." However, in an earlier-related story entitled "Prelude," Mansfield focuses on the relationship shared by the parents, Linda and Stanley Burnell, and describes the event of their moving from a house in town to one in the country—a move urged onto the family by Stanley.[4] In "Prelude," Linda's sense of not belonging in the new house, or even in her family, is made clear when, the morning after the move, she awakes and wishes "that she was going away from this house, too. And she saw herself driving away from them all in a little buggy, driving away from everybody and not even waving" (Mansfield 66). In another fantasy, she imagines that she is being rowed far away from the house in a flying ship, that she is crying "'Faster! Faster!'" to the boatmen, and that no one from the family "would dare to come near the ship or to follow after." Roused from her reverie, she thinks "How much more real this dream was than . . . the house where the sleeping children lay" (Mansfield 92–93). Thinking of her obligation to them, she becomes like the rigid toy mother of the sleeping doll children in "The Doll's House."

The unnatural doll family unfortunately mars the miniature vision and detracts from the dollhouse's aim to portray "nothing of the grotesque absurdity of a scene that does not resemble life and has only the interest of a caricature."[5] Ironically, these stiff dolls that reside so uneasily in the glamorous dollhouse serve as reminders of the world of the body and the reality of lived experience, which is never immune from the grotesque and the absurd. The family conflict embodied in the misfit dolls provides a telling example of the uncanny; their discomfort should have remained private, but it is now on display. Usually withdrawn from the eyes of strangers, the uneasiness of the family is revealed when the *heimlich* façade of the house is disturbed. The dis-ease of the family is the *unheimlich* at the heart of the *heimlich*, the center within the center.

Typically, however, even the revealing world of the dollhouse strives to protect the most secret centers of the house. In this way, the dollhouse is both a representation of propriety and a "version of property which is metonymic to the larger set of property relations [and social codes] outside its boundaries"; these boundaries are observed and respected in the domestic model of the dollhouse as well as in the human dwelling: "the dollhouse erases all but *the frontal view*; its appearance is the realization of the self as property, the body as container of objects, perpetual and incontaminable."[6] Thus the body, like the house, has its hidden center and its secrets of interiority. Yet, the promise of perpetuity described here is countered by the threat of uncanniness that also exists in the container of the body. Just as the house may be haunted and the inviolable somehow contaminated, so may the body be "*heimlich* and full of terrors" for its owner (Freud 226). In respect to this betrayal of the exterior by the interior, Freud mentions the uncanny effect of epilepsy and madness, which "excite in the spectator the impression of automatic, mechanical processes at work behind the ordinary appearance of mental activity. . . . The layman sees in them the working of forces hitherto unsuspected in his fellow-men, but at the same time he is dimly aware of them in remote corners of his own being" (Freud 243). The functions and malfunctions of the body are often secret and largely unfamiliar, concealed behind the frontal view—as the dysfunctional family is shielded by the walls of the home.

Stewart calls the dollhouse "a materialized secret," and the Burnell sisters are certainly anxious to share the secret of their new possession. They are instructed that they may bring their friends from school, two at a time, to view the splendid toy. These visits are to be allowed, however, with the specific condition that the visitors are "not to stay to tea, of course, or to come traipsing through the house" (Mansfield 320). That is, the girls may share with outsiders the secrets of the miniature house but not those of the life-size house. The privacy and the sanctity (and the secrets) of the home are to be protected from intrusion and idle curiosity. Nor are the guests invited to actually play with the dollhouse; they are asked merely to admire it, "to stand quietly in the courtyard while Isabel pointed out the beauties and Lottie and Kezia looked pleased" (Mansfield 320). This restriction is in keeping with Stewart's explanation that "even the most basic use of the toy object—to be 'played with'—is not often found in the world of the dollhouse. The dollhouse is consumed by the eye." The transcendent vision offered by the dollhouse, "the most consummate of miniatures," can be known through visual apprehension alone.[7]

The assertion that "the dollhouse within the dollhouse" is what the viewer seeks as the promise of interiority explains why doll-makers often create for their dolls even smaller dolls—miniaturized miniatures—for the larger creations to hold. It also reinforces the connection between the threat of the uncanny and the promise of the interior as perpetual and inviolate. "Center within center, within within within"—this motif of repetition is one of the elements that Freud associates with the uncanny. He stresses, however, that it is *involuntary* repetition that makes an object, an event, or a sensation seem both familiar and unfamiliar (the paradox of the uncanny). But the repetition of the doll-maker, creating diminutive dolls or smaller and smaller dollhouses, is intentional. These objects of receding size are products of *voluntary* repetition. Yet they are still perceived as simultaneously known and unknown because they typify "the structure of memory, of childhood, and ultimately of narrative's secondary . . . relation to history."[8] Freud likewise locates the compulsion to repeat in the infantile unconscious; his thinking about repetition figures in both "The 'Uncanny'" and *Beyond the Pleasure Principle*. His focus is on "repeated and repeating phenomena" in dreams, neurotic symptoms, behavior patterns, and the transference of unconscious wishes: "the task of his two interacting principles of mental functioning—the pleasure principle, and its more sober partner, the reality principle" was to explain the recurring nature of such phenomena. Like the Uncanny, the repetition-compulsion is both known and unknown, "at once mobile and concealed in its operation."[9] This compulsion, well able to take on a life of its own, is the invisible energy that informs the uncanny.

In Mansfield's story, the compulsion to repeat is found not in language, dreams, or behavior patterns, but in an artifact of material creation. Within the dollhouse of the Burnell children there is no tiny doll or miniature dollhouse. There is only the awkward doll family, whose members are too large for the house, reminders of an exteriority that must be held at bay. Instead, it is a little lamp that represents, especially to Kezia, the "promise of an infinitely profound interiority":

> But what Kezia liked more than anything, what she liked frightfully, was the lamp. It stood in the middle of the dining-room table, an exquisite little amber lamp with a white globe. It was even filled all ready for lighting, though, of course, you couldn't light it. But there was something inside that looked like oil, and that moved when you shook it. . . . [T]he lamp was perfect. It seemed to smile at Kezia, to say "I live here." The lamp was real. (Mansfield 319)

When Isabel, the most boastful of the sisters, describes the wonders of the dollhouse to their admiring schoolmates, Kezia interrupts, reminding her not to forget the lamp: "'The lamp's best of all.'" Isabel gives her audience a thorough description of it, mentioning its tiny glass shade and the fact that "'you couldn't tell it from a real one.'" Yet, Kezia still feels that the lamp is not receiving its due: "Isabel wasn't making half enough of the little lamp" (Mansfield 322).

The lamp represents both the promise of interiority and the erasure of the uncanny. In "Prelude," a friend of the family drives Lottie and Kezia to the new country house in the evening, the others having departed earlier in the day to supervise the move and unpack their belongings. Being outside after dark is a new experience for the children, and they find that the world has been transfigured by the distortion of the miniature (the closure of the domestic interior) and the gigantic (the unwieldiness of the overly natural). In the moonlight, these perceptual modes seem even more exaggerated than usual: "Everything looked different—the painted wooden houses far smaller than they did by day, the gardens far bigger and wilder" (Mansfield 57). When the buggy arrives in the drive, the first thing Kezia sees is her grandmother "walking through the empty rooms carrying a lamp. From a window downstairs the light of a fire flickered. A strange beautiful excitement seemed to stream from the house in quivering ripples" (Mansfield 59).

The grandmother, Mrs. Fairfield, is the embodiment of every agreeable, comforting, and domestic connotation of *heimlich*. She carries the lamp out onto the porch, lighting the way for the belated travelers and asking if they made their way safely through the dark. Mrs. Fairfield must lift the sleeping Lottie and so entrusts the lamp to Kezia. Carrying "the bright breathing thing," Kezia leads the way into a place that, though strange and unknown to her, has already been made familiar by her grandmother's efforts. The rest of the family is relaxing in the dining-room, and again it is the lamp that dispels the unfamiliar and wards off the encroachment of the big, wild gardens: "Outside the pool of lamp and firelight the room stretched dark and bare to the hollow windows." Though Kezia is ordered by her aunt to "'put down the lamp . . . or we shall have the house on fire before we are out of the packing cases,'" she does not forget that moment of trust when her grandmother allowed her to hold the bright and breathing source of light (Mansfield 60).

The lamp, then, with its special significance, is the miniature within the miniature that most profoundly affects Kezia's sensibility. The promise that it holds for her is rooted in nostalgia. In fact, nostalgia is one of the two dominant motifs attributed to the dollhouse. Its quaint charm and old-fashioned qualities are echoes of this nostalgic strain. The second motif that informs the tradition of the dollhouse is wealth, and this trait too is exhibited in the attitudes that the Burnell children hold toward the extravagant toy. David Simpson discusses "trinkets and baubles" and "the worship of ornament" in a way that clarifies the significance of the lamp, especially when viewed as merely decorative rather than functional. In fact, Simpson's remarks are equally applicable to the dollhouse itself, whose function is purely ornamental. He points out that the imaginative, aesthetic, and pleasure-giving appeal of the decoration or the decorative image provides an attraction that goes beyond convenience or utility. One of the attractions of furs over sackcloth (the example he gives) is, of course, the obvious wealth that the first choice represents. Just as wealth and nostalgia can be identified as the dominant motifs of the dollhouse, Simpson says that both economic and imaginative trends inform the appeal, the history, and the worship or "fetishization" of ornament.[10]

Not only is the dollhouse itself a display of idealized upper-middle class life, but it also represents the relative affluence of the Burnells themselves. Choosing which playmates may or may not see the remarkable exhibition, the children impose the same social class barriers observed by their elders. The two girls who are excluded from the joy of viewing the dollhouse are "the two who were always outside, the little Kelveys. They knew better than to come anywhere near the Burnells" (Mansfield 320).

Because they attend a country school, the only one for miles around, all of the neighborhood children, regardless of their parents' professions are "forced to mix together." Lil and Else Kelvey are shunned because their mother is a "washerwoman" who works in other people's homes, their father is rumored to be in prison, their wardrobe is made up of hand-me-downs from their mother's various employers, and their lunches consist of messy jam sandwiches wrapped in old newspaper. They are thin, quiet, shy, and strange-looking to the other children, who taunt them mercilessly. Their one strength seems to be that they "never failed to understand each other" (Mansfield 320–21). Lil and Else know, of course, about the magical dollhouse, and they accept without question the fact that, though all the other girls have been to see it, they will not be invited.

Kezia, however, decides to question the unwritten and sometimes unspoken social code by which the Kelveys are ostracized. When she asks if she might possibly invite them, her mother responds, "'Certainly not, Kezia.'" She persists, "'But why not?'" only to be told, "'Run away, Kezia; you know quite well why not'" (Mansfield 322–23). Mrs. Burnell speaks less from conviction than from an unquestioned compliance with an abstract standard for which the dollhouse provides an objective correlative; it is a "monument against instability, randomness, and vulgarity."[11] The disgust directed against the innocent and hapless Kelvey children is motivated by a fear of these very forces. These are the factors that Mr. Burnell hopes to counter by moving his family to the country and from which Mrs. Burnell seeks to shield her children by monitoring their guests. But Kezia does not defer to the peer pressure, the social anxiety, or the parental authority that results in such aversion to Lil and Else.

Any class snobbery that she harbors is vanquished when the opportunity arises to treat the Kelveys to a view of the dollhouse. They, on the other hand, long accustomed to perceiving themselves in the despised position, are doubtful—astounded even—when Kezia extends to them the privilege of an invitation: "'You can come see our doll's house if you want to.'" Lil, the older of the two sisters, is hardly bold enough to defy convention; she flushes, gasps, and murmurs her refusal: "'Your ma told our ma you wasn't to speak to us.'" Kezia is initially at a loss for words at this abrupt rejoinder but soon decides to brush the warning aside: "'It doesn't matter. You can come and see our doll's house all the same. Come on. Nobody's looking'" (Mansfield 324). Finally, to placate little Else, Lil is persuaded to give in. When Kezia opens the hinge and the interior of the house swings into view, Lil and Else are overwhelmed by the same marvelous despair that first swept over the Burnell children. Kezia points out "'the drawing-room and the dining-room, and that's the—'" (Mansfield 325). The unfinished thought was undoubtedly to be "and that's the *little lamp*." But before Kezia can finish the tour of the house or even her sentence, the cold, furious voice of reprimand is heard in the doorway.

It is not Kezia's mother but her stern Aunt Beryl who issues the demand that Lil and Else leave at once: "'How dare you ask the little Kelveys into the courtyard? . . . You know as well as I do, you're not allowed to talk to them. Run away, children, run away at once. And don't come back again. . . . Off you go immediately!'" Whereas Kezia's mother scolded earlier out of unthinking acquiescence to the social hierarchy, Beryl scolds not so much to enforce the class system as to regain some sense of order and control over her own confusing personal life. For she has just that afternoon received a "terrifying, threatening letter" from one of her suitors, Willie Brent: "The afternoon had been awful. . . . But now that she had frightened those little rats of Kelveys and given Kezia a good scolding, her heart felt lighter" (Mansfield 325). Exercising her power over the small children and over the miniature world of the dollhouse is a substitute for taking control of the situation with Willie.

"Worlds of inversion, of contamination and crudeness, are controlled within the dollhouse by an absolute manipulation and control of the boundaries of time and space."[12] Beryl, who lives with her sister's family, feels isolated and lonely in the country. In some ways, she herself is the doll, stuck within the confining boundaries of the dollhouse, under the absolute control of an unkind fate. In the story "Prelude," Beryl's unhappiness is described at some length. Yes, she is shielded from the contamination and crudeness she might be exposed to if she had to live on her own and fend for herself; but she is also shielded from experience and happiness: "If she had been happy and leading her own life, her false life would cease to be" (Mansfield 98). She feels trapped by a false self, suffocated by the restraints of time and space, angry that her beauty, her youth, her charm, her exquisitely fashionable outfits all go unappreciated—"there was nobody to see, nobody." She fears that her destiny is to remain unmarried, to become "a most awful frump" (Mansfield 80, 95). She is able to meet only the young men invited to the house by her brother-in-law, Mr. Burnell, who is well-meaning but does not understand her tastes and desires. Unable to eliminate the lack of graciousness that contaminates her social life, Beryl fills this need by manipulating and controlling her niece Kezia and eliminating the intruders Lil and Else, who seem to embody the crudeness and vulgarity from which Beryl feels she suffers. The two Kelvey children represent to Beryl (as well as to the class-conscious school children, their teacher, and the larger community) Kristeva's concept of abjection. Beryl herself is caught in an attitude of abjection, "one of those violent, dark revolts of being, directed against a threat that seems to emanate from an exorbitant outside or inside, ejected beyond the scope of the possible, the tolerable, the thinkable." Beryl finds the presence of Lil and Else intolerable and unthinkable because they remind her of those elements in her own life that she would rather cast off than assimilate into her own being. The abject, like the uncanny and the secret of the dollhouse, is an issue of interiority/exteriority, and the Kelveys are to Beryl an exterior manifestation of the abject. The interior manifestation is the false self that Beryl feels dominates her personality. Kristeva explains the power of the other, who resides within the subject as an alter ego to point the way toward abjection: "I experience abjection only if an Other has settled in place and stead of what will be 'me.'"[13]

The children themselves, small and dependent, are miniatures compared to Beryl, and the dollhouse is an even further reduction of their small world. It is the miniature belonging to the miniatures. Beryl imposes her will on the world of the miniature, which "linked to nostalgic versions of childhood and history, presents a diminutive, and thereby manipulatable, version of experience, a version which is domesticated and protected from contamination."[14] In fact, Kezia does not need Beryl's protection from the Kelveys, and they are merely a metaphor for the true fear of instability that threatens Beryl—the anxiety of living with her married sister, of having no husband and no house of her own. This frustration finds an outlet when Beryl sees that Kezia has disobeyed a rule of the same social code by which she herself is hampered: "'Wicked, disobedient little girl!' said Aunt Beryl bitterly to Kezia, and she slammed the doll's house to" (Mansfield 325). The bitterness she feels toward the reality of her life is vehemently displaced, directed instead toward a more diminutive and manipulatable version of experience—the world of small children and even smaller houses.[15] Her righteous outburst relieves the "ghastly pressure" of her inner turmoil, and she is able to return to her own less manageable life in the big house, relaxed and humming a tune (Mansfield 325).

As the doors slam shut, Lil and Else are not surprised that their glimpse inside of Kezia's dollhouse has been so brief. They shrink away from the courtyard, not stopping to rest alongside the road until they are well away from the scene of their humiliation. Lil, who is described as "like her mother," still feels the shame burning in her cheeks, but Else soon forgets "the cross lady," remembering only the privilege of the moment. The narrator attempts to read their thoughts as they look "dreamily" into the distance, but Lil's remain private. Beryl's unkindness has struck her as a much deeper rejection than Else can perceive. Not only are they denied a view of the dollhouse, they are also barred from the vision that it represents—the comfort and security of a middle-class home. No four walls protect them from the instability, the randomness, and the vulgarity of life. Else, on the other hand, smiles "her rare smile." Even if only for a moment, she has been illuminated by that infinite promise of profound interiority that resides within the dollhouse. Kezia's admonitions on the playground that everyone pay attention to the lamp were not wasted on Else, who remembered every word and, in the few seconds given her, witnessed the symbolic object. Now, softly, she says to her sister Lil, "'I seen the little lamp'" (Mansfield 325–26).

For Else as for Kezia, the vision of the little lamp obliterates the distress of the unhomelike. Kezia experiences this distress most distinctly in "Prelude" when she and Lottie are left behind on the day of the move, to stay with the neighbors until evening. Kezia strays from the safety of the neighbors' nursery and returns one last time to her own family's now empty house. As she wanders through the bare rooms, cluttered with obscure and miscellaneous items—a piece of soap, a pill box, a needle—inadvertently left behind, she is frightened by the uncanny, "that class of the frightening which leads back to what is known of old and long familiar" (Freud 220). The house, once known to her, has been made strange, and such homely and familiar items as a discarded "hair-tidy with a heart painted on it" serve only to heighten the discrepancy between the familiar and the frightening. As daylight changes to dark and a fierce wind shakes the roof, walls, floors and windows of the empty house, Kezia is paralyzed by fear and uncertainty: "She wanted to call Lottie and to go on calling all the while she ran downstairs and out of the house. But IT was just behind her, waiting at the door, at the head of the stairs, at the bottom of the stairs, hiding in the passage, ready to dart out at the back door" (Mansfield 56). In fact Lottie is waiting at the door for Kezia, and the eerie sensation dissipates as they prepare for their journey to the new house.

In the new house, Kezia's mother is the one who experiences sensations of uncanniness and fear. The possibility that a lifeless object might in fact be animate is a condition for the uncanny that Freud calls "intellectual uncertainty" (Freud 226, 230).[16] But, in fact, Linda Burnell feels quite positively that "things had a habit of coming alive like that. Not only large substantial things like furniture, but curtains and the patterns of stuffs and fringes of quilts and cushions" (Mansfield 68). Her sensations express the haunting power of the *unheimlich* to pervade the very corners of a house, a negative displacement of the intimate serenity of the *heimlich*. She senses that these things in her house—like the quilts and the medicine bottles—listen and smile and "swell out with some mysterious important content. . . . But it was not for her, only, their sly secret smile; they were members of a secret society and they smiled among themselves." The mysterious capital letters of the "IT" that spooks Kezia appear also in Linda's account of an uncanny "THEY" with which she must contend:

> But the strangest part of this coming alive of things was what they did. . . . Sometimes . . . she woke and could not lift a finger, could not even turn her eyes to left or right because THEY were there; sometimes when she went out of a room and left it empty, she knew as she clicked the door to that THEY were filling it. And there were times . . . when she could hardly escape from them. . . . THEY were not deceived. THEY knew how frightened she was; THEY saw how she turned her head away as she passed the mirror. What Linda always felt was that THEY wanted something of her, and she knew that if she gave herself up and was quiet, more than quiet, silent, motionless, something would really happen. (Mansfield 68)

The power that this uncanny THEY has to frighten Linda Burnell can be explained somewhat by looking at Kristeva's observations on abjection, pre-objectal relationships, and violence. It is up to the subject, Linda

Burnell in this case, to confront the unnerving THEY with something called the "*heterogeneous 'I,'*" to persist until assimilation is accomplished, to determine the meaning of the fearful law, to produce the sign equivalent to the mysterious and unnamed effect, and to create for herself "a space out of which signs and objects arise."[17] For Linda, the one thing that staves off these uncanny forces and prevents something from really happening is the presence of her mother, Mrs. Fairfield, in the house. Just as Mrs. Fairfield vanquishes Kezia's fears by illuminating the night, she calms Linda's anxiety by creating order out of chaos and exercising an authority over the inanimate household objects that Linda herself can never quite muster.

In the kitchen of the new house, for example, Mrs. Fairfield "put the crocks away with a sure, precise touch . . . looking into the pantry and the larder as though there were not an *unfamiliar* corner. When she had finished, everything in the kitchen had become part of a series of patterns" (Mansfield 70, emphasis added). Mrs. Fairfield simply does not allow the *unheimlich* to lurk within her territory or to "destroy the *Heimlichkeit* of the home" (Freud 222). Freud explains, in his history of the term, that *Heimlichkeit, heimelich,* and *heimeleg* all share with *heimlich* the meaning of "belonging to the house, not strange, familiar." To illustrate these words in context, he supplies such samples as: "'We pictured it so comfortable, so nice, so cosy and *heimlich*.' 'In quiet *Heimlichkeit*, surrounded by close walls.' 'A careful housewife, who knows how to make a pleasing *Heimlichkeit* (*Häuslichkeit* [domesticity]) out of the smallest means'" (Freud 222, parentheses and brackets Freud's).

Mrs. Fairfield, shooing the unfamiliar out of every corner, imparting order and pattern, has rendered the room *heimlich* in every detail. Her command of domesticity is apparent not only in the new house but also in the one just vacated. When Kezia wanders through the empty house surveying the abandoned knick-knacks and litter, she does not even check the room that had been Mrs. Fairfield's because "she knew there was nothing in her grandmother's room; she had watched her pack" (Mansfield 56). Under Mrs. Fairfield's watchful eye, no inanimate object is left to its own device. No pincushion, ottoman, or milk-jug springs to life unbidden. Her control is absolute. Nor is this feat of calmly and competently establishing "a pleasing *Heimlichkeit*" lost on her appreciative daughter, Linda, who declares upon entering the newly organized kitchen: "'It says "mother" all over; everything is in pairs'" (Mansfield 71). Likewise, her son-in-law, Stanley, surveys the kitchen, concluding, "'You seem pretty snug, mother,'" and Mrs. Fairfield agrees with him: "'We are, Stanley. We are very snug'" (Mansfield 78). In *The*

Magic Toyshop, the apparent *Heimlichkeit* of the kitchen is described in terms of *smugness* rather than *snugness*: "Melanie was by herself in the kitchen, which was warm and *smug* and complacent since its work was finished for the day. The pots on the dresser and the straight-backed, hard-backed chairs and the rag rug all seemed to be at peace with the world."[18]

The interior of Mrs. Fairfield's "warm, tidy kitchen" is a world of near perfection in itself, offering respite from the distressing imperfections of reality (Mansfield 87). Her kitchen, like the dollhouse, is a tribute to the small details of everyday life. Like Hannele and Mitchka in their shop, Mrs. Fairfield is a participant in what Schor has called the "larger semantic network" of the detail, "bounded on one side by the *ornamental*, with its traditional connotations of effeminacy and decadence, and on the other by the *everyday* whose 'prosiness' is rooted in the domestic sphere of social life presided over by women."[19] Comfort and familiarity prevail here, an antidote of sorts to the tension that afflicts Linda, Beryl, and Stanley. Unlike the secret recesses of their hearts, the pantry doors conceal nothing that ought to remain secret. In the children's dollhouse, a world bound by space and time, perfection is a given. It is the condition of the miniature, and the immutable secrets of perfection and interiority are surely there for those like Kezia Burnell and little Else Kelvey, who are willing to look closely enough. But in the larger world without, the miniature represents not just a timeless ideal but a mode of exaggeration beside which the gigantic also holds sway. Both the miniature figure and the gigantic form are located on a scale of exaggeration, and both are processes of measurement that alienate the subject from the single "given notion of the normal" that is privileged as constant—the site of the human body.[20]

Linda Burnell detects the *unheimlich*—itself an exaggeration of the *heimlich*—in things both large and small. In the house, not only has the uncanny breathed life into the large, heavy pieces of furniture, but "everything had come alive down to the minutest, tiniest particle." She is not comforted but threatened by the interior of her home. The consolation of the little lamp escapes her as she fearfully awaits the uncanny, awaits the appearance of something that should have remained secret and hidden but has come to light, revealing itself in the animated objects of her house. Such revelation, despite her watchfulness, is allusive: "Only she seemed to be listening with her wide open watchful eyes, waiting for someone to come who just did not come, watching for something to happen that just did not happen" (Mansfield 69).

Linda relies upon her mother's skill to maintain the *Heimlichkeit* of the home and to protect her from the ubiquitous "THEY" who so subtly terrorize and threaten her. The need she feels for her mother is in direct proportion to the extent of her fear: "There was something comforting in the sight of her that Linda felt she could never do without" (Mansfield 72). When they walk together in the garden, Linda daydreams of escape, but even her mother's fantasies are firmly rooted in reality. Mrs. Fairfield, when Linda asks what she has been thinking of, confesses only to wondering about "'the splendid healthy currant bushes in the vegetable garden. . . . I should like to see those pantry shelves thoroughly well stocked with our own jam'" (Mansfield 94).

Unlike her mother, Linda is not able to maintain a clear and steady focus on the *heimlich* nature of such things as fruits, vegetables, jams, and jellies but is soon distracted by the most *unheimlich* plant in the garden—the gigantic aloe, with its mysterious property of blooming once every hundred years and its associations of superstition and grief. She says, "'I like that aloe. I like it more than anything here. And I am sure I shall remember it long after I've forgotten all the other things'" (Mansfield 92). But despite the attraction it holds for her, uncanniness hovers over the huge and ancient aloe, whose thorny, cruel, and curving leaves "seemed to be hiding something" (Mansfield 75). Somehow the stark plant, whose eerie presence governs the night, represents for Linda a certain antipathy that she feels toward Stanley; at the sight of its long sharp thorns, "her heart grew hard." The plant's tenacity seems to offer her protection from Stanley's frightening virility, and she imagines the garden growing "'bigger and bigger, with whole fleets of aloes . . . for me to choose from'" (Mansfield 93, 94).

Just as Beryl searches for the true self trapped inside the false, Linda stands trembling in the garden, "mocking and laughing" and asking herself: "And why this mania of hers to keep alive at all? . . . 'What am I guarding myself for so preciously?'" (Mansfield 94). In fact, what they both strive to keep alive is the sign of a light flickering on the dark porch; they search for a miniature amber lamp within a dollhouse, a materialized promise of interiority. What Beryl yearns for when she asks, "Shall I ever be that Beryl for ever? Shall I? How can I?" is a glimpse of—not the doll-like young woman before the mirror but—the true self within and a chance to bear witness to that integral self with the same confidence that prompts Else to claim, "I seen the little lamp" (Mansfield 98, 326). What Linda guards so preciously is the profound interiority of her own integrity and identity, the self within the self.

Linda's belief that the new house is haunted by a nameless "THEY" is linked with her old, established fears of Stanley's strength, of his desire to have more children than their three daughters, of the tenuous coexistence of her own identity and her intimate relationship with her husband.

The "THEY" for whom she holds so still, in silent apprehension, is none other than Stanley—or rather her fear of his energy and vigor: "He was too strong for her; she had always hated things that rush at her. . . . There were times when he was frightening—really frightening" (Mansfield 93). She has displaced this complex of emotions into the house (which is itself concrete evidence of Stanley's ability to accomplish his desires), and the anxiety that she experiences as a result of this displacement is, according to Freud, properly classed as repression: "It may be presumed that when people . . . feel an obscure fear—a dread of rousing something that, so they feel, is better left sleeping—what they are afraid of is the emergence of [the repetition-] compulsion with its hint of possession by some daemonic power."[21] He explains how "something repressed which *recurs*" not only constitutes an instance of the frightening but also captures the secret nature of the uncanny and demonstrates why linguistic usage would extend *das Heimliche* into its opposite: " for this uncanny is in reality nothing new or alien, but something which is familiar and old-established in the mind and which has become alienated from it only through the process of repression" (Freud 241). Thus the chairs and sofa cushions in Linda's new house are not animated by anything new or alien but by her contradictory feelings for Stanley, which have, through repression, been transformed into anxiety.[22] Any small reminder can call forth in her this nameless dread, this obscure fear that has lain sleeping for so long: "The feeling of the uncanny would seem to be generated by the being-reminded-of-the-repetition-compulsion, not by being-reminded-of-whatever-it-is-that-is-repeated. It is the becoming aware of the process that is felt as eerie, not the becoming aware of some particular item in the unconscious, once familiar, then repressed, now coming back into the consciousness."[23]

On the evening of her walk in the garden with her mother—the night she imagines floating away in a ship, under the protection of the aloe plant—she finally bears witness to the content of her repressed emotions and achieves the revelation for which she had earlier waited in vain:

> It had never been so plain to her as it was at this moment. There were all her feelings for him, sharp and defined, one as true as the other. And there was this other, this hatred, just as real as the rest. She could have done her feelings up in little packets and given them to Stanley. She longed to hand him that last one, for a surprise. She could see his eyes as he opened that . . . (Mansfield 93–94, ellipses Mansfield's)

She desires to shock him, not with the unfamiliar, but as she has shocked herself by giving audience to the ever-present repressed and familiar voices of her own secret heart, by admitting her secret grief. Her urge to wrap these "materialized secrets" up as surprise packages suggests, once again, that the *unheimlich*, the ugly and unnerving emotion of hate, is found within the *heimlich*, the ostensible gift of love. Linda's long-secret feelings are uncanny because they no longer remain hidden but have surfaced—and not just by inhabiting the recesses of her house or possessing everything from the largest piece of furniture to the smallest fringe. Instead, they have come to light in her consciousness, whether or not they ought to.

Thus, swinging back the front of the house, the viewer, the voyeur, the narrator, the reader, all discover what they long to know about the secret interior of another's house. When the cover is lifted and light admitted, the connected and unconnected dramas that would otherwise remain private are revealed and discovered. In one room, a tiny lamp promises perpetuity, infinity, and the ever-receding perfection of the miniature to two curious children while the parent dolls sit stiffly on the small sofa. In another, the two parents exchange gifts. The father presents the mother with a large bottle of oysters, a pineapple, a basket of fresh black cherries, and his secret desire for a son. The mother offers a little wrapped package from which looms, along with "her love and respect and admiration," her fear of further childbearing, and her secret hate (Mansfield 93). The contents of the package threaten to disrupt, perhaps irrevocably, the apparent perfection and the "snugness" of the Burnell household. At the center of the house and in the heart of its inhabitants, the promise of interiority and the power of the uncanny quietly, secretly coexist. The openly familiar and the secretly familiar hang in a delicate, precarious balance, the *heimlich* threatening to extend into its opposite, and the *unheimlich* held at bay by such unlikely talismans as a little lamp.

Angela Carter: Within the Toyshop

Angela Carter's *The Magic Toyshop* is another drama of interiority that examines not only the impact of the miniature on human consciousness but also the uncanniness lurking in the ostensibly safe confines of the home. In this novel, as well as in Mansfield's stories, "the interior space of the home and the interiority of emotion provide a narrative scenario for a female protagonist with minimal outlets for exterior cathartic action."[24] The female protagonist of Carter's novel is Melanie, a girl of fifteen, who, along with her Aunt Margaret, lives as a captive in the toyshop of her uncle, Philip Flower. The novel opens with the revelation that "the summer she was fifteen, Melanie discovered she was made of flesh and blood" (Carter 5). The tale's focus is on her Uncle Philip's struggle to capitalize on the flesh-and-blood existence of those around him while simultaneously sapping their humanity and automating them to his own ends. His single-minded work as a master craftsman has skewed his perception of the distinct differences between living people and the dolls, puppets, and automated creatures of his toyshop.

A sense of the uncanny pervades the humble yet macabre dwelling that the family inhabits behind the dark facade of the shop: "TOYS PHILIP FLOWER NOVELTIES" (Carter 40). Melanie's uneasy life here begins when she and her younger siblings, Jonathon and Victoria, are suddenly left orphaned and unprovided for. From their secure, even plush, middle-class life in the country, they are shunted to the care of their mother's only brother, the mysterious and unsavory Uncle Philip. Melanie has never seen this man but knows him as the one unsmiling guest in her parents' wedding photograph. The only memory she associates with him is of a jack-in-the-box that he had sent one year for her Christmas present. As a small girl, she had been frightened by the toy, and reasonably so: "a grotesque caricature of her own face lurked from the head that leaped out at her. That year her parents had sent him one of their printed Christmas cards showing themselves and Melanie . . . And in return came this horrid toy." After causing the child months of nightmares, the jack-in-the-box is thrown away, and the family decides to exchange no further Christmas greetings with Uncle Philip: "The tenuous contact was lost for good" (Carter 15).

As suggested by this incident, in which the three-dimensional representation is sent in response to the two-dimensional, *The Magic Toyshop* is filled with descriptions of the power of photographs, mirrors, masks, puppets, statues, and automated toys—all creations that yield an image of the human body. The first of these images is that of Melanie before the mirror. Having discovered that she is "made of flesh and blood" and is "no longer a little girl," Melanie spends hours staring at her naked body in the mirror. "O, my America, my new-found land," the narrative voice exclaims, capturing the rapture that Melanie experiences (Carter 5). She enjoys numerous fantasies, dancing for her own reflection, posing in Pre-Raphaelite attitudes, or imagining her wedding night; she entitles each pose as if it were "a photograph in her own photograph album. 'Myself at fifteen.'" She searches in the mirror for a confirmation of perfection, unable to bear the thought that "she might not be already perfect" (Carter 10, 12).

The narcissism of these exercises can be more accurately understood according to Lacan, as the subject's attempt to identify the ego ideal and the ideal ego. For Lacan, "the kernel of the ego ideal" to which the subject clings is found in "the field of desire" and in "the field of the Other." The vision in the mirror is one level at which the relation of the subject to the other is established. The child/subject sees in her own reflection the ego ideal, and in the reflection of the parent/other she sees the ideal ego: "By clinging to the reference-point of him who looks at him in a mirror, the subject sees appearing, not his ego ideal, but his ideal ego, that point at which he desires to gratify himself in himself." Lacan elaborates upon this concept in his description of the girl who said "that it was about time somebody began to look after her so that she might seem lovable to herself."[25]

Melanie, for example, prays, "Please God, let me get married. Or let me have sex." She thinks of Juliet, "married and dead of love at fourteen," and laments that she herself has never even been out with a boy (Carter 12). Like Lacan's case study, she longs for someone to make her "seem lovable to herself." The ego ideal that Lacan describes is the "privileged signifier," and the subject, in order to feel "satisfactory and loved," seeks a relationship with the ego ideal that moves beyond narcissistic identification.[26] Despite the handsome princes who inhabit Melanie's private fantasies, she is able to name herself as this central signifier: "Since she was thirteen, when her periods began, she had felt she was pregnant with herself, bearing the slowly ripening embryo of Melanie-grown-up inside herself for a gestation time the length of which she was not precisely aware" (Carter 22).

Melanie is the subject who makes herself an object by displaying herself before the mirror, a stance that is "passifying" yet ultimately frustrating because it is based on "misapprehension." Lacan says that even if such a subject "achieved his most perfect likeness in that image, it would still be the *jouissance* of the other that he . . . recognized in it."[27] According to Lacan, the mirror phase is a moveable point. Sometimes he writes of it occurring as a stage in the newborn infant's perceptual development; at other times he dates it later in infancy. Other writers have argued for the significance of an adolescent mirror stage. La Belle, for example, says that the first encounter with the mirror may occur later: "For most females, at least those created in fiction, the memorable scene is not in infancy as Lacan indicates. Neither is it necessarily a singular incident; indeed, many characters experience a succession of 'primal' confrontations with the mirror at various stages in their development, from childhood through adolescence."[28] What Melanie experiences during the summer of her fifteenth year is an adolescent stance before the mirror. Her self-perception edges from chaos and discord to harmony in the artistic poses that she strikes. As with the infant, the mother represents wholeness and order to Melanie while she herself remains bewildered by a confusion of drives and functions.

The infant, unable to stand before the mirror without the mother's support, "finds in the mirror image 'already there,' a mastery that she will actually learn only later"; aligning herself with her mother's image, the child "appears *already* to be what she will *only later become*."[29] All of Melanie's mirror selves are illusion, based on "an already anticipated maturity."[30] In each pose, she appears already to be what she might later become. Wondering how she will look "in her grown-up photograph album," what her children will be like, what pets they will have, and where they will all go for summer vacation, she impetuously wishes that she were "forty and it was all over and I knew what was going to happen to me" (Carter 10).

Her boldest venture of self-discovery is to model her mother's wedding dress one restless night while her parents are away on a lecture tour in America. Standing in their moonlit bedroom, Melanie observes that "familiar things seemed exotic and curious in the light of the moon" (Carter 13). The ordered *heimlichkeit* of the familiar environment has been replaced by a sensation of uncanniness that touches the clocks, knick-knacks, and family portraits in the room. After studying the wedding photograph for many long moments, Melanie dreamily imagines herself surrounded by the wealth of satin from which the bridal gown was made. The temptation soon becomes irresistible, and she opens the trunk that holds the "epiphany of clothing" that had been her mother's wedding finery (Carter 14). Overwhelmed by what she sees— first in her mother's long mirror and then in her own—she leaves the house, wearing the unwieldy dress, for a solitary walk in the moonlight, an adventure that ends in destruction (of the dress) and despair. The largeness of the night, which at first had filled her with ecstasy, soon becomes, like the dress, "too big for her. . . . Too much" (Carter 21).

She has ventured into the territory of the *unheimlich* and is engulfed by an "alien loneliness, and terror" against which she is defenseless: "The garden turned against Melanie when she became afraid of it." Her only hope, she feels, is to return as quickly as possible to the familiar, to the *heimlich*: "She had to get back to the front door and closed-in, cozy, indoors darkness and the smell of human beings. . . . [T]he worst thing was sitting outside of the house and not being able to get in" (Carter 21). Melanie cannot bear being barred from the comfort of her accustomed surroundings. Locked out of the sleeping house, surrounded by "the treacherous and deceitful night," she is overwrought by the unknown. Only the purring cat offers "a domestic sound, unexpected and reassuring.. . . . as if someone had lit a small fire for her" (Carter 23). Like the beckoning lamp of Mrs. Fairfield and the tiny dollhouse lamp in Mansfield's fiction, the cat provides a temporary reminder of the snug and *heimlich* interior of the home.

Just as Mrs. Fairfield imparts domesticity to the Burnell home, it is the housekeeper, Mrs. Rundle, who dispels the uncanny for Melanie's family. Mrs. Rundle speaks with "an Old-World, never-never-land stateliness," is "very much at home," cooks bread pudding "plain and fancy," and sings sentimental old songs. Melanie thinks of her as "a fixed point . . . the mother hen" (Carter 7, 30). The morning after Melanie's escapade, she wakes to another sign of Mrs. Rundle's stability—the aroma of toast and bacon floating through the house, signifying that "life went on" (Carter 25).

By climbing up a tree and through a window the night before, Melanie had finally reached the safety of her own room and slept in exhaustion. Upon waking, she stuffs the tortured remains of the dress back into its trunk and resolves to confess all upon her mother's return. She is, however, to be denied this chance to explain and beg forgiveness. The previous night's folly turns out to be more than just one night of destruction and bewilderment; it heralds the onset of irreparable loss, damage, and confusion.

Still sickened from the events of the night before, Melanie breaks completely when news arrives of her parents' death in an air crash. Superstitious and guilty, she cries, "'It is my fault, because I wore her dress. If I hadn't spoiled her dress, everything would be all right. Oh, Mummy!'" In anger she shatters her beloved bedroom mirror, flinging the hairbrush at her reflected face and revealing the wood upon which the glass had been mounted: "She was disappointed; she wanted to see her mirror, still, and the room reflected in the mirror, still, but herself gone, smashed" (Carter 27). Writing of the subject's frustration and "dispossession of being," Lacan says that the subject "ends up by recognizing that this being has never been anything more than his construct in the imaginary and that this construct disappoints all his certainties." He describes the "sincere portraits which leave [the idea of the subject] no less incoherent" and "the defences that do not prevent his statue from tottering." It is by these portraits and defenses that Melanie feels betrayed, and her goal is to eradicate the sentiment of self which she had seen in her own mirror image.[31]

In grief she goes to her parents' room and, in a trance, destroys everything in her path, first tearing the wedding photograph into tiny bits. Destroying the picture is the most tangible way in which she can express her despair, for only the night before it had occurred to her, while gazing at it, that "photographs are chunks of time you can hold in your hand; this picture was a piece of her mother's best and most beautiful time" (Carter 15–16). Photographs are one way in which the body is made miniature and imaginary; the photograph is "a depiction of an event effected through a reduction of physical dimensions, a picture which becomes both the occasion for the event and a replacement for it. The photographs of the event themselves speak its effort toward transcendence: front is behind, behind is front, and all of history is stopped."[32]

Indeed, it was Melanie's admiration of her mother's effort toward transcendence that had inspired her to model the wedding dress for herself: "On her mother's wedding day she had had an epiphany of clothing. So extravagantly, wholeheartedly had she dressed herself. . . . Her smile was soppy and ecstatic and young and touching" (Carter 14). The simplicity of this smile grounds the complication of transcendent clothing and expresses the sentiments that make the photograph an object of desire, longing, and nostalgia. As such an object, the photograph becomes a souvenir of the occasion it depicts, "the preservation of an instant in time through a reduction of physical dimensions." Equally important, the significance of the ever-silent photograph is always supplied by means of narrative. Thus, telling the story of the occasion of the photograph renders the narration itself an object of nostalgia. Without an accompanying narrative line, the ancestors captured on the surface of the film "become abstractions, losing their proper names."[33] The wedding photo that Melanie shreds is a "fragment of her mother's happy time" (Carter 16), and it is the poignancy of her parents' tragic narrative that makes the sight of it suddenly unbearable to her. She cannot allow the existence of a souvenir that captures the memory of a bride and bridegroom—and even a bridal gown—that are now lost to her forever. She can relish the sight of the miniature only when its original is accessible to her. With her parents gone, the picture is ineffective as a replacement of their past happiness. Months later, Melanie is shocked to see an identical copy of the wedding portrait on her Uncle Philip's mantelpiece. She fears that his "house is haunted" and that "the figures in the photograph might come alive" (Carter 177). Now her parents, along with the miscellaneous collection of dimly remembered relatives represented in the print, have been rendered abstract.

After tearing up the wedding photograph and breaking the frame that held it, Melanie moves automatically to clothing, bedding, the contents of drawers: "She neither saw nor heard anything, but wrecked like an *automaton* . . . unbending as wood, and wailing." This stiff and automated Melanie, her face smeared with the remains of her mother's make-up, "a formalized mask of crimson and black," prefigures the Melanie of Uncle Philip's contorted vision (Carter 28–29, emphasis added). Her sudden transformation suggests the life of artificiality and imposed control that she is soon to enter.

With these deliberate acts of destruction, she brings to a close her adolescent mirror stage. Fulfilling Lacan's prediction of inevitable dissatisfaction, Melanie is now forced to acknowledge her own youth and inadequacy. The subject identified and developed in her summer-long mirror stage is one who "must defend against natural chronology in favor of the future perfect": "Any 'natural maturation' simply proves that the self was not mature before, and since the self was founded upon an assumption of maturity, the discovery that maturity was prematurely assumed is the discovery that the self is built on hollow ground."[34] But Melanie admits defeat in the face of the natural chronology that has brought about the unexpected death of her parents. The shift in her thinking is obvious in the thoughts that run through her mind after her parents' death. Instead of wondering whether her breasts will ever grow, her musings run toward the new roles she must assume in relation to Jonathon and Victoria: "A little mother. I am responsible. . . . 'I am no longer a free agent.'" She feels that "a tender, budding part" of herself has been killed (Carter 33). She does not fail, however, to appreciate the thought of her ghost remaining to haunt the huge country house, emanating in the form of one her many mirror images.

Gallop's analysis of Lacan's "Le Stade du miroir" focuses on the manifestation of "the specular self" or the phantom, a figure that seems to explain the ghost that preoccupies Melanie's thoughts. Gallop interprets the mirror stage as "the moment when the infant proleptically takes on a totalizing/totalized shape—a cohesive identity—through the mediation of a mirror, . . . This alienation in the constitution of a self . . . will later serve as the basis for the alienation of the specular self in the social self." Gallop is interested in the "exteriority" of this self and in the "phantoms" it leaves behind: "what is left out, not properly *buried* and contained, by the necessity of constituting a well-composed, presentable self."[35]

Interestingly enough, when Melanie is able to cope with the reality of her parents' death and the unpleasant memory of her moonlit adventure, she removes the tattered dress from its old trunk and actually buries it beneath the tree outside her window. For her, burying the dress properly is necessary if she is to accept the dissolution of all her former certainties and present a well-composed self: "She . . . buried the wedding dress decently under the apple tree. Her breast felt hollow, as if it were her heart she had buried; but she could move and speak still" (Carter 30).

Along with the dress, she has laid to rest the ideal of her romantic, imaginary constructs. In order to develop a social self (who is responsible, though not necessarily a free agent), she sacrifices the specular self (the constructed subject of her own fantasies). Gallop explains how it is that "alienation is the necessary obverse of the self's integrity": "The social self (self tainted by the world) is grounded in the specular self (assumption of the fictionally solid cohesive body—total shape, well-defined and firm). Alienation/violation cannot be avoided without calling into question the specular self, the fictional unity of the body."[36]

Replacing the specular with the social self is one of the most painful elements of Melanie's discovery that she is made of flesh and blood and that her many mirror images were never anything more than imaginary constructs. Lacan outlines the way in which human development "is conditioned by the priority of imaginary forms of the body over the control of the body and by the defensive power the subject gives these forms to protect it against the terror of bodily rending."[37] Having relinquished the defensive power of the imaginary, Melanie now stands vulnerable and unprotected. While the evolution from a fictional phantom to an integrated self-image may be a positive transition, it is not accomplished without a sense of loss, especially considering that the second stage is dependent upon developing and then relinquishing the first—watching the specular statue totter defenselessly. Stewart, in her discussion of the imaginary body, explains that "during the mirror phase the child acquires an imaginary identification of the real, corporeal image as a unified image. In this creation of the unified subject, the self begins to be positioned in sociality and is available to the further modifications made possible by language and the symbolic."[38] To realize that closure of the body is no more than a fictional unity seems a hard price to pay for the attainment of a more intellectual integrity whose manifestation, in fact, is not even sensed immediately. Melanie recalls her fall from innocence to experience, from specular to social, with resolution and regret:

> A black bucket of misery tipped itself up over Melanie's head. Part of herself, she thought, was killed, a tender, budding part; the daisy-crowned young girl who would stay behind to haunt the old house, to appear in the mirrors where the new owner expected the reflection of his own face, to flash whitely on dark nights out of the prickly core of the apple tree. An amputee, she could not yet accustom herself to what was lost and gone, lost as her parents scattered in fragments over the Nevada desert. (Carter 33)

With their parents gone and no inheritance left behind, the three children are turned over to their sinister and "churlish" uncle whom they had safely supposed they would never meet (Carter 15–16). The tenuous contact is reestablished, after all.

Beginning with the invasion of the uncanny on the wedding-dress night, Melanie's safe and ordered existence has evaporated. Her longing to escape from the shadowy garden into the familiarity behind her own front door is soon replaced with a harsh knowledge of how suffocating the "cozy, indoor darkness" is to one who is confined there against her will and can find no escape from "the interior space of home and the interiority of emotion."[39] The mirror of her childhood irrevocably broken, Melanie finds herself trapped in a house with no mirrors at all, a place where "she could not bear to feel such a stranger, so alien, and somehow so insecure in her own personality, as if she found herself hard to recognize" (Carter 57). Although she had felt angry at her mirror image and ready to live without it, without a mirror, she is unable to "effectively evolve a persona" from her predicament.[40] She senses that the same is true for her brother as well, for he "hardly seems to be there. As though the real Jonathon is somewhere else and has left a copy of himself behind so that no one notices he's gone" (Carter 110).

Begrudgingly but stoically, Melanie relinquishes her imaginary body for one of flesh. The strength and perseverance that this resolve requires is exemplified in Carter's description of the sorry facilities available to Melanie in Uncle Philip's bathroom, that space where the physical body is restored, repaired, and prepared each day. It is here that the lack of mirrors in her new surroundings becomes evident. The first morning at Uncle Philip's, she surveys the dingy room in dismay: no hot water, no bath soap, one soiled towel for use by all, a malfunctioning flush toilet, and sheets of torn newspaper instead of tissue. The sight of the dark narrow room fills her with homesickness, and her eyes brim with tears. Having already imagined, in her mind's eye, "The Last Meal in the Old Home," she now envisions "The Last Wash":

> Not a genre picture at all, but a photograph from an advertising book on bathrooms. Porcelain gleamed pink, and the soft, fluffy towels and the toilet paper were pink to match. Steaming water gushed plentifully from the dolphin-shaped taps, and jars of bath essence and toilet water and aftershave glowed like jewelry; and the low lavatory tactfully flushed with no noise at all. It was a temple to cleanness. (Carter 56)

Melanie realizes the truth that the "simple, cozy, homely things" that she had only so recently taken for granted "were, in fact, great luxuries"

(Carter 56). The *heimlich* scenes of domestic comfort provided by her
mother and by Mrs. Rundle are now only memories. Adjusting to the
harshness of life in the "chilly, high, inconvenient house" behind the
toyshop, Melanie likens herself to Eve, cast out of Eden with only herself
to blame (Carter 90). She now experiences the "inevitable anxiety" that
sets in after the "fleeting moment of jubilation" provided by the mirror
stage. Gallop interprets this disillusionment as "high tragedy: a brief
moment of doomed glory, a paradise lost," comparing it to the dilemma
of Adam and Eve, who, despite the fact of their humanity, do not truly
"enter the human condition until [they are] expelled from Eden."[41]
Melanie discovers that she is human (made of flesh and blood) when she
sees herself in the mirror; but not until she is cast into the wilderness of
the bizarre toyshop does she become aware of the human condition.

In her new, inhospitable environment, a horrid gargoyle takes the
place of the old bathroom's gleaming dolphins. The murky bathwater
erupts from a large metal geyser, a "banging, popping, gangrenous, gas-
flaring monster" with a "brutish snout." Melanie never attempts to use
the "rusty, maniacal" device, relying instead on splashes of cold water
from the sink or sponge baths in the kitchen when a kettle of hot water
and a moment of privacy are available. She remembers with longing
"how she had submerged herself in scented water every day and
sometimes twice in the sticky summertime and never would again, until
she grew up and had a bathroom of her own" (Carter 111–12). Despite
the new reality of caring for herself, body and soul, Melanie fears that
her flesh and blood self has disappeared along with her mirror image.
She feels that she is suspended "in limbo and would be for the rest of her
life. . . . It was the fault of the wedding-dress night, when she married the
shadows and the world ended" (Carter 74–76). Bereft of her specular
self, she has been given no outlet for developing the social self that
should replace it. Action and anything resembling objective, external
reality have given way to what Mulvey calls a "domestic interior which
acts as a space that confines rather than providing a wide terrain for
escape and realised conflict. The space of the home can then relate,
metaphorically, to the inside space of human interiority, emotions and the
unconscious."[42] In her uncle's house, her alienation is complete. The
family seem to have no friends, receive no visitors, watch no television;
they exist in a world of confining restrictions. At times, Melanie feels
drawn toward her Aunt Margaret and Margaret's two brothers, Finn and
Francie Jowle, who complete the odd family: "But did she really want to
belong to them?" This is the question she asks herself, trying to
overcome the revolting conviction that they were "dirty and common":
"And the holes in Aunt Margaret's stockings. And no lavatory paper. It

was all disgusting. They lived like pigs. But in spite of all that they were red and had substance and she, Melanie, was forever gray, a shadow" (Carter 75).

Neither of Melanie's lives, former nor present, seems real to her. She thinks of her past as "rich, strange and remote, as if it had never happened or had happened to another person. . . . [T]he tenderness of the lavish past was tenuous, insubstantial." Yet when she considers her present life at the toyshop, it seems that "the change in her way of living was so vast she could scarcely credit it; she would stop, sometimes . . . and say aloud, 'But this can never be me, not really me!' But it was" (Carter 90, 87). She wonders if she might wake, as from a long dream, and find herself in her own room, looking into an unbroken mirror. Recalling that she has not seen her reflection since the day she shattered the mirror, she is "seized with panic, remembering that she had not seen her face for so long. Do I still look the same? Oh, God, could I still recognize myself?" (Carter 99).

Her question is answered one evening when she and Finn go for a walk through the ruins of a park that he calls "the graveyard of a pleasure ground." Neglected statues from the National Exposition of 1852 litter the area, and Melanie senses "the uncanny blindness of statues, who seem always to be perceiving another dimension where everything is statues." A toppled Queen Victoria, whom Finn calls "The Queen of the Waste Land," lies "face down in a puddle, narcissistically gazing at itself" (Carter 97, 100). Finn approaches Melanie in the deserted park, coming close enough to her face that she can see her reflection in his eyes. Although she feels no romantic response when he attempts to kiss her, she is comforted to see herself reflected "as she thought she looked" and intrigued by the idea of turning them into one of her portraits or poses:

> She thought vaguely that they must look very striking, like a shot from a new-wave British film, locked in an embrace beside the broken statue in this dead fun palace. . . . She wished someone was watching them, or that she herself was watching them, Finn kissing this black-haired young girl, from a bush a hundred yards away. Then it would seem romantic. (Carter 101–2)

She views herself in Finn's arms from the perspective of the ego ideal, the point "from which the subject will see himself . . . *as others see him*—which will enable him to support himself in a dual situation that is satisfactory from the point of view of love." Lacan makes this observation as part of a general discussion of the state of being in love, claiming that the specular image of love is a deceptive mirage, "centered on the Ideal point . . . somewhere in the Other, from which the Other sees me, in the form I like to be seen."[43]

In addition to the many mirror images in the novel, *The Magic Toyshop* contains a number of other instances of self-imaging, both two- and three-dimensional. Set in the house, shop, and workroom of a toymaker, the novel lends itself to an abundance of such imagery. Carter's surreal and gothic portrayal of the unconscious, as revealed in self-created concrete figures, is well understood in the light of Lacan's discourse of the other. Miniature toys and life-size puppets make up two groups in which the other is manifested, and a third group consists of the human characters who are gradually transformed into mechanized versions of themselves.

The toyshop is described as "a dark cavern" containing "the vague outlines [of] . . . stiff-limbed puppets" (Carter 40). Melanie detects "a grotesque inventiveness, a deliberate eccentricity" in Uncle Philip's disconcertingly life-like mechanical inventions, and his animated creations give her "a twinge of discomfort" (Carter 59, 64). Finn explains to Melanie that Uncle Philip is a master of his art and craft, a genius. But she sees him as a "Beast of the Apocalypse," making "toys that parodied [his wife's] innocent amusements and those of her brothers" (Carter 76). Although she loathes Uncle Philip, the shop itself holds for her a peculiar charm: "all the tempting boxes gave it a night-before-Christmas look, a richly expectant atmosphere of surprise packages. She was happier in the shop than in the house. She was happy to be near a door into the street, where she could see passers-by and know that other lives went on in their placid courses." It is only in the house that she expects to see at any moment "some clockwork horror rolling hugely on small wheels, some terrifying joke or hideous novelty" (Carter 82, 80). In the shop, the aura of uncanniness is dissipated by her contact, however slight, with the outside world. When a customer calls the shop "charming" and "Kind of Dickensian," Melanie realizes "how profitably the shop purveyed old-fashioned charm" (Carter 131).

The old-fashioned store, especially during the Christmas season, is run like those of a century earlier described by Christian Bailly in *Automata: The Golden Age.* Before 1850, artisans who made children's toys did not manufacture on a large scale. Instead, "they lived and worked in one or two rooms. The tasks to be accomplished were divided among members of the family. . . . Unsure of being able to sell, unable and indeed not daring to produce their goods in advance, they worked resolutely through the November and December nights without stopping to rest."[44] Working through the busy weeks, Melanie begins to think of herself as a salesgirl, observing the differences between herself and the customers, who resemble her parents' stylish friends from the past. One customer, "an expensive woman, all in suede," requests "something little and gay. . . . Something to make my friends say, 'Wherever did you find that?'" (Carter 91–92). An American shopper purchases one of the costliest toys in the store—and Melanie's favorite: a Noah's Ark—six inches high, carved from wood, and painted by Finn. The set contains an ark, scores of animals, and a curious Noah family. Melanie notices that Finn has designed one of Noah's sons to resemble himself: "Japhet (she knew it was Japhet, for the name was printed in little letters on his tee shirt) was nobody but Finn himself, perfect down to the squint, in blue jeans. He had signed himself as a signature on the ark." This signature is one of Finn's doubles, the presence of his other, in a piece of miniature handiwork. Melanie finds all of the animals "so little, so pretty," and, after setting out the pieces one by one on the counter, she "found she was thinking small, on the scale of the ark, seeing her own hands huge as those of Gulliver in Lilliput" (Carter 83–84).

The "toy world," which captures Melanie's imagination while she works, "presents a projection of the world of everyday life; this real world is miniaturized or giganticized in such a way as to test the relation between materiality and meaning."[45] This relation is also tested by the pleasure- or use-value of the toy world and by the toymaker's motivation for re-creating the perspective from which the real world is viewed. Uncle Philip reprimands Melanie: "'And kindly put those things away, miss. I don't like people playing with my toys. . . . You be careful with them things. They're your bread and butter now'" (Carter 84). While this remark suggests that he sees the miniatures as an economic commodity, in fact, he is not inclined to have his creations admired or purchased any more than he likes to see them toyed with. He loathes the elite shoppers who are attracted to his elaborate toys and does not relish the thought of them "buying his gear for conversation pieces" (Carter 92).

In his study of the labor-intensive automata of the nineteenth century, Bailly says that they were masterpieces of invention and execution, "too luxurious and complex to be real toys." He also stresses the "elitism of automata" and the fact that prohibitive prices made them inaccessible to most families.[46] The same is true of the miniature masterpieces for sale in Philip Flower's shop. Though Uncle Philip is disdainful of his elite clientele, they are among the few who can afford his luxurious inventions. The intensity of disdain he feels is evident in his treatment of the reporter who hoped to write a photo-feature of the shop. Finn recounts the unfortunate visit: "'Toys for grownups. He said we—your uncle and me—were a unique fusion of folk art and pop art'" (Carter 92). Bailly draws a similar parallel, claiming that the automaton, "neither purely toy nor *objet d'art* but partaking of the qualities of both, embodies in a wonderfully immediate fashion the artistic and cultural atmosphere of its time."[47]

But Uncle Philip has little time for popular advertising, whether or not it aspires or appeals to art and culture. Smashing the reporter's camera in a fury, he refuses the offer, unwilling to have his three-dimensional creations reduced to a series of glossy photographs. He does not want his work displayed in the newspaper, not even in the more sophisticated color supplement, as novelties for consumption by collectors. He resents any popular appeal that the consumer might find in his creations, just as he resents the thought of children playing with them. What Melanie resents is the fact that in a house full of toys, there are none for Victoria to play with. Even Finn explains that certain of the toys are "too good for children." But Melanie finds it difficult to understand that Uncle Philip creates from a motivation that is unrelated to the amusement of children (Carter 92). "It must be remembered," writes Stewart, "that the toy moved late to the nursery, that from the beginning it was adults who made toys, and not only with regard to their other invention, the child." Likewise, Bailly points out that automata "are clearly products of children's imagination, but as they might be remembered by adults."[48]

Much more eerie than the shop's interior is Uncle Philip's basement, where the uncanny truly prevails. He spends long evenings here in his workroom, making human-sized puppets that are not for sale and writing shows in which they perform. Although he prefers to keep his hobby to himself, he has conscripted Finn as his apprentice, not only to learn the craft of toymaking but also to assist him in painting sets and pulling strings for the puppet theater he has devised for his productions. The sense of power that Philip derives from his obsessive involvement with the puppets is suggested in the title announcing one of his productions: "'GRAND PERFORMANCE—FLOWER'S PUPPET MICROCOSM'" (Carter 120). He is the supreme being of the puppet world that he has created and over which he has complete control.

Finn gives Melanie a tour of the basement, showing her an array of partially assembled puppets, some without arms and legs, some blind, some unclothed—but "all with a strange liveliness as they dangled unfinished from their hooks." The most uncanny sight of all is the puppet she sees when Finn opens the curtains of the makeshift stage: "Lying face downward in a tangle of strings was a puppet fully five feet high, a sylphide in a fountain of white tulle, fallen flat down. . . . She had long black hair down to the waist of her tight satin bodice." Dismayed by this reminder of her own abandoned past, she utters, "'It is too much. . . . There is too much,'" the same words that marked the night of her misadventure (Carter 66). Reminded of herself, stranded in her mother's ill-fated wedding dress, Melanie can hardly bear the sight of this stricken doll:

> "There is too much," she repeated. This crazy world whirled about her, men and women dwarfed by toys and puppets, where even the birds were mechanical and the few human figures went masked and played musical instruments in the small and terrible hours of the night into which again she had been thrust. She was in the night again, and the doll was herself. (Carter 67)

The fallen puppet is for Melanie "the object that cannot be swallowed, as it were, which remains stuck in the gullet of the signifier. It is at this point of lack that the subject has to recognize himself."[49] In fact, it is only a matter of time before Melanie does become a doll, stranded in the middle of the stage as this one is, dressed in white chiffon, her face covered with greasepaint. As subject, she is forced not only to recognize herself in the unpalatable object but actually to become the other. Implementing his latest creative scheme of placing people on stage beside his puppets, Uncle Philip chooses Melanie—because she is "not too big" and "won't be out of scale"—to act upon the stage as Leda, opposite his newly designed swan puppet (Carter 126).

The poster for Philip's production of "Leda and the Swan" once again reveals his inflated intentions; it proclaims: "'GRAND XMAS NOVELTY SHOW—Art and Nature combine with Philip Flower to bring you a Unique Phenomenon'" and is illustrated with a drawing of Uncle Philip, surrounded by a "dwarfish" ring of dancing girls and holding a swan above his head (Carter 155). A combination of stilted, mundane narration and excerpts from Tchaikovsky's *Swan Lake*, Philip's "play" is little more than a vehicle for displaying the huge swan that he believes to be an exceedingly handsome creation. To Melanie, however, the ungainly puppet is "a grotesque parody . . . nothing like the wild, phallic bird of her imaginings. It was dumpy and homely and eccentric" (Carter 157). Despite its lumpish appearance, she is quite frightened by its attempted rape of her, and the very thought of the production makes her feel "infinitely small, furious, reluctant . . . minute" (Carter 154). The final performance takes shape as a terrifying disaster:

> Like fate or the clock, on came the swan. . . . She thought of the horse of Troy, also made of hollow wood; if she did not act her part well, a trapdoor in the swan's side might open and an armed host of pygmy Uncle Philips, all clockwork, might rush out and savage her. This possibility seemed real and awful. . . . [S]he felt herself not herself, wrenched from her own personality. . . . [T]he mocked up swan might assume reality itself and rape this girl in a

blizzard of white feathers. The swan towered over the black-haired girl who was Melanie and who was not. (Carter 157)

Not until the swan is once again hanging limply from its backstage strings, the "motive power" of the puppet gone and that of the puppet master temporarily suspended, does the distraught, detached Melanie begin to feel real again: "She put Melanie back on like a coat, slowly. . . . She was trembling and sick with anticlimax. . . . She felt she cast no shadow" (Carter 158–60).

Incapable of understanding the extent of her distress, Uncle Philip is angry with his niece, ordering her off his stage and criticizing her performance. He compliments the swan, "'Well done, old fellow,'" but to Melanie he complains, "'You overacted. . . . You were melodramatic. Puppets don't overact. You spoiled the poetry'" (Carter 159). Melanie has already sensed the inevitable failure of Uncle Philip's plan to stage her amidst his passive and custom-made puppets, knowing how easily she would be upstaged by them in his eyes. During rehearsal, he had expressed his dissatisfaction with the size of her breasts, feeling that they were too large for those of the nubile Leda of his imagination. He approved her long, dark hair and shapely legs as right for the part; yet she knew then that "he was resenting her because she was not a puppet" (Carter 137).

Finn has long understood Philip's resentment of human beings and his desire to turn them into objects under his control, and he tries to convince Melanie of her uncle's insidiousness. Because Philip wanted Melanie's response to the swan to be spontaneous, it did not appear at rehearsal. Instead, Philip decided that Finn should stand in for the swan and demonstrate to Melanie what to expect. Finn saw through this staged charade, protecting both himself and Melanie from Philip's manipulations: "'He's pulled our strings as if we were his puppets, and there I was, all ready to touch you up just as he wanted. He told me to rehearse Leda and the swan with you. Somewhere private. Like your room, he said. Go up and rehearse a rape with Melanie in your bedroom. Christ. He wanted me to do you and he set the scene. Ah, he's evil!'" (Carter 144).

Finn perceives the latent sexual threat in Philip's suggestion. Initially, Melanie had received this explanation with some incredulousness, but Finn becomes her hero the day the swan attacks her. While Uncle Philip rails at her, Finn is solicitous, straightening her clothes and helping her to her feet. To vindicate Melanie and to vent his own suppressed anger, Finn plots revenge against Philip and the outrageous power that he wields over the household. In their subservience to Philip, Finn and

Melanie are bound together by "the problems, contradictions and irreconcilable demands made by the acquisition of sexual identity, family structures and historical conditions [that] surface in collectively held desires, obsessions and anxieties."[50]

Sneaking to the basement, Finn chops the ludicrous and obscene swan into small pieces then carries the remains to the deserted park and buries them beside Queen Victoria's statue. Like Melanie, Finn has something to bury if he is to assert a well-composed social self—and wrongs to redress if he is to be free of haunting phantoms. Just as Melanie could not properly leave the tattered wedding dress hidden away in the storage trunk, Finn feels that although he "'could have put the bits of swan into the dustbin . . . it seemed best of all to bury it in the pleasure garden'" (Carter 164). The swan—like the wedding dress, the dark night, and the basement workshop—is overwhelming. "'Finn, the *enormity* of it!'" is Melanie's amazed response. "The swan was *too big, too potent*, to all at once stop being" (Carter 162, 165, emphasis added).

After the burial, Finn comes to Melanie's room in the dark of night to tell of her of his conquest and of the uneasy confrontation with the *unheimlich* that his heroic gesture demanded: "'It is much better now. Dear God, I thought I'd never be easy again. I was burning and freezing at the same time. It was like dying. . . . God preserve me from the perils of the night.'" She is surprised when he makes the sign of the cross as a safeguard against the memory of uncanniness, but she empathizes completely with his predicament: "It must have been like the wedding-dress night. In the pleasure garden, Finn had walked in the forests of night where nothing was safe. I have been in that place, too, she thought. She could have cried for them both" (Carter 162–63). Although she had seen herself in Finn's eyes months before, while standing in the park, it is not until now that she sees him as her double, her counterpart. She feels "that somehow their experience ran parallel. She understood his frenzy." She shudders to think of Finn's daring descent into "the workroom which was so full of the sense of Uncle Philip, surrounded by *severed limbs* and watching masks" (Carter 164; 162, emphasis added).

In "The 'Uncanny,'" Freud devotes several paragraphs to the uncanniness of severed limbs (relating them, as might be expected, to the castration complex): "Dismembered limbs, a severed head, a hand cut off at the wrist . . . feet which dance by themselves . . . all these have something peculiarly uncanny about them (Freud 244). When her parents were killed, Melanie herself felt like "an amputee" unable to adjust "to what was lost and gone" (Carter 33). Lacan explains the fragmented body as either a precursor to or a reversal of the mirror stage. He says that the mirror stage is dependent upon a "succession of phantasies that extends from a fragmented body-image to a form of its totality that I shall call orthopaedic—and, lastly, to the assumption of an alienating identity, which will mark with its rigid structure the subject's entire mental development." At any stage in this process, however, the fragmented body can manifest itself, signaling "a certain level of aggressive disintegration in the individual. It then appears in the form of disjointed limbs, or . . . organs."[51] Thus, when Melanie's progress toward totality is suspended—when she breaks the looking-glass and discontinues her romantic posing—she feels that some part of her body has been amputated. Lost in a house without mirrors and unprotected by any imaginary forms of the body, the bolder Melanie of the summer does indeed disintegrate to some degree. The extent of this disintegration is made clear, even to her, one evening when she opens a dresser drawer and sees "a freshly severed hand, all bloody at the roots" (Carter 112). Lacan says that such fantasms of dismemberment "have no connection with any real body; rather, they are associated with a disjointed mannikin, a grotesque doll, an accumulation of limbs in which we recognize the narcissistic object."[52] Like the fantasies described by Lacan, it is the obvious unreality of Melanie's hallucination that renders it so striking:

> It was a soft-looking, plump little hand with pretty tapering fingers the nails of which were tinted with a faint pearly lacquer. There was a thin silver ring of the type small girls wear on the fourth finger. . . . From the raggedness of the flesh at the wrist, it appeared that the hand had been hewn from its arm with a knife or ax that was very blunt. Melanie heard blood fall *plop* in the drawer.
>
> "I am going out of my mind," she said aloud. (Carter 112–13)

Unable to maintain her composure, Melanie faints, and Francie appears, to revive her with whisky and strong tea. The strain of living for months in an interior where "nothing was ordinary, nothing was expected" is allayed somewhat by Francie's comforting presence (Carter 60). Grateful for his predictability after the uncanny sight of the bloody hand, she says to him, "'You are ordinary,'" and he agrees "'So I am. . . . Just an ordinary chap.'" He assures her that the drawer contains nothing out of the ordinary and offers an explanation that echoes Lacan's hypothesis for the appearance of severed limbs in dreams and nightmares: "'Nothing . . . you might think was a hand unless it is still your distress. The distress of your loss might make you see things. It is only natural'" (Carter 113, 115). As Gallop points out, the violently unorganized image of the body in bits and pieces *"only comes after* the mirror stage so as to *represent what came before."*[53]

For Finn, the midnight confrontation with the severed limbs that Philip has strewn about the place and the determination with which he dismembers the swan suggest not "aggressive disintegration" so much as his assumption of an "alienating identity" (see Lacan above). Irrevocably alienating himself from Philip's favor is an essential step in the process of forming the "rigid structure" of his "mental development." When Melanie inquires how Uncle Philip will react to the destruction, Finn— willing to accept the consequence of his action—says "'I can't tell. . . . Only surmise. . . . He put himself into it. That is why it had to go'" (Carter 165).

Finn's defiance is the first step toward reestablishing an atmosphere of normalcy in the home behind the toyshop and freeing the family from Uncle Philip's desire to control and automate them. Philip is caught up in what Lacan calls "the lure of spatial identification." But because of his aversion to mirrors, his fascination has never taken its place in the drama of the mirror stage, "whose internal thrust is precipitated from insufficiency to anticipation."[54] Instead, he remains locked at a level of insufficiency, forever striving to attain spatial identification through the creation and manipulation of the other rather than through the development of self. Melanie thinks of Philip as an alchemist, able to transform one thing to another, and she feels that the rest of the household are "flattened to paper cutouts by [his] personified gravity" (Carter 160). He seems to have the sinister ability to turn not only wood but also human beings into puppets, and he exercises this alchemy particularly over Margaret, Finn, and Melanie.

Melanie perceives Aunt Margaret to be "a wispy appendage of the toymaking uncle" and describes the good-night kiss Margaret bestows as "a stiff, Dutch-doll embrace; her arms were two hinged sticks" (Carter 39, 49). She observes that when Finn dances, "his body hung strangely limp, his arms dangled loosely by his sides; all his personality seemed concentrated in his fleet, dextrous feet, which moved in a complex and various sequence." After suffering a fall at the hands of the abusive Philip, Finn "creaked, indeed, like a puppet. . . . [H]is grace was all gone" (Carter 52, 141). Melanie herself, while drying dishes, feels that she has become "a wind-up putting-away doll, clicking through its programmed movements. Uncle Philip might have made her over already. She was without volition of her own. . . . [She] hung cups on hooks on the dresser; her arm went up and down, up and down. She watched it with mild curiosity; it seemed to have a life of its own." She even develops a stance—"stiff, wooden and unresponsive"—that is similar to Aunt Margaret's Dutch-doll embrace (Carter 74, 76, 101).

More intriguing than the subtle mechanization of Philip's family, however, is his own resemblance to the puppets he creates. Melanie's first observation of Uncle Philip's artificiality and automation is the sight of his false teeth, which rest each night in a tumbler in the bathroom. Next, she notices with astonishment that "his head is quite square! . . . His head was a jack-in-a-box" (Carter 136). When he stands proudly displaying the star puppet of one of his shows, the similarity is more marked than ever. His shark-like grin reminds Melanie of "the barren, professional, show-biz smiles on the faces of the toy acrobats." Like a marionette, he bows from the waist, dressed up in his "rusty finery." Melanie observes that "all the clothes were unused-looking and old, as if kept for years in jars of formaldehyde. This was his puppet master's outfit" (Carter 122). This vision of Philip standing next to his wooden nymph, the Melanie look-alike, vividly captures what Mulvey describes as a gender-based dichotomy of property and power: "It is as though man, in exercising patriarchal power and freezing woman into spectacle, has also turned himself into a masquerade that can crack. . . . Power is a trap that alienates, both into the making of history and transforming the other into pose."[55] Creating the wood nymph to resemble Melanie is his initial attempt to transform his niece into pose; and, in forcing her to play a puppet's role of portraying Leda, he moves one step further in the process of freezing her into spectacle.

In an attempt to reverse the power struggle and transform the puppet master himself into a pose, Finn and Francie create a miniature of Philip, a small carved doll similar to the clockwork pygmy of Melanie's fearful vision. Dressed in miniature imitation of Philip's finery, the doll wears "a small dandyish white shirt with a bootlace tie" (Carter 149). Seeing the brothers with their diminutive creation, Melanie imagines with what difficulty Margaret must have stitched the small, fine clothes for this occasion. Not content to *freeze* Philip's sacrificial double into spectacle, they instead apply matches to its various parts, burning it voodoo style.

In *The Magic Toyshop*, the puppet spectacle is played out against a backdrop of family drama and melodrama. Uncle Philip, likened by Melanie to a "Beast of the Apocalypse," embodies what Lacan terms the "Name-of-the-Father," the symbolic signifier of both the Law and Death. Lacan points out that for Freud, the symbolic Father is equivalent to the dead Father.[56] Melanie (whose own father is dead) makes a similar connection, wondering if her uncle's ominous power resides in the possibility of his nonbeing. What if her strange, fat uncle of today is an impostor who somehow substituted himself for the thin Uncle Philip in the wedding photo: "what if Uncle Philip of the iron fists is not my mother's brother at all?" (Carter 151).

But this same Philip, whoever he may be, exercises the Law of the Father while his wife Margaret is mute. Communicating with the family by writing messages on chalkboards and note pads, she is unable to talk. Silenced by Philip, not only symbolically but also psychosomatically, she is the Mother who cannot speak. In a discussion of various sensory drives, Lacan distinguishes between *making oneself heard* and *making oneself seen*: "In the field of the unconscious the ears are the only orifice that cannot be closed. Whereas *making oneself seen* is indicated by an arrow that really comes back towards the subject, *making oneself heard* goes towards the other."[57] Philip is the self-oriented subject, manipulating his automated microcosm and demanding to be seen as the figure of unquestioned authority that he perceives himself to be. In contrast, Margaret is other-oriented, mothering the orphaned children, interjecting herself as a buffer between her brusque husband and her defiant brother Finn, and relying on gesture in every effort to make her messages heard.

Although Philip is the authoritarian father and Margaret the silent mother, the drives to be seen and to be heard are not necessarily rooted in sexual difference. According to Mulvey, Lacan emphasizes "the fictional, constructed nature of masculinity and femininity, the results of social and symbolic, not biological, imperatives." Mulvey describes motherhood as it exists under the cultural patriarchy spelled out by Lacan: "access to the symbolic order is achieved by crossing the frontier, out of the imaginary, the dyadic world of mother and child, into recognition of the Father's Name and his Law. That is, out of a body-based, maternal relationship into one created by social exchange, culture and legal taboos (of which the first, of course, is the incest taboo)." The "most sophisticated means of symbolic articulation" is language, and without speech, Margaret is deprived of this method of exchange.[58] On the other hand, she also refuses to recognize the Father's Name and Law. Despite her fear and trembling at Philip's wrathful orders, she lives in violation of the primal taboo. What Finn calls "our secret . . . our heart's core . . . the thing that makes us different from other people, Francie and Maggie and I" is the incestuous love shared by his older siblings Francie and Margaret (Carter 184).

Melanie, however, fails to perceive this relationship, sensing only the oppression and humiliation symbolized by Margaret's muteness: "She was wrung with pity for her aunt, whose silence was so haunted when her brothers were not there." She thinks of herself and her aunt as "poor women pensioners, planets around a male sun" (Carter 118, 134). Aunt Margaret bows constantly to Philip's commands, crying in silent anguish when she cannot still the conflict between the furious Philip and the resentful Finn. She appeases Philip and contributes to the family shop by sewing "clothes for toys or puppets, tiny dresses and jackets for anthropomorphic bears and monkeys" and creating the costumes for her husband's puppet plays (Carter 88). All her work is done by hand, for Philip denies her the expense of a sewing machine. A master at automating his subjects, he is unwilling to share his expertise. Thus she is allowed neither the artificial assistance of machinery nor the speed of automation.

Considering her own role in this tortured family, Melanie feels "too young, too soft and new, to come to terms with these wild beings whose minds veered at crazy angles from the short, straight lines of her own experience" (Carter 129). Initially, she tried to cope with the violence and sadness in her usual fashion, transforming the reality before her into artistic media: "she found it made things easier if she dramatized them. Or melodramatized them. It was easier, for example, to face the fact of Uncle Philip if she saw him as a character in a film, possibly played by Orson Welles. She was sitting in a cinema watching a film" (Carter 74–75). Although this trick of the imagination fails her, it is significant that she chooses cinema, a genre born in silence and melodrama. Like Aunt Margaret, these early movies were mute, "distanced from language by technology rather than the *law*."[59] This distance was covered by the exaggerated gestures and visual expression of theatrical melodrama.

Mulvey compares the "melodramatic mode of expression and the language of the unconscious which must speak through symptom, on the knife-edge between meaning and silence, demanding interpretation rather than a direct, unmediated understanding of what is said."[60] Claiming that women have been gagged and "left largely without a voice," she identifies the strength of the melodramatic aesthetic as "its displacement of the power of the word" and its ability, through gesture and theatrical spectacle, to depict "a whole terrain of the 'unspeakable.'"[61] In Carter's novel, Margaret and Melanie are both women gagged and without voice. In Margaret's experience, gesture displaces the direct word, and the language of the unconscious must displace the silence into which she is locked by her disability and by her unhappy marriage. The melodrama that Melanie witnesses when she finally sees Margaret and Francie slip to the floor in a lovers' embrace derives from that unspeakable terrain of primeval passion and primal taboo.

Pointing out that "the melodrama drew its source material from unease and contradiction within the very icon of American life, the home, and its sacred figure, the mother," Mulvey equates the ideological function of melodrama with the ideology of the family in a manner that clearly illuminates the conflicts that pervade the Flower/Jowle household and the tension from which Melanie longs for escape, cinematic or otherwise.[62] In another of her fantasies, for example, Melanie sees her hand as "wonderful and surprising, an object which did not belong to her and of which she did not know the use. The fingers were people, the members of a family. . . . She flexed her hand, and, obligingly, the family performed a brief dance for her. Then she was horrified. I must be going crazy! In this crazy house" (Carter 153). In this imaginary family, which in some ways resembles her own family of origin, the mother—the index finger—predominates. But her game of dramatizing Uncle Philip's family becomes redundant to the melodrama that is already inherent in their complicated dance of conflict. Mulvey explains the basis of this dance in her summary of the melodramatic style:

> The social sphere of the family provides a ready-made *dramatis personae* of characters whose relations are by very definition overdetermined and overlaid with tension and contradiction, destined to act out Oedipal drama, generational conflict, sibling rivalry, the containment and repression of sexuality. The family is the socially accepted road to respectable normality, an icon of conformity, and at one and the same time, the source of deviance, psychosis and despair.[63]

The setting for familial melodrama is, of course, the home, that private realm where "the text of muteness [like Margaret's] is produced not by the material constraints of the law or technology but by a proximity to the mechanisms of repression [like Philip's practice of puppetry]."[64] Instead of locating her despairing, adopted family on the larger-than-life, two-dimensional screen, Melanie finds them distorted into a curved miniature. They are reduced yet "monstrously swollen" in the reflection she catches in the glass "witch ball" that sits on the dining room sideboard. Instead of popcorn and candy at the movies, the family is eating Christmas cake at a "warped white table that stretched forever." Because "the company around the tea table was as distorted and alien as its miniature in the witch ball," Melanie finds its difficult to distinguish between the reality and the reflection (Carter 147, 159). Gathered around the holiday table, they may faintly resemble the socially acceptable family unit; yet, in the glass ball, the monstrous tension of their deviance, psychosis, and despair is captured, clearly contradicting any pretense of normality. Melanie finds it difficult to believe that her mother, who "could never have been eccentric," was ever a member of the same family as Uncle Philip; and she wonders if there was some time, in the "distant past when the Flowers had been just an ordinary family?" (Carter 151).

However, at the heart of even the most "ordinary family," such as Katherine Mansfield's Burnells, the dark secrets of interiority lurk, waiting to take their place. They embody the *unheimlich*, which becomes "not really a member of the family" but a concept that presents itself as "a unit in the 'family.'"[65] Melanie's first encounter with this presence was the uncanny jack-in-the-box that she was given as a child. Uncle Philip's earliest attempt to freeze his niece into spectacle, the grotesque head, embodied all of the *unheimlich* potential that can lie in wait behind an innocently familiar exterior. The unnerving caricature hidden within the brightly colored box is like the distorted family portrait captured in the crystal witch ball—or like the repressed fear and hatred that Linda Burnell longs to wrap up in paper for her husband, Stanley. The little boxes of grief, which Linda wants to give away, and the ugly jack-in-the-box shunned by Melanie are reminiscent of Pandora's mythological, iconographical box. A "motif of inside/outside" informs this myth, and a shift in perspective or interpretation, through the centuries, has caused the magical container "to shrink from a very large jar or urn . . . to a small box she could carry in her hand."[66]

This shift in perspective, from the gigantic to the miniature, is consistent with Stewart's placement of the promise of interiority inside one's heart, inside of a locket, or inside the dollhouse within the dollhouse: "center within center, within within within."[67] This secret promise, whether one of dread or hope, is ever looming large in some uncanny manifestation, yet ever receding: "What one cannot keep outside, one always keeps an image of inside."[68]

Thus Finn, who had at one time looked to Melanie "like a death mask of himself," finally dazzles her as "a small precious statuette, a chessman" (Carter 142, 175). Melanie has seen Aunt Margaret, as well as Finn, wearing the aspect of death: "Her face was a tragic mask, that of a woman who has sent all her sons to a war and waits hourly for the death telegram" (Carter 128–29). The motif of the mask—luridly colored, death-like, and terrifying—is a recurring one in Carter's novel. When Melanie visits the basement workshop with Finn, he frightens her by donning a snarling mask of Mephistopheles. Working in the shop during the Halloween season, Melanie finds herself "repelled yet attracted by the ferocious masks" on display, most of which are depictions of wild, scary animals. She tries on one or two for herself, and, though there is no mirror in which to view herself, she feels "peculiarly feline or vulpine according to the mask she wore" (Carter 82). In *The Violent Effigy*, John Carey reports how Charles Dickens, as a child, was affected by the threatening visage of a repellent mask that had somehow found its away into his toy box and "pretended to be dead with alarming ill-success."[69]

Just thinking of the frightening mask apparently gave Dickens intolerable nightmares as a child. The trauma Carey describes seems to support Melanie's conclusion that the "bestial, ferocious" masks, "burning bright with phosphorescent paint" were not "nice toys for young children" (Carter 78).

After the threat Finn initially held for Melanie has dissipated, his aspect changes from the grotesque gigantic mask to the miniature chess piece, perfect in every detail. While for Kezia Burnell it is a miniature lamp, for Melanie it is this miniaturized image of Finn's body that becomes the talisman enabling her to confront the *unheimlich* that pervades the atmosphere of the toyshop. Lacan, in fact, calls the body a "monument" where one can rediscover the "truth" that has been displaced by falsehood, censored, or repressed in the unconscious.[70] This is the body that, unlike the *jouissance* of the other in the mirror, can fulfill the desire for spatial identification. This body is a three-dimensional figure rather than a two-dimensional reflection; it signifies realized experience rather than imaginary construct; it is a newfound land of flesh and blood, living and animated, rather than an artificial form, inanimate except for the machinations of a tortured and torturous creator. The charm of Finn as a precious statuette holds truth for Melanie precisely because she has begun to love and accept the larger Finn. In their struggle to break free from the tangled strings of Philip's control, they reestablish the boundaries between the automated creatures of toyshop and puppet show and the human subjects—in whose image those figures were created.

Conclusion

The emergence of the doll as a manifestation of the other, the double, and the uncanny is founded on the tension between the mechanical automaton and the subject of flesh and blood. The literary automaton, however, is more than just a machine that simulates life. Bailly says that such a limited definition, "although certainly accurate, addresses only the mechanical aspect of the automaton," ignoring the more essential quality that is "without a doubt the power to fascinate and mystify, common to all automata of all epochs."[71] The dream of animation originates in the human subject's fascination with creating likenesses in his own image. While this dream, desire, or fantasy seems to have long inspired the human consciousness, Bailly focuses specifically on the motivation that spurred the magnificent androids of the eighteenth century, the labor-intensive mannequins filling E. T. A. Hoffmann and his fictional characters with such nameless dread: "Why did the android so fascinate the eighteenth century? Surely because the *siecle des lumierès* saw in it a symbol of the triumph of human reason over ignorance."[72]

Reason over ignorance, order over chaos, perfection over imperfection—these are a few of the triumphs that the body of the created other can symbolize, as it does in the textual search for an ideal shape. These are the shapes or self-images that give "the greatest degree of narcissistic gratification."[73] Narcissism is thus intrinsic to the desire to achieve an ideal form, to create an ideal shape. This search is nowhere more evident than in Victor Frankenstein's attempt to breathe the breath of life into an android of his own making. His effort to re-create life, to animate clay, illustrates a number of conflicts that informed the nineteenth-century view of automata.

First, as George Levine observes, "the terrible threat of the nonrational violence built into that machine lurks behind the human ideals that give meaning to the lives of fiction's protagonists." Second, the terms of moral judgment and divine order are shifted by the "transposition of the creator from God to man, the secularization of the means of creation from miracle into science."[74] And third, Frankenstein is mistaken in his dream "that the world is rational and comprehensible" and in the assumption on which his monster is built—"that there is no mystery in vitality, nothing sacred in life." Thus, his creation "is evil not because he is irrational, but because he is constructed entirely out of rational, mechanical principles. He is the embodiment of the idea that mind can control matter, that thought is more important than flesh, and he is the revenge of the flesh on the arrogant mind." Frankenstein overlooks the "metahuman possibilities" of his action, but he has an equally limited view of his creature's *human* potential and misunderstands the cost to his own humanity which his deed will exact.[75] Frankenstein has given away a large part of himself in exchange for imparting life to his creature. The loss of self is the price Frankenstein pays for having created life: "It is as if one cannot *give* life or add to the existing limited vital resources, only *redistribute* the available stocks by making over part of one's life to another."[76] According to this principle of redistribution, the self—at least a part of it—is hidden inside the other, particularly if the other in question is created in the image of the subject. Thus the created other is the subject's double—sharing enough essential properties to be nearly the same as the subject—but also the abject, the undesired poacher of the ego.

The fear of losing any of one's limited vital resources so that another may exist is what so angers the dolls in Yeats's "Dolls" and what threatens Alexander Hepburn in Lawrence's "Captain's Doll." Creators such as Yeats's dollmaker, Lawrence's Hannele, and Carter's Uncle Philip take the liberty of transferring this vital life force from one form to another. Sometimes it is a bit of themselves they impart to their creations, but at other times they consign a part of someone else's life to their automata. More often than android or giant, the artistically created double in modern and contemporary narrative takes the form of idealized miniature, as it does in these works by Yeats, Lawrence, and Carter. Likewise, in O'Brien's "Doll," Atwood's "Resplendent Quetzal," and Mansfield's "Dollhouse" the other is contained within the miniaturized body of the doll. As these narratives suggest, the double in this form conveys an uncanny, at times even sinister, power over the original in whose image it has been created.

Coates suggests that the double's impact has been weakened for the contemporary reader, that the appearance of one's own image has "become a banal and casual punctuation of everyday life":

> Meanwhile, as the multiplication of reflecting surfaces, mirrors and plate glass in modern architecture enhances the self-consciousness of society, the sight of one's own image ceases to harbinger death [see Freud and Rank] or trigger a devastating flash of self-knowledge but pops up fleetingly and irritatingly wherever one walks, a slow seepage of identity.[77]

While this banality may be true of the mirror image (although Lacan suggests differently) it is not true of the three-dimensional image whose disconcerting appearance continues to evoke flashes of self-knowledge, self-consciousness, and self-awareness. For example, the sight of Melanie's own image in the form of jack-in-the-box or life-like puppet is a harbinger of death and fear to her in *The Magic Toyshop*. The forceful surge of identity that this particular group of literary automata continues to exert is perhaps best described by Rilke, who defines the other lurking inside the self-created miniature as "the doll-soul."

In Rilke's 1930 essay "Puppen" (translated "Some Reflections on Dolls"), *doll-soul* is his term for the importance taken on by "grown-up versions" of the "plump, unchanging dolls of childhood." He describes this soul as "an invisible Something, which we held high above you [the sexless dolls of childhood] and ourselves, secretly and with foreboding, and for which both we and you were, so to say, merely pretexts, we were thinking of a soul: the doll-soul."[78] For Rilke, the truths of lived experience are carried in the doll's "uncanny loneliness" and in the elusive doll-soul.[79] Like Naomi Schor, Rilke lends the miniature an epistemological dignity and invests the detail with "a truth-bearing function" because he sees the significance of their function in larger semantic, domestic, and social networks.[80] Rilke feels that souls may be found not only in dolls but also in objects such as rocking-horses, domino pieces, school satchels, balls, and other "quite simple things": "a sewing clamp, a spinning-wheel, a domestic loom, a bridal glove, a cup, the binding and the leaves of a Bible; not to mention the mighty will of a hammer, the self-surrender of a violin, the friendly eagerness of horn spectacles . . . that pack of cards on the table." What gives these items a soul is their "beautiful participation in human living."[81]

As Rilke's essay and the fictional narratives treated here illustrate, the body of the doll is often invested with a "truth-bearing function," perhaps even with a soul. The handcrafted miniature is designed to serve as "the guarantor of meaning . . . constantly threatened by falsification and misprison."[82] Or it may be the object constantly threatening its subject with falsification, the double, other, or imitation threatening to imprison its original. Advancing a feminine (and detailed) aesthetic similar to Schor's, Valie Export writes that the "actual double of the real is the body": "In ego stagings via the body or in feminine objects (like the bed), one is able to recognize how the feminine tries to escape that ambivalence of the work of culture . . . in order to achieve a specific feminine aesthetic."[83] The doll, like the bed mentioned by Export, is one of those objects whose traditional connotations are effeminate or child-like, domestic, and trivial. Yet, as Freud points out in his essay, such seemingly innocent objects are easily invested with an uncanny truth, powerful in its ability to unsettle and transform the subject.

Rilke places the doll at a border that conscribes existence much as the Kristevan border protects the subject from uncanniness and abjection. He describes dolls who "lay there on the border of the children's sleep, filled, at most, with the rudimentary idea of falling down, allowing themselves to *be dreamed*; as it was their habit, during the day to be lived unwearyingly with energies not their own."[84] This vision is the uncanny and "inhuman spectacle of a dream no longer in need of its dreamer," a doll no longer in need of a dollmaker, an object no longer in need of a subject.[85] Like the three-dimensional dolls of childhood, the doll-soul too eventually appears then vanishes at its own uncanny border, "the quiveringmost borders of our vision. . . . Reflecting thus and looking up, one is confronted and almost overwhelmed by their waxen nature."[86]

Rilke does not overlook the abject nature of these waxen bodies nor the potential imperfection that lurks beneath their seamless perfection. Even the doll's "extreme state of well-enough known solidity" is gradually worn away in time by the "consuming caress" of its owner.[87] In such a way, the doll's body is aligned with the human body—and with the most abject form of the body, the corpse. Rilke claims also that the subject's relation to the doll is sustained in part by an unacknowledged anger. Hidden behind the doll's seamless solidity, waiting to be unmasked, is the "horrible foreign body on which we had wasted our purest ardour . . . the externally painted watery corpse, which floated and swam on the flood-tides of our affection."[88] Once on dry land again, Rilke concludes his metaphor, the subject discards the doll in the undergrowth. The doll is necessary to the subject because of its acquiescence, because it forces the subject to be assertive and allows him to feel superior. In this role, the doll is no more than a "half-object" with no imagination: "But this being less-than-a-thing, in its utter irremediability, is the secret of its superiority."[89] Although she is a miniature person rather than a doll, it is as a "half-object" or "less-than-a-thing" that Lispector's Little Flower is viewed. Her story reminds one reader of the fate of another "half-object," a tale she once heard of a corpse in an orphanage: "The orphans had no dolls, and, with terrible maternity already throbbing in their hearts, the little girls kept hidden the death of one of the children from the nun. . . . [T]hey played with the dead child, giving her baths and things to eat, punishing her only to be able to kiss and console her."[90]

The girls' devotion to their "doll" is like the misplaced and hopeless early affections that Rilke says we are content to lay before the silent and "motionless mannequins" of childhood. It is this devotion that situates the subject before the doll, "facing it, expecting something from it": "We took our bearings from the doll. . . . But soon we realized that we could not make a person or a thing of it, and all the confidences we had poured into and over it became foreign to us."[91] It is for this reason that Captain Hepburn mourns the disappearance of his little doppelgänger and that Hannele decides to burn the painting of it. As Landolfi's Gogol learns when his marvelous Caracas disappoints him so utterly, the doll—the half-object—no matter how life-like, can never be made into a person. Therein lies both its power over the human subject and its inevitable downfall. In the end, the doll cannot share one's confidence, and all of those conversations—"the most intense and the most incriminating of all" (O'Brien 49)—have really with been with one's self.

To construct the doll, to gain power over a double created in the subject's image, lends the fictional character a sense of control that may distract her from a pervasive sense of powerlessness—as Hannele gains some control over her situation with Hepburn by "making a doll of him" or as Atwood's Marian takes charge of her life by re-creating herself as a miniature sponge cake. In each of the cases studied here, the subjects must relinquish the sense of self that they have invested in the double, as

Frankenstein has with his monster and as Nathanael has with Olimpia, and reclaim this power for themselves. The lives of Frankenstein and Nathanael, in fact, end in despair because they are able to begin but unable to complete this process. Those characters who do successfully confront themselves in miniature, conquering uncanniness and abjection, are rewarded by control over their essential selves.

Notes

1. Created in Our Image

1. Sigmund Freud, "The 'Uncanny'" (1919), in *The Standard Edition of the Complete Psychological Works*, trans. and ed. James Strachey (London: Hogarth Press, 1953–74), 17:235. All further references to Freud's "The 'Uncanny'" will appear parenthetically in the text, marked by author's name and page number. See also Otto Rank, *The Double: A Psychoanalytic Study*, trans. and ed. Harry Tucker Jr. (Chapel Hill: University of North Carolina Press, 1971).

2. Masao Miyoshi, *The Divided Self: A Perspective on the Literature of the Victorians* (New York: New York University Press, 1969), xii.

3. Ibid., x.

4. Ibid., 291.

5. Ibid., xi.

6. Tzvetan Todorov, *The Fantastic: A Structural Approach to a Literary Genre*, trans. Richard Howard (Cleveland: Case Western Reserve University Press, 1973), 120, 139.

7. Robert Rogers, *Psychoanalytic Study of The Double in Literature* (Detroit: Wayne State University Press, 1970)), 2.

8. Ibid.

9. See Paul Coates, *The Double and the Other: Identity as Ideology in Post-Romantic Fiction* (New York: St. Martin's Press, 1988). Coates devotes a very brief section to "The Double and the Doll."

10. Karl Miller, *Doubles: A Study in Literary History* (New York: Oxford University Press, 1985), 416.

11. G. Stanley Hall and A. Caswell Ellis, *A Study of Dolls* (New York: E. L. Kellogg and Co., 1897), 3.

12. Ibid., 4.

13. Ibid., 48.

14. Angela Carter, "The Loves of Lady Purple," in *Wayward Girls and Wicked Women: An Anthology of Subversive Stories*, ed. Angela Carter (Harmondsworth, Middlesex, England: Penguin, 1988), 254. All further references to this story will appear parenthetically in the text, marked by author's name, the shortened title "Lady Purple," and page number.

15. Susan Stewart, *On Longing: Narratives of the Miniature, the Gigantic, the Souvenir, the Collection* (Baltimore: Johns Hopkins University Press, 1984), 172.

16. Ibid., xii.

17. Jonathan Swift, *Gulliver's Travels* (Boston: Houghton Mifflin, 1960), 70. All further references to this work will appear parenthetically in the text, marked by author's name and page number.

18. Stewart, 71.

19. Loren Eiseley, "The Bird and the Machine," in *The Immense Journey* (New York: Random House [Vintage], 1959), 181.

20. See Carole Fabricant, *Swift's Landscape* (Baltimore: Johns Hopkins University Press, 1982). Fabricant identifies confinement as a central feature of the Swiftian landscape. Each of Gulliver's four journeys is marked by a falling into captivity followed by a prolonged endeavor to obtain freedom. Fabricant suggests that the various architectural structures that Gulliver inhabits provide the objective correlative for the mental entrapment with which Swift is concerned. She identifies first "the house in Lilliput that he got into 'with some difficulty'"; then "the box in Brobdingnag, 'close on every Side' . . . the 'wooden Chamber of Sixteen Foot square' built by the Brobdingnag Queen's personal cabinetmaker, for whose door Gulliver, in an ironically self-imprisoning gesture, demands a lock; and the 'travelling closet' he occupies accompanying Glumdalclitch" (46–47). See also William Bragg Ewald Jr., *The Masks of Jonathan Swift* (Oxford: Blackwell, 1954). Ewald discusses the size relationships between Gulliver and his various hosts.

21. Stewart, 94.

22. Ibid., 147.

23. Ibid., 172.

24. Lewis Carroll, *The Annotated Alice* (New York: Penguin, 1978), 31, 35. Alice, on the other hand, remains in the same world (though an odd one it is), and the objects there, such as the Rabbit's gloves by which she measures her hands and the glass table by which she measures her height, become the constant measure while her body shifts in size. Though not a doubled character, "this curious child was very fond of pretending to be two people"; and her experience in the fluctuating world of the miniature and the gigantic leads her to an emotional, if not a psychological, crisis in identity: "'But if I'm not the same, the next question is, "Who in the world am I?" . . . Who am I then? Tell me that first, and then, if I like being that person, I'll come up: if not, I'll stay down here till I'm somebody else.'" It is the sage Caterpillar who says to her "'So you think you're changed, do you?'" and informs her that one side of the mushroom will make her grow taller, the other side shorter (Carroll 37, 39, 69). Now able to govern her size, depending on what the situation calls for, Alice "finds that she can become a *giantess* or a *pygmy* by nibbling alternate sides of a magic mushroom" (William Rose Benét, et. al., *Benét's Reader's Encyclopedia* [New York: Dover, 1967], 25, emphasis added). A true participant in the world of miniature and gigantic, she embodies the fantasy of changing size at will rather than the charm of the ideal miniature.

25. Stewart 67, 101.

26. Ibid., 133.

27. Johann Wolfgang von Goethe, "The New Melusina," in *The Sorrows of Young Werther and Selected Writings* (New York: New American Library [Signet], 1962), 216. All further references to this story will appear parenthetically in the text, marked by author's name and page number.

28. In "The New Melusina," Goethe offers this analogy for the traveling casket's transformation: "Whoever may have seen a trick writing desk made by Röntgen, with springs and secret drawers that can be set in motion, whereupon writing space, paper, letters, pigeon-holes, and money compartment are revealed, all at once or one at a time, will have some idea of how this palace unfolded before our eyes." A footnote identifies David R.

Röntgen (1745–1807) as "a fine cabinetmaker in Neuwied, whom Goethe probably met on his Rhine journey with Lavater" (Goethe 216, 255 n32).

Goethe's fascination with such curiosities is well documented. Hall and Ellis mention that "Goethe reproduced dramas with puppets in a doll theatre" (Hall and Ellis 53–54); and Stewart reports the following anecdote concerning "the little guillotines that were sold in France during the time of the Revolution. In 1793 Goethe wrote to his mother in Frankfurt requesting that she buy a toy guillotine for his son, August. This was a request she refused, saying that the toy's maker should be put in stocks" (Stewart 57–58).

29. Leo Tolstoy, "The Porcelain Doll," trans. Aylmer Maude, in *Magical Realist Fiction, An Anthology*, ed. David Young and Keith Hollman (New York: Longman, 1984), 35. All further references to this story will appear parenthetically in the text, marked by author's name and page number.

30. Hall and Ellis, 44.

31. Clarice Lispector, "The Smallest Woman in the World," trans. Elizabeth Bishop, in *Magical Realist Fiction, An Anthology*, ed. David Young and Keith Hollman (New York: Longman, 1984), 385. All further references to this story will appear parenthetically in the text, marked by author's name and page number.

32. Hall and Ellis, 48, 41.

33. Stewart, 23.

34. Ibid., 87.

35. Hall and Ellis, 48–49.

36. Margaret Atwood, "Five Poems For Dolls," in *Selected Poems II: Poems Selected and New, 1976–1986* (Boston: Houghton Mifflin, 1987), 7–9.

37. Miyoshi, 335.

2. Creating/Erasing the Other

1. Hélène Cixous, "Fiction and Its Phantoms: A Reading of Freud's *Das Unheimlich*," *New Literary History* 7 (1976): 525, a translation of an article originally published in *Poetique* 10 (1972): 199–216. The reading of Freud's "Uncanny" and Hoffmann's "Sandman" presented here has been informed particularly by the work of Cixous and that of Françoise Meltzer. See Meltzer, "The Uncanny Rendered Canny: Freud's Blind Spot in Reading Hoffmann's 'Sandman,'" in *Introducing Psychoanalytic Theory*, ed. Sander L. Gilman (New York: Brunner/Mazel, 1982), 218–39.

In my discussion of Hoffmann's story, I have used the spellings of such proper names as *Clara, Nathanael, Olimpia, Sand-man*, and *Spalanzani* as they appear in E. F. Bleiler's translation of the story, from which all references in the text are drawn. However, any spelling variations used by Cixous, Meltzer, or any other critics have been retained in material quoted directly from these secondary sources.

2. Mary K. Patterson Thornburg, *The Monster in the Mirror: Gender and the Sentimental Gothic Myth in Frankenstein* (Ann Arbor: University of Michigan Research Press, 1987), 6.

3. Coates, 2; E. F. Bleiler, "Introduction," in *The Best Tales of Hoffmann* (New York: Dover, 1967), xxi–xxii; Christian Bailly, *Automata: The Golden Age, 1848–1914* (New York: Harper and Row [Sothebys], 1987), 14; Valie Export, "The Real and Its Double: The Body," *Discourse: Journal for Theoretical Studies in Media and Culture* 11.1 (fall–winter 1988–89): 19.

For more on the history of automata, see Bailly's impressive pictorial history of this artform. The creation of automata has proved to be a captivating occupation in the world of art as well as a recurring motif in the world of literature. Bailly, one of the world's most important dealers in automata, identifies the heyday of a movement that had been gathering strength since at least the early 1700s and provides a history of the tradition by outlining the careers of master automaton creators, most of whose shops and traveling shows were flourishing in the 1890s, in both America and Europe.

4. Carl F. Keppler, *The Literature of the Second Self* (Tucson: University of Arizona Press, 1972), 70.

5. George Levine, *The Realistic Imagination: English Fiction from Frankenstein to Lady Chatterley* (Chicago: University of Chicago Press, 1981), 31.

6. Cixous, 542–43.

7. Levine, *Realistic Imagination*, 31.

8. See Freud, "The 'Uncanny,'" 219 n. 1, 222 n. 2, and 225 n. 1.

9. Anthony Wilden, "Lacan and the Discourse of the Other," in *Speech and Language in Psychoanalysis* by Jaques Lacan, trans. and ed. Anthony Wilden (Baltimore: Johns Hopkins University Press, 1981), 166.

10. Jacques Lacan, *Écrits: A Selection*, trans. Alan Sheridan (New York: Norton, 1977), 2.

11. E. T. A. Hoffmann, "The Golden Flowerpot," trans. Thomas Carlyle, in *The Best Tales of Hoffmann*, ed. E. F. Bleiler (New York: Dover, 1967), 41. All further references to the following stories from *Best Tales of Hoffmann* will appear parenthetically in the text, marked by the following shortened titles and page numbers:
"Automata": "Automata"
"Flower Pot": "The Golden Flower Pot"
"Nutcracker": "Nutcracker and the King of Mice"
"Sand-Man": "The Sand-Man."

12. Lacan, *Écrits*, 134.

13. John P. Muller and William J. Richardson, *Lacan and Language: A Reader's Guide to Écrits* (New York: International University Press, 1982),133.

14. Meltzer, 221–25. Todorov says "that in Hoffmann it is not vision itself that is linked to the world of the marvelous, but rather eyeglasses and mirrors, those symbols of indirect, distorted, subverted vision" (Todorov 122). Cixous also stresses the concrete objects (or symbols) of vision as inextricably linked to "vision itself" or "scopic knowledge." She imagines a "dangerous eye-glass which passes from the narrator to the unfortunate protagonist . . . [to] the reader, and exposes him to the horrible peculiarity of the world of doubles" and the *Unheimliche* (Cixous 527).

15. Bernard Rubin, "Freud and Hoffmann: 'The Sandman,'" in *Introducing Psychoanalytic Theory*, ed. Sander L. Gilman (New York: Brunner/Mazel, 1982), 209, 217 n. 6.

16. Mary Shelley, *Frankenstein* (New York: Signet [New American Library] 1965), 114. All further references to this story will appear parenthetically in the text, marked by author's name and page number.

17. Peter Brooks, "'Godlike Science/Unhallowed Arts': Language, Nature, and Monstrosity," in *The Endurance of Frankenstein: Essays on Mary Shelley's Novel*, ed. George Levine and U. C. Knoepflmacher (Berkeley: University of California Press, 1979), 215.

18. Jaques Lacan, "The Family Complexes," *Critical Texts* 5.3 (1988): 16.

19. Wilden, 165.

20. Todorov, 155.

21. Thornburg, 86.

22. Cixous, 540.

23. Keppler, 98.

24. Jenijoy La Belle, *Herself Beheld: The Literature of the Looking Glass* (Ithaca: Cornell University Press, 1988) 104. La Belle compares the experience of Frankenstein's "synthetic creation" to that of women in contemporary society. The monster is an artificial construct "much as the self-conception of females and their role in society are in many ways male inventions. In this sense, the monster (like his actual creator, Mary Shelley) has a feminine, exterior notion of self in which mirroring can play a key role. The creature's idea of himself is totally different from what he sees in the mirror, just as many women have a sense of that difference" (104).

25. Ibid., 104–5.

26. Thornburg, 4–6.

27. Cixous, 539–40.

28. Thornburg, 120.

29. Coates, 43; Brooks, 205; James B. Twitchell, *Dreadful Pleasures: An Anatomy of Modern Horror* (New York: Oxford University Press, 1985), 165. Brooks explains further that "each tale interlocked within tale touches its listener with the taint of monsterism." This "textual monsterism" informs the self's "lack of being," the narrative's "lack of ultimate reference," and "language's murderous lack of transcendent reference." He offers an intriguing connection between his concept of "textual monsterism" and the epistolary nature of the novel's development (see Brooks 219–20). Stewart echoes this assessment in her description of the postcard as an object of desire and a textual signifier of the experience of mortality. For her, any narrative's lack of reference is evidenced in the subject's desire to produce "a referent with no representation" or "a representation with no referent" (Stewart 173).

30. Coates, 40.

31. William Veeder, *Mary Shelley and "Frankenstein": The Fate of Androgyny* (Chicago: University of Chicago Press, 1986), 89–91. Veeder concludes that Victor has created "not an androgyne but a hermaphrodite" (Veeder 98). On this same subject, Twitchell attributes the horror of Frankenstein to "unnatural creation" and to the creator's spurning of his creature (Twitchell 160).

Similarly, see Anne K. Mellor, "Possessing Nature," in *Romanticism & Feminism*, ed. Anne K. Mellor (Bloomington: Indiana University Press, 1988); she says that Frankenstein first "fails to feel empathy for the creature he is constructing . . . then fails to love or feel any parental responsibility for the freak he has created" (Mellor 227); and Peter Dale Scott, "Vital Artifice: Mary, Percy, and the Psychopolitical Integrity of *Frankenstein*," in *The Endurance of Frankenstein: Essays on Mary Shelley's Novel*, ed. George Levine and U. C. Knoepflmacher (Berkeley: University of California Press, 1979), 172–202. Scott interprets "the great mythic innovation of the frightful but sympathetic man-made Monster" as a construction of "vital artifice" (174, 176).

32. Anne K. Mellor, "*Frankenstein*: A Feminist Critique of Science," in *One Culture: Essays in Science and Literature*, ed. George Levine (Madison: University of Wisconsin Press, 1987), 299.

33. Mellor, "Possessing Nature," 230. Mellor points out that Frankenstein and Walton both fail to maintain proportion and thus violate Mary Shelley's ethical/aesthetic norm of keeping balance between large and small objects. Their "dream of breaking boundaries is explicitly identified as both evil and ugly" (230).

34. Stewart, 88.

35. Ibid., 89.

36. Mellor, "Possessing Nature," 221.

37. Stewart, 88, 103.

38. Levine, *Realistic Imagination*, 28; Coates, 40.

39. Brooks, 215, 214.

40. Levine, *Realistic Imagination*, 27, 322; Bailly, 22–23.

41. Stewart, 60, 171.

42. William G. Plank, "The Imaginary: Synthesis of Fantasy and Reality," in *The Scope of the Fantastic—Theory, Technique, Major Authors: Selected Essays from the First International Conference on the Fantastic in Literature and Film*, ed. Robert A. Collins and Howard D. Pearce (Westport, Conn.: Greenwood Press, 1980), 78.

43. Levine, *Realistic Imagination*, 29–30.

44. Kenneth Negus, *E. T. A. Hoffmann's Other World: The Romantic Author and his "New Mythology"* (Philadelphia: University of Pennsylvania Press, 1965), 91–92.

45. Cixous, 533, 538. For more on Clara's role in the triangle, see Meltzer (229–30, 230–34); and Lee B. Jennings, "Blood of the Android: A Post-Freudian Perspective on Hoffmann's *Sandmann*," *Seminar* 22.2 (1986): 101–5.

46. Cixous, 537–38. See also Malcolm V. Jones, "'Der Sandmann' and 'The Uncanny': A Sketch for an Alternative Approach," *Paragraph* 7 (1986): 77–101; and Elizabeth Wright, *Psychoanalytic Criticism: Theory in Practice* (New York: Methuen, 1984). Jones and Wright share the view that Freud's analysis of Hoffmann is not necessarily "the last word on the uncanny" (Wright 143; see also Jones 77).

47. Meltzer, 227–28.

48. Ibid., 231.

49. Ibid., 228, 233.

50. Jennings, 97, 105.

51. Ibid., 105–6, 110.

52. Sherry Turkle, "Lacan and America: The Problem of Discourse," in *Introducing Psychoanalytic Theory,*. ed. Sander L. Gilman (New York: Brunner/Mazel, 1982), 253.

53. Meltzer, 231, emphasis added.

54. See Neil Hertz, "Freud and the Sandman," in *Textual Strategies: Perspectives in Post-structuralist Criticism*, ed. Jouse V. Harari (Ithaca: Cornell University Press, 1979), 296–321. Hertz provides an outline of the "repetition-compulsion" as it is treated by Freud in both "The 'Uncanny'" and *Beyond the Pleasure Principle*.

55. Rubin, 215.

56. Nathaniel Hawthorne, "Feathertop: A Moralized Legend," in *Mosses From An Old Manse*, The Centenary Edition of the Works of Nathaniel Hawthorne, X (Columbus: Ohio State University Press, 1974), 223. All further references to this story will appear parenthetically in the text, marked by author's name and page number.

57. For another comparison of Hoffmann and Hawthorne, see Allienne R. Becker, "'Alice Doane's Appeal': A Literary Double of Hoffman's [sic] *Die Elixiere des Teufels*," *Comparative Literature Studies* (1986): 1–11.

58. Shelley L. Frisch, "Poetics of the Uncanny: E. T. A. Hoffmann's 'Sandman,'" in *The Scope of the Fantastic—Theory, Technique, Major Authors: Selected Essays from the First International Conference on the Fantastic in Literature and Film*, ed. Robert A. Collins and Howard D. Pearce (Westport, Conn.: Greenwood Press, 1980), 50.

59. Cixous, 538.

60. Todorov, 47.

61. Meltzer, 235–36.

62. Thornburg, 7. See also James M. McGlathery, *Mysticism and Sexuality: E. T. A. Hoffmann; Part One: Hoffmann and His Sources* (Las Vegas: Peter Lang, 1981). Like

Thornburg, McGlathery notes the sexual element in the dreams that figure in Hoffmann's stories of automata (see 178).

63. Lacan, "Family," 21.

64. Thornburg, 11.

65. E. T. A. Hoffmann, "The Doubles," in *Selected Writing of Hoffmann*, trans. and ed. Leonard J. Kent and Elizabeth C. Knight (Chicago: University of Chicago Press, 1969), 287. All further references to this story will appear parenthetically in the text, marked by the shortened title "Doubles" and page number.

66. Lacan, *Écrits*, 19.

67. In Hoffmann's *Serapion Brethren* cycle, to which "Automata" (as well as "Nutcracker and the King of Mice") belongs, the members of the brotherhood—Lothair, Ottmar, Theodore—discuss each tale at its conclusion. Theodore compares the fantastic effect of the Talking Turk in "Automata" to "The New Melusina." He says that Goethe's "'most delightful tale of the little lady whom the traveller always carried about with him in a little box always exercises an indescribable charm upon me.'" See E. T. A. Hoffmann *The Serapion Brethren*, trans. Major Alex Ewing (London: George Bell, 1886), 382.

68. Jane Gallop, *Reading Lacan* (Ithaca: Cornell University Press, 1985), 109.

69. Lacan, *Écrits*, 287.

70. Gallop, *Reading Lacan*, 109.

71. Lacan, *Écrits*, 285.

72. Jane Gallop, *Thinking Through the Body* (New York: Columbia University Press, 1988), 126.

73. Ibid.

74. Stewart, 56–57.

75. Ibid., 57. Stewart, considering the toy's relation to the "problems of the inanimate and the animate," says that "the toy is the physical embodiment of the fiction: it is a device for fantasy, a point of beginning for narrative. The toy opens an interior world, lending itself to fantasy and privacy in a way that the abstract space, the playground, of social play does not" (56).

76. Negus, 121.

77. Miyoshi, 294. For a study of the nineteenth-century double as Lacanian Other and Kristevan Abject, see William Veeder and Gordon Hirsch, *Dr. Jekyll and Mr. Hyde: After One Hundred Years* (Chicago: Chicago University Press, 1988).

78. Oscar Wilde, "The Harlot's House," in *The Poems of Oscar Wilde*, *The Collected Works of Oscar Wilde*, ed. Robert Ross (London: Routledge/Thoemmes Press, 1993), 9:249–50.

79. Charles Dickens, *Bleak House* (Boston: Houghton Mifflin [Riverside], 1956), 11–13.

80. John Carey, *The Violent Effigy: A Study of Dickens' Imagination* (London: Faber and Faber, 1973), 88. Covering numerous representations of literary automata in the works of Dickens, Carey points out that "Dickens plainly wants us to feel that it's a grand thing that men can be converted into automatons so effectively" (41). He attributes Dickens's fascination with effigies and literary automata to "their silent watching" and to the fact that "they ape human gestures" (89).

81. Ibid., 88–89. Also helpful in analyzing these and other pertinent incidents is Robert Newsom, *Dickens on the Romantic Side of Familiar Things: "Bleak House" and the Novel Tradition* (New York: Columbia University Press, 1977). See particularly the third chapter, for Newsom's study of The Uncanny in *Bleak House*, in which he compares Dickens's use of the word *familiar* with the German *heimlich* and *unheimlich*, using the history of these words as provided by Freud in "The 'Uncanny.'"

82. Hall and Ellis, 48.

83. Nicolas J. Perella, "An Essay on *Pinocchio*," in *The Adventures of Pinocchio: Story of a Puppet*, by Carlo Collodi (Berkeley: University of California Press, 1986), 50.

84. Ibid., 2.

85. Cixous, 541.

86. Carlo Collodi (Carlo Lorenzini), *The Adventures of Pinocchio: Story of a Puppet*, trans. and ed. Nicolas J. Perella (Berkeley: University of California Press, 1986), 377, ellipses Collodi's. All further references to this story will appear parenthetically in the text, marked by author's name and page number.

87. Around her neck this Fairy wears "a thick gold chain from which hung a medallion. On the medallion was the portrait of a puppet" (Collodi 399). This keepsake is the miniature of what is already a miniature, a further reduced Pinocchio, an artificial representation of what is already an artifact.

88. Perella, 21.

89. Ibid., 49, 45.

90. Stewart, 60.

91. Perella, 27.

92. Ibid., 49.

93. Ibid., 17, 51.

94. Ibid., 48.

95. Stewart, 57.

96. Cixous, 548.

97. Perella, 54, 57.

98. Cixous, 544–45.

3. The Doll as Icon

1. Naomi Schor, *Reading in Detail: Aesthetics and the Feminine* (New York: Methuen, 1987), 138, 140. For more on the sculptures of Duane Hanson, see Stewart 27.

2. Umberto Eco, *A Theory of Semiotics* (Bloomington: Indiana University Press, 1976), 191–92, emphasis Eco's.

3. Ibid., 207.

4. Ibid., 193.

5. Stewart, 172.

6. William Butler Yeats, *The Poems: A New Edition*, ed. Richard J. Finneran (New York: Macmillan, 1983), 126–27. All further references to these poems will appear parenthetically in the text, marked by author's name and page number.

7. Stewart, 124.

8. Eco, *Theory of Semiotics*, 210, 200.

9. Ibid., 202, emphasis added.

10. Umberto Eco, *Semiotics and the Philosophy of Language* (Bloomington: Indiana University Press, 1984), 210.

11. See David Lynch Simpson, *Yeats: The Poetics of the Self* (Chicago: Chicago University Press, 1979), 101. Simpson analyzes the impact of various familial relationships in Yeats's poetry but mentions "The Dolls" only in passing, commenting on tone rather than on the role of the father.

12. Stewart, 133, emphasis Stewart's.

13. Gallop, *Thinking Through the Body*, 163.

14. Stewart, xiii.

15. Schor, 6, 7, 4.

16. Julia Kristeva, *Powers of Horror: An Essay on Abjection*, trans. Leon S. Roudiez (New York: Columbia University Press, 1982), 1.

17. Terry Eagleton, *Literary Theory: An Introduction* (Minneapolis: University of Minnesota Press, 1983), 174.

18. Kristeva, *Horror*, 1, 6.

19. Ibid., 2.

20. Ibid.

21. Ibid.

22. Ibid., 3.

23. Julia Kristeva, *Desire in Language: A Semiotic Approach to Literature and Art*, ed. Leon S. Roudiez, trans. Thomas Gora, Alice Jardine, and Leon S. Roudiez (New York: Columbia University Press, 1980), 18.

24. Eagleton, 188.

25. Ibid., 186.

26. Kristeva, *Horror,* 3. Concerning the essential elements of defilement, uncleanness, impropriety, etc., Kristeva draws various connections between the subject of abjection and purification, the history of religion, and art as catharsis (see *Horror,* 17). See also Jaques Lacan, *The Four Fundamental Concepts of Psycho-Analysis*, ed. Jaques-Alain Miller, trans. Alan Sheridan (New York: Norton, 1978). Lacan says that "up until the advent of psycho-analysis, the path of knowledge was always traced in that of a purification of the subject, of the *percipiens*. Well! We would now say that we base the assurance of the subject in his encounter with the filth that may support him, with the *petit a* of which it would not be untrue to say that its presence is necessary" (*Concepts* 258).

27. Kristeva, *Horror*, 4.

28. Kristeva, *Desire*, 240.

29. Kristeva, *Horror*, 4, emphasis added.

30. Ibid.

31. Ibid., 2.

32. Ibid., 5.

33. Kristeva, *Desire*, 128. Here Kristeva contrasts the "me, miserable treasure" with the "transcendental ego."

34. Ibid., 132.

35. Kristeva, *Horror*, 8, emphasis and parentheses Kristeva's.

36. Ibid., 1.

37. Stewart, 124.

38. D. H. Lawrence, *Psychoanalysis and the Unconscious* (London: Martin Secker, Ltd., 1923), 48, 124.

39. D. H. Lawrence, *The Fox, The Captain's Doll, The Ladybird*, in *The Cambridge Edition of the Letters and Works of D. H. Lawrence*, ed. Dieter Mehl (Cambridge: Cambridge University Press, 1992), 151. All further references to this story will appear parenthetically in the text, marked by author's name and page number.

40. F. R. Leavis, *D. H. Lawrence: Novelist* (New York: Knopf, 1956), 259.

41. Janice Hubbard Harris, *The Short Fiction of D. H. Lawrence* (New Brunswick, N.J.: Rutgers University Press, 1984), 158. Harris's description of Hepburn as a "closed end" is drawn from the text of the story: "He is at a closed end. I don't know where I can get to with him. . . . Ach, like a closed road! (Lawrence 77).

42. Harris, 159.

43. Lawrence, *Psychoanalysis and the Unconscious*, 124, 128.

44. Harris, 159.

45. D. H. Lawrence, *The Rainbow* (New York: Penguin, 1981), 149, 174.

46. Stewart, xii.

47. Ibid., xiii.

48. Eugene W. Dawson, "Love Among the Mannikins: *The Captain's Doll*," *The D. H. Lawrence Review* 1.2 (summer 1968): 144. Dawson's article is prefaced by the following passage, which he attributes to Lawrence:

> The ego . . . that doll-like entity, that mannikin made in ridiculous likeness of the Adam which I am: am I going to allow that that is *all* of *me*? . . .
>
> Of course, if I am nothing but an ego, and woman is nothing but another ego, then there is really no vital difference between us. Two little dolls of conscious entities, squeaking when you squeeze them. And with a tiny bit of an extraneous appendage to mark which is which. (Taken from "Love Was Once a Little Boy")

49. Stewart, 133, 134, 152.

50. Dawson, 144.

51. Ibid., 143.

52. Michael Riffaterre, *Semiotics of Poetry* (Bloomington: Indiana University Press, 1978), 86.

53. Harris, 158.

54. Riffaterre, 86.

55. Ibid.

56. Leavis, 51; Stewart, 68.

57. Dawson, 145.

58. Eco, *Theory of Semiotics*, 179.

59. Ibid., 183.

60. Ibid., 181.

61. Dawson, 145. Dawson draws here on the psychology of the American psychoanalyst Trigant Burrow.

62. Stewart, 171.

63. Ibid., 61–62.

64. Ibid., 149.

65. Dawson, 140.

66. Stewart, 74.

67. Ibid., 70.

68. Ibid., 71.

69. Ibid., 102.

70. Ibid., 69.

71. Ibid., 71.

72. Leavis, 267.

73. Dawson, 147, see also 140.

74. Stewart, 101, 102.

75. Ibid., xiii.

76. Dawson, 145.

77. Freud associates such sphinx-like stillness with The Uncanny. One of the etymological derivations he provides is "*Unheimlich* and motionless like a stone image" (Freud 224).

78. See "A Prayer for My Daughter":

> Considering that, all hatred driven hence,
> The soul recovers radical innocence
> And learns at last that it is self-delighting,
> Self-appeasing, self-affrighting,
> And that its own sweet will is Heaven's will.
>
> (Yeats 93–94)

4. Contemporary Narratives of Abjection and Imperfection

1. Kristeva, *Horror*, 2.
2. Lacan, *Écrits*, 2–3.
3. Gallop, *Thinking Through the Body*, 18–19; Laura Mulvey, *Visual and Other Pleasures* (Bloomington: Indiana University Press, 1989), 148.
4. Todorov, 23.
5. Lacan, *Écrits*, 11.
6. Tommaso Landolfi, "Gogol's Wife," trans. Wayland Young, in *Gogol's Wife and Other Stories*, trans. Raymond Rosenthal, John Longrigg and Wayland Young (Norfolk, Conn.: New Directions, 1963), 1. All further references to this story will appear parenthetically in the text, marked by the author's name and page number.
7. Stewart, 133, 124.
8. Jane Gallop, *The Daughter's Seduction: Feminism and Psychoanalysis* (Ithaca: Cornell University Press, 1982), 70.
9. Kristeva, *Horror*, 8.
10. Stewart observes that in certain works of the gigantic "the major victories against the giants . . . are made through the use of fire, a quantity and quality which, like any element, cannot be permanently miniaturized, and which presents the ultimate image of consumption" (Stewart 87). For more on the body's role as a self-determining (and self-consuming) signifier, see the essays in *Discourse* 11.1 (fall–winter 1988–89), a special issue on "Body / Masquerade"; and Susan Rubin Suleiman, *The Female Body in Western Culture: Contemporary Perspectives* (Cambridge, Mass.: Harvard University Press, 1986), a collection of essays that look at both the poetics and the politics of body.
11. Edna O'Brien, "The Doll," in *A Fanatic Heart*, (New York: Plume [New American Library], 1985), 48. All further references to this story will appear parenthetically in the text, marked by the author's name and page number.
12. Stewart, 61.
13. Kristeva, *Horror,* 17.
14. Ibid., 8, emphasis Kristeva's.
15. Ibid.
16. Ibid.
17. Ibid., 6.
18. Margaret Atwood, *Surfacing* (New York: Fawcett, 1972), 35.
19. In a moment of disillusion, Hannele says of Hepburn: "He was a nullus, in reality. . . . and even when she looked at his doll she saw nothing but a barren puppet. And yet for this dead puppet she had been compromising herself" (Lawrence 90).

20. Stewart, 126.

21. Kristeva, *Horror,* 12, emphasis Kristeva's.

22. Ibid., 11–12.

23. Ibid., 8, emphasis Kristeva's.

24. This motif appears also in "The Captain's Doll": "you always feel you would be happy somewhere else, and not just where you are. Isn't that it?" (Lawrence 88).

25. Kristeva, *Horror,* 12.

26. Ibid., 8.

27. Ibid., 6, 12.

28. Lawrence, *Psychological Unconscious*, 99–100.

29. Ibid., 100–101.

30. Kristeva, *Desire*, 237–42.

31. Ibid., 253–54. See also "Giotto's Joy" (in Kristeva's *Desire*), which deals with how the body or subject is signified in pictorial narrative episodes.

32. Margaret Atwood, "The Resplendent Quetzal," in *Dancing Girls and Other Stories* (New York: Simon and Schuster, 1982), 154. All further references to this story will appear parenthetically in the text, marked by author's name and page number.

33. See also Carlos Fuentes, "The Doll Queen," in *Burnt Water: Stories by Carlos Fuentes*, trans. Margaret Sayers Peden (New York: Noonday Press), 115–33. In this work, a couple struggle to deal with the fate of their child, Amilamia, who was born healthy but developed a handicap. Entirely unable to deal with the reality of her imperfect body, they mark their daughter's life as having ended when the crippling disease or accident struck her. Although she still resides in their house, a stunted adult in a wheelchair, they eerily worship Amilamia's past self and body before a funeral shrine that they maintain in their attic. Incense, flowers, and used toys and shoes surround an elaborate coffin in which rests a "sham cadaver" of their child. In disbelief, the narrator confronts this "petrified doll," the morbid double of his childhood friend: "I reach out my hand and run my fingers over the porcelain face of my little friend. I feel the coldness of those painted features of the doll queen who presides over the pomp of this royal chamber of death. Porcelain, wax, cotton" (Fuentes 131, see also 132).

34. Marilyn French, *The Women's Room* (New York: Jove/HBJ, 1978), 135.

35. Margaret Atwood, *Cat's Eye* (New York: Doubleday, 1988), 135–36.

36. Ibid., 256.

37. Kristeva, *Desire,* 237.

38. Stewart, 131.

39. Atwood, *Surfacing*, 104–5.

40. Ibid., 28.

41. Atwood, "Five Poems For Dolls," 10.

42. Lacan, *Écrits*, 2–3.

43. Kristeva, *Horror*, 3.

44. Lacan, *Écrits*, 2–3.

45. Kristeva, *Horror*, 8, emphasis Kristeva's.

46. Ibid., 9.

47. Kristeva, *Desire*, 239.

48. Kristeva, *Horror*, 10.

49. Ibid., 3–4.

50. Jane Gallop, *Thinking Through the Body*, 8, emphasis added.

51. Ibid., 8–9.

52. Ibid., 93.

53. Kristeva, *Horror*, 3.

54. Margaret Atwood, *The Edible Woman* (New York: Warner, 1969), 274. All further references to this story will appear parenthetically in the text, marked by author's name, title, and page number.

55. Gallop, *Thinking Through the Body*, 132.

56. Gallop, *Reading Lacan*, 59.

57. Ibid.

5. *Heimlich/Unheimlich*

1. Stewart, 61.

2. Katherine Mansfield, "The Doll's House," in *Stories*, ed. Elizabeth Bowen (New York: Vintage, 1956), 318. All further references to this story and to "Prelude" (also drawn from *Stories*) will appear parenthetically in the text, marked by author's name and page number.

3. Stewart, 70–71.

4. Though the three stories are not presented as a sequence, "Prelude," "The Doll's House," and another story, "At the Bay" (see Mansfield, *Stories*, 99–137), all feature this same family.

5. Arthur Benson, *The Book of the Queen's Dolls' House* (London: Methuen, 1924), 5.

6. Stewart, 62, emphasis Stewart's. See also David Simpson, *Fetishism and Imagination: Dickens, Melville, Conrad* (Baltimore: Johns Hopkins University Press, 1982). Simpson describes "the usurpation of the inner by the outer qualities." He discusses the house as "a form of fetishism, in the broader sense of the word"; for the mansion's artificial facade is an exhibition of wealth representing "the thing endowed with value and inviting envy . . . the focus of immediate attention and also of subsequently active and energetic meditation" (Simpson 25–27). In fact, Mansfield concludes "The Doll's House" with Lil and Else Kelvey engaged in this kind of intense meditation, following their viewing of the enviable dollhouse.

7. Stewart, 62, 61.

8. Ibid., 171–72.

9. Hertz, 299–300.

10. Simpson, 20. See especially chap. 1, sec. 3 ("Trinkets and Baubles") and 4 ("Commodities and Money"), 20–38.

11. Stewart, 62.

12. Ibid., 63.

13. Kristeva, *Horror*, 1, 10.

14. Stewart, 69. Kristeva, too, identifies childhood as a version of experience that should be protected from the contamination of death and abjection. In a particularly poignant passage, she isolates the time or condition of childhood as a stable factor in the living universe, and one that should protect the subject:

> In the dark halls of the museum that is now what remains of Auschwitz, I see a heap of children's shoes, or something like that, something I have already seen elsewhere, under a Christmas tree, for instance, *dolls* I believe. The abjection of Nazi crime reaches its apex when death, which, in any case, kills me, interferes with what, in my living universe, is supposed to save me from death: *childhood*, science, among other things. (Kristeva, *Horror*, 4, emphasis added)

The now useless shoes, a metonymic representation of the children who wore them, stand as reminders of the vulnerability of the manipulatable body and the tragedy of lived reality. Likewise, the dolls, who are interchangeable with the shoes in Kristeva's dark vision, represent the children whom they have replaced. But unlike the children, the dolls are members of a world not only diminutive but also removed from lived experience; only in this realm are the small not subject to contamination and death.

15. See Naomi Schor, *Reading in Detail*, for a discussion of the concept of displacement and the position of the detail in Freud's tropological system. Her analysis clarifies not only Beryl's unduly angry reaction here but also the intensity of Kezia's focus on the lamp and the power of Linda's interior decoration to rise up against her peace of mind (Schor 71).

16. See also Sigmund Freud, *Beyond the Pleasure Principle* (1920), in *The Standard Edition of the Complete Psychological Works*, trans. and ed. James Strachey (London: Hogarth Press, 1953–74), vol. 28. Freud explains the complex relation between the ego-instincts, the coming to life of inanimate matter, and the restoration of the inanimate state: "If we are to take it as a truth that knows no exception that everything living dies for *internal reasons*—becomes inorganic once again—then we shall be compelled to say that '*the aim of all life is death*' and, looking backwards, that '*inanimate things existed before living ones*'" (emphasis Freud's, 38).

17. Kristeva, *Horror*, 10, emphasis Kristeva's.

18. Angela Carter, *The Magic Toy Shop* (New York: Simon and Schuster, 1962), 112, emphasis added. All further references to this story will appear parenthetically in the text, marked by author's name and page number.

19. Schor, 4.

20. Stewart, xiii.

21. Freud, *Pleasure*, 36.

22. See Robert Newsom for a treatment of similar themes in the work of Charles Dickens. Newsom speaks of developments in *Bleak House* that "strike us with a sense at once of familiarity and inevitability"; and he describes the "continual peripety" of the opening chapters of *Bleak House*, the "falling round and round and round . . . that continually makes the familiar strange and the strange familiar" (Newsom 41, 45). Concerning "Dickens' pyrotechnic toying with uncanny effects" he concludes that Dickens creates a world that is characterized by repression and suppression: "And in Dickens, as in Freud, the repressed returns, and returns, and returns" (Newsom 92).

23. Hertz, 301.

24. Mulvey, xi.

25. Lacan, *Concepts*, 256–57.

26. Ibid.

27. Lacan, *Écrits*, 42.

28. La Belle, 83.

29. Gallop, *Reading Lacan*, 78.

30. Ibid., 83.

31. Lacan, *Écrits*, 41–42.

32. Stewart, 123.

33. Ibid., 138.

34. Gallop, *Reading Lacan*, 83.

35. Gallop, *Daughter's Seduction*, 80, emphasis added.

36. Ibid., 81.

37. Lacan, "Family," 20.

38. Stewart, 117.

39. Mulvey, xi.

40. This passage is from Angela Carter, *The Infernal Desire Machines of Doctor Hoffmann* (London: Rupert Hart-Davis, 1972), 190. See David Punter, "Angela Carter: Supersessions of the Masculine," in *The Hidden Script: Writing and the Unconscious* (London & Boston: Routledge & Kegan Paul, 1985), 28–42. Punter says that Carter's novels *Doctor Hoffmann* and *The Passion of the New Eve* [and *The Magic Toyshop* could well be added to this list] are "dramatisations of the constructed subject . . . specifically about the exact point at which gender enters as a structuring principle. 'You could effectively evolve a persona from your predicament, if you tried,' Desiderio is admonished in *Doctor Hoffmann* at one point, although Carter does not here go in for easy answers" (Punter 29).

41. Gallop, *Reading Lacan*, 85.

42. Mulvey, 74.

43. Lacan, *Concepts*, 268, emphasis Lacan's.

44. Bailly, 14.

45. Stewart, 57.

46. Bailly, 18.

47. Ibid., 9.

48. Stewart, 57; Bailly, 19.

49. Lacan, *Concepts*, 270.

50. Mulvey, 175.

51. Lacan, *Écrits*, 4.

52. Lacan, "Family," 20.

53. Gallop, *Reading Lacan*, 80, emphasis Gallop's.

54. Lacan, *Écrits*, 4.

55. Mulvey, 130.

56. Lacan, *Écrits*, 199.

57. Lacan, *Concepts*, 195.

57. Mulvey, 165.

59. Ibid., 73, emphasis added.

60. Ibid., 72.

61. Ibid., 39, 72–73.

62. Ibid., 64.

63. Ibid., Mulvey, 73–74. Similarly, Twitchell writes of Mary Shelley's *Frankenstein* that "it is a horror novel not because there is a huge, violent, mindless destructive monster lumbering about the countryside, but because human desire, our desire, has made this protoplasm and is strangely motivating it to play out roles in the family romance" (178). See also Lacan, "The Family Complexes."

64. Mulvey, 74.

65. Cixous, 528.

66. Mulvey, xi.

67. Stewart, 61.

68. Lacan, *Concepts*, 243.

69. Carey, 85.

70. Lacan, *Écrits*, 50.

71. Bailly, 13.

72. Ibid., 14.

73. Rubin, 211.

74. Levine, *Realistic Imagination*, 19, 27.

75. Ibid., 320.

76. Coates, 44.

77. Ibid., 35.

78. Rainer Maria Rilke, "Some Reflections on Dolls," in *Rilke: Selected Works, Prose,* I, trans. G. Craig Houston (Norfolk, Conn.: New Directions, 1960), 47–48, see also 43.

79. Ibid., 44.

80. Schor, 7, see also 3–6.

81. Rilke, 45, see also 48.

82. Schor, 7.

83. Export, 19, 23.

84. Rilke, 44.

85. Stewart, 172.

86. Rilke, 50.

87. Ibid., 43.

88. Ibid., 45.

89. Ibid., 47.

90. Lispector, 387. See also Judith Thurman, *Isak Dinesen: The Life of a Storyteller* (New York: St. Martin's Press, 1982). Thurman describes a similar kind of "terrible maternity" in her biography of Isak Dinesen: "There was something of a lonely child playing with a doll in all her [Dinesen's] relations with the Africans: the extreme tenderness, the maternal solicitude, the sense of power and responsibility that distracted her from her own feelings of helplessness and despair" (Thurman 269).

91. Rilke, 46–47.

Works Cited

Atwood, Margaret. *Cat's Eye*. New York: Doubleday, 1988.

———. *The Edible Woman*. New York: Warner, 1969.

———. "Five Poems For Dolls." In *Selected Poems II: Poems Selected and New, 1976–1986*, 7–10. Boston: Mass., 1987.

———. "The Resplendent Quetzal." In *Dancing Girls and Other Stories*, 144–59. New York: Simon and Schuster, 1982.

———. *Surfacing*. New York: Fawcett, 1972.

Bailly, Christian. *Automata: The Golden Age, 1848–1914*. New York: Harper and Row (Sothebys), 1987.

Becker, Allienne R. "'Alice Doane's Appeal': A Literary Double of Hoffman's [sic] Die Elixiere des Teufels." *Comparative Literature Studies* (1986): 1–11.

Benét, William Rose, et. al. *Benét's Reader's Encyclopedia*. New York: Harper and Row, 1987.

Benson, Arthur. *The Book of the Queen's Dolls' House*. London: Metheun, 1924.

Bleiler, E. F. "Introduction." In *The Best Tales of Hoffmann*, v–xxxiii. New York: Dover, 1967.

Brooks, Peter. "'Godlike Science/Unhallowed Arts': Language, Nature, and Monstrosity." In *The Endurance of Frankenstein: Essays on Mary Shelley's Novel*, edited by George Levine and U. C. Knoepflmacher, 205–20. Berkeley: University of California Press, 1979.

Carey, John. *The Violent Effigy: A Study of Dickens' Imagination*. London: Faber and Faber, 1973.

Carroll, Lewis. *The Annotated Alice*. New York: Penguin, 1978.

Carter, Angela. *The Infernal Desire Machines of Doctor Hoffman*. London: Rupert Hart-Davis, 1972.

———. "The Loves of Lady Purple." In *Wayward Girls and Wicked Women: An Anthology of Subversive Stories*, edited by Angela Carter, 254–66. Harmondsworth, Middlesex, England: Penguin, 1989.

———. *The Magic Toy Shop*. New York: Simon and Schuster, 1962.

Cixous, Hélène. "Fiction and Its Phantoms: A Reading of Freud's Das Unheimlich." *New Literary History* 7 (1976): 524–48. A translation of an article originally published in *Poetique* 10 (1972): 199–216.

Coates, Paul. *The Double and the Other: Identity as Ideology in Post-Romantic Fiction.* New York: St. Martin's, 1988.

Collodi, Carlo (Carlo Lorenzini). *The Adventures of Pinocchio: Story of a Puppet.* Translated and edited by Nicolas J. Perella. Berkeley: University of California Press, 1986.

Dawson, Eugene W. "Love Among the Mannikins: *The Captain's Doll.*" *The D. H. Lawrence Review* 1.2 (summer 1968): 137–48.

Dickens, Charles. *Bleak House.* Boston: Houghton Mifflin (Riverside), 1956.

―――. *Our Mutual Friend.* Edited by Michael Cotsell. New York: Oxford University Press, 1989.

Eagleton, Terry. *Literary Theory: An Introduction.* Minneapolis: University of Minnesota Press, 1983.

Eco, Umberto. *Semiotics and the Philosophy of Language.* Bloomington: Indiana University Press, 1984.

―――. *A Theory of Semiotics.* Bloomington: Indiana University Press, 1976.

Eiseley, Loren. "The Bird and the Machine." In *The Immense Journey,* 179–93. New York: Random House (Vintage), 1959.

Eliot, George. *The Mill on the Floss.* Edited by Gordon S. Haight. New York: Oxford University Press, 1980.

Ewald, William Bragg Jr. *The Masks of Jonathan Swift.* Oxford: Blackwell, 1954.

Export, Valie. "The Real and Its Double: The Body." *Discourse: Journal for Theoretical Studies in Media and Culture* 11.1 (fall-winter 1988–89): 3–27.

Fabricant, Carole. *Swift's Landscape.* Baltimore: Johns Hopkins University Press, 1982.

French, Marilyn. *The Women's Room.* New York: Jove/HBJ, 1978.

Freud, Sigmund. "The 'Uncanny'" (1919). In *The Standard Edition of the Complete Psychological Works,* translated and edited by James Strachey, 17:217–56. London: Hogarth Press, 1953–74.

―――. *Beyond the Pleasure Principle* (1920). In *The Standard Edition of the Complete Psychological Works,* translated and edited by James Strachey, 18:3–64. London: Hogarth Press, 1953–74.

Frisch, Shelley L. "Poetics of the Uncanny: E. T. A. Hoffmann's 'Sandman.'" In *The Scope of the Fantastic—Theory, Technique, Major Authors: Selected Essays from the First International Conference on the Fantastic in Literature and Film,* edited by Robert A. Collins and Howard D. Pearce, 49–55. Westport, Conn.: Greenwood Press, 1980.

Fuentes, Carlos. "The Doll Queen." In *Burnt Water: Stories by Carlos Fuentes,* translated by Margaret Sayers Peden, 115–33. New York: Noonday Press.

Gallop, Jane. *The Daughter's Seduction: Feminism and Psychoanalysis.* Ithaca: Cornell University Press, 1982.

―――. *Reading Lacan.* Ithaca: Cornell University Press, 1985.

―――. *Thinking Through the Body.* New York: Columbia University Press, 1988.

Gilman, Sander L., ed. *Introducing Psychoanalytic Theory.* New York: Brunner/Mazel, 1982.

Goethe, Johann Wolfgang von. "The New Melusina." In *The Sorrows of Young Werther and Selected Writings,* 201–19. New York: New American Library (Signet), 1962.

Hall, G. Stanley, and A. Caswell Ellis. *A Study of Dolls*. New York: E. L. Kellogg and Co., 1897.

Hardy, Thomas. *The Return of the Native*. Edited by Simon Gatrell. New York: Oxford University Press, 1990.

Harris, Janice Hubbard. *The Short Fiction of D. H. Lawrence*. New Brunswick, N.J.: Rutgers University Press, 1984.

Hawthorne, Nathaniel. "Feathertop: A Moralized Legend." In *Mosses From an Old Manse*, The Centenary Edition of the Works of Nathaniel Hawthorne, 10:223–46. Columbus: Ohio State University Press, 1974.

Hertz, Neil. "Freud and the Sandman." In *Textual Strategies: Perspectives in Post-structuralist Criticism,* edited by Jouse V. Harari, 296–321. Ithaca: Cornell University Press, 1979.

Hoffmann, E. T. A. "Automata." Translated by Major Alexander Ewing. In *The Best Tales of Hoffmann,* edited by E. F. Bleiler, 71–103. New York: Dover, 1967.

———. "The Doubles." In *Selected Writing of Hoffmann,* translated and edited by Leonard J. Kent and Elizabeth C. Knight. Chicago: University of Chicago Press, 1969.

———. "The Golden Flowerpot." Translated by Thomas Carlyle. In *The Best Tales of Hoffmann,* edited by E. F. Bleiler, 1–70. New York: Dover, 1967.

———. "Nutcracker and the King of Mice." Translated by Major Alexander Ewing. In *The Best Tales of Hoffmann,* edited by E. F. Bleiler, 130–82. New York: Dover, 1967.

———. "The Sand-Man." Translated by J. T. Bealby. In *The Best Tales of Hoffmann,* edited by E. F. Bleiler, 183–214. New York: Dover, 1967.

———. *The Serapion Brethren.* Translated by Major Alex Ewing. London: George Bell, 1886.

Jennings, Lee B. "Blood of the Android: A Post-Freudian Perspective on Hoffmann's *Sandmann." Seminar* 22.2 (1986): 95–111.

Jones, Malcolm V. "'Der Sandmann' and 'The Uncanny': A Sketch for an Alternative Approach." *Paragraph* 7 (1986): 77–101.

Keppler, Carl F. *The Literature of the Second Self.* Tucson: University of Arizona Press, 1972.

Kristeva, Julia. *Desire in Language: A Semiotic Approach to Literature and Art.* Edited by Leon S. Roudiez. Translated by Thomas Gora, Alice Jardine, and Leon S. Roudiez. New York: Columbia University Press, 1980.

———. *Powers of Horror: An Essay on Abjection.* Translated by Leon S. Roudiez. New York: Columbia University Press, 1982.

La Belle, Jenijoy. *Herself Beheld: The Literature of the Looking Glass.* Ithaca: Cornell University Press, 1988.

Lacan, Jacques. *Écrits: A Selection.* Translated by Alan Sheridan. New York: Norton, 1977.

———. "The Family Complexes." *Critical Texts* 5.3 (1988): 12–29.

———. *The Four Fundamental Concepts of Psycho-Analysis.* Edited by Jaques-Alain Miller. Translated by Alan Sheridan. New York: Norton, 1978.

Landolfi, Tommaso. "Gogol's Wife." Translated by Wayland Young. In *Gogol's Wife and Other Stories,* translated by Raymond Rosenthal, John Longrigg, and Wayland Young, 1–16. Norfolk, Conn.: New Directions, 1963.

Lawrence, D. H. *The Fox, The Captain's Doll, The Ladybird.* In *The Cambridge Edition of the Letters and Works of D. H. Lawrence,* edited by Dieter Mehl. Cambridge: Cambridge University Press, 1992.

———. *Psychoanalysis and the Unconscious.* London: Martin Secker, Ltd., 1923.

———. *The Rainbow.* New York: Penguin, 1981.

Leavis, F. R. *D. H. Lawrence: Novelist.* New York: Knopf, 1956.

Levine, George. *The Realistic Imagination: English Fiction from Frankenstein to Lady Chatterley.* Chicago: University of Chicago Press, 1981.

Levine, George, and U. C. Knoepflmacher, eds. *The Endurance of Frankenstein: Essays on Mary Shelley's Novel.* Berkeley: University of California Press, 1979.

Lispector, Clarice. "The Smallest Woman in the World." Translated by Elizabeth Bishop. In *Magical Realist Fiction, An Anthology,* edited by David Young and Keith Hollman, 385–90. New York: Longman, 1984.

Mansfield, Katherine. "At the Bay." In *Stories,* edited by Elizabeth Bowen, 99–137. New York: Vintage, 1956.

———. "The Doll's House." In *Stories,* edited by Elizabeth Bowen, 318–26. New York: Vintage, 1956.

———. "Prelude." In *Stories,* edited by Elizabeth Bowen, 52–99. New York: Vintage, 1956.

McGlathery, James M. *Mysticism and Sexuality: E. T. A. Hoffmann; Part One: Hoffmann and His Sources.* Las Vegas: Peter Lang, 1981.

Mellor, Anne K. "*Frankenstein*: A Feminist Critique of Science." In *One Culture: Essays in Science and Literature,* edited by George Levine, 287–312. Madison: University of Wisconsin Press, 1987.

———. "Possessing Nature." In *Romanticism & Feminism,* edited by Anne K. Mellor, 220–32. Bloomington: Indiana University Press, 1988.

Meltzer, Françoise. "The Uncanny Rendered Canny: Freud's Blind Spot in Reading Hoffmann's 'Sandman.'" In *Introducing Psychoanalytic Theory,* edited by Sander L. Gilman, 218–39. New York: Brunner/Mazel, 1982.

Miller, Karl. *Doubles: A Study in Literary History.* New York: Oxford University Press, 1985.

Miyoshi, Masao. *The Divided Self: A Perspective on the Literature of the Victorians.* New York: New York University Press, 1969.

Muller, John P., and William J. Richardson. *Lacan and Language: A Reader's Guide to Écrits.* New York: International University Press, 1982.

Mulvey, Laura. *Visual and Other Pleasures.* Bloomington: Indiana University Press, 1989.

Negus, Kenneth. *E. T. A. Hoffmann's Other World: The Romantic Author and His "New Mythology."* Philadelphia: University of Pennsylvania Press, 1965.

Newsom, Robert. *Dickens on the Romantic Side of Familiar Things: "Bleak House" and the Novel Tradition.* New York: Columbia University Press, 1977.

O'Brien, Edna. "The Doll." In *A Fanatic Heart,* 48–54. New York: Plume (NAL), 1985.

Perella, Nicolas J. "An Essay on *Pinocchio*." In *The Adventures of Pinocchio: Story of a Puppet,* by Carlo Collodi, 1–69. Berkeley: University of California Press, 1986.

Plank, William G. "The Imaginary: Synthesis of Fantasy and Reality." In *The Scope of the Fantastic—Theory, Technique, Major Authors: Selected Essays from the First International Conference on the Fantastic in Literature and Film,* edited by Robert A. Collins and Howard D. Pearce, 77–82. Westport, Conn.: Greenwood Press, 1980.

Punter, David. "Angela Carter: Supersessions of the Masculine." In *The Hidden Script: Writing and the Unconscious,* 28–42. London & Boston: Routledge & Kegan Paul, 1985.

Rank, Otto. *The Double: A Psychoanalytic Study.* Translated and edited by Harry Tucker, Jr. Chapel Hill: University of North Carolina Press, 1971.

Riffaterre, Michael. *Semiotics of Poetry.* Bloomington: Indiana University Press, 1978.

Rilke, Rainer Maria. "Some Reflections on Dolls." In *Rilke: Selected Works, Prose,* I, translated by G. Craig Houston. Norfolk, Conn.: New Directions, 1960.

Rogers, Robert. *A Psychoanalytic Study of the Double in Literature.* Detroit: Wayne State University Press, 1970.

Rossetti, Dante Gabriel. "Sister Helen." In *The Poetical Works of Dante Gabriel Rossetti,* edited by William M. Rossetti, 66–74. 1903. Reprint, New York: Folcroft Library Editions, 1977.

Rubin, Bernard. "Freud and Hoffmann: 'The Sandman.'" In *Introducing Psychoanalytic Theory,* edited by Sander L. Gilman, 205–17. New York: Brunner/Mazel, 1982.

Schor, Naomi. *Reading in Detail: Aesthetics and the Feminine.* New York: Methuen, 1987.

Scott, Peter Dale. "Vital Artifice: Mary, Percy, and the Psychopolitical Integrity of *Frankenstein.*" In *The Endurance of Frankenstein: Essays on Mary Shelley's Novel,* edited by George Levine and U. C., 172–202. Knoepflmacher. Berkeley: University of California Press, 1979.

Shelley, Mary. *Frankenstein.* New York: Signet (NAL), 1965.

Simpson, David. *Fetishism and Imagination: Dickens, Melville, Conrad.* Baltimore: Johns Hopkins University Press, 1982.

Simpson, David Lynch. *Yeats: The Poetics of the Self.* Chicago: University of Chicago Press, 1979.

Stewart, Susan. *On Longing: Narratives of the Miniature, the Gigantic, the Souvenir, the Collection.* Baltimore: Johns Hopkins University Press, 1984.

Suleiman, Susan Rubin. *The Female Body in Western Culture: Contemporary Perspectives.* Cambridge, Mass.: Harvard University Press, 1986.

Swift, Jonathan. *Gulliver's Travels.* Boston: Houghton Mifflin, 1960.

Thornburg, Mary K. Patterson. *The Monster in the Mirror: Gender and the Sentimental Gothic Myth in Frankenstein.* Ann Arbor: University of Michigan Research Press, 1987.

Thurman, Judith. *Isak Dinesen: The Life of a Storyteller.* New York: St. Martin's Press, 1982.

Todorov, Tzvetan. *The Fantastic: A Structural Approach to a Literary Genre.* Translated by Richard Howard. Cleveland: Case Western Reserve University Press, 1973.

Tolstoy, Leo. "The Porcelain Doll." Translated by Aylmer Maude. In *Magical Realist Fiction, An Anthology,* edited by David Young and Keith Hollman, 33–36. New York: Longman, 1984.

Turkle, Sherry. "Lacan and America: The Problem of Discourse." In *Introducing Psychoanalytic Theory,* edited by Sander L. Gilman, 240–54. New York: Brunner/Mazel, 1982.

Twitchell, James B. *Dreadful Pleasures: An Anatomy of Modern Horror.* New York: Oxford University Press, 1985.

Veeder, William. *Mary Shelley and "Frankenstein": The Fate of Androgyny.* Chicago: University of Chicago Press, 1986.

Veeder, William, and Gordon Hirsch. *Dr. Jekyll and Mr. Hyde: After One Hundred Years.* Chicago: University of Chicago Press, 1988.

Wilde, Oscar. "The Harlot's House." In *The Poems of Oscar Wilde, The Collected Works of Oscar Wilde,* 9:249–50. London: Routledge/Thoemmes Press, 1993.

Wilden, Anthony. "Lacan and the Discourse of the Other." In *Speech and Language in Psychoanalysis,* by Jaques Lacan, translated and edited by Anthony Wilden, 159–311. Baltimore: Johns Hopkins University Press, 1981.

Wright, Elizabeth. *Psychoanalytic Criticism: Theory in Practice.* New York: Methuen, 1984.

Yeats, William Butler. *The Poems: A New Edition.* Edited by Richard J. Finneran. New York: Macmillan, 1983.

Index

197